MODERNIZATION OF THE LAW IN ARAB STATES

An Investigation into Current Civil Criminal and Constitutional Law in the Arab World

George N. Sfeir

MODERNIZATION OF THE LAW IN ARAB STATES

An Investigation into Current Civil Criminal and Constitutional Law in the Arab World

George N. Sfeir

Austin & Winfield, Publishers
San Francisco - London - Bethesda
1998

Library of Congress Cataloging-in-Publication Data

Sfeir, George N.
Modernization of the law in Arab states : an investigation into current civil, criminal and constitutional law in the Arab world / George N. Sfeir.
p. cm.
Includes bibliographical references and index.
ISBN 1-57292-103-X (hardcover : alk. paper). -- ISBN 1-57292-102-1 (paper : alk. paper)
1. Law--Arab countries--Codification. I. Title
KMC128.S45 1997
349'.14927--dc21 ISBN: 978-0-57292-102-3 97-37076
CIP

Editorial Inquiries:
Austin & Winfield, Publishers
7831 Woodmont Avenue, #345
Bethesda, MD 20814
(301) 654-7335

To Order: (800) 99-AUSTIN

To *Carola*

for her unfailing support

TABLE OF CONTENTS

INTRODUCTION

The Move from Medieval to Modern

The roots of the law in the Near East go back to antiquity, to the transcendental, the customary and the codified rules of behavior by which people there lived since recorded time. They are the same roots which, by different means and in varying degrees, fed and sustained the well-known classical and modern legal systems from Babylonian to Biblical to Byzantine. Even those who for reasons of convenience or certainty prefer to trace modern European civil law to a single source, that of Roman law, admit that law was nothing but a mixture of Roman, Greek, Near Eastern, and Christian elements.[1] Its final configuration, the Corpus Juris of Justinian, was compiled in the 6th century by legal scholars from the law schools of Constantinople and Berytus, that is modern Beirut, which Justinian called "the mother and nurse of the law."[2] The proximity of the Beirut law school to the birth place of Islam and the early Islamic jurisconsults in Arabia, Syria and Iraq, was one of the factors which led European legal historians in the 19th century to speculate about the extent of the influence of Roman law on Islamic law which displaced it the following century in the Roman provinces of the Near East;[3] a speculation which Muslim scholars heatedly refuted[4]

Nevertheless, elements of the customary, the religious, and the imperial coexisted in the law of all universal states in the region as evidenced by the Syrian-Roman Law Book which became predominant in the Byzantine and even the Sassanid areas of the Near East. As Toynbee has pointed out, the drive for an authoritative, unified, imperial law was a common trait of universal states as these states came to reckon with the living legacies of the conquered peoples and the parochial states they brought under their control.[5]

But the universal state in the Near East would acquire a decidedly religious complexion, whether it was Byzantine, Sassanid, or Islamic. This led Oswald Spengler to muse that the cultural development of the Near East has taken place in terms not of nations but of churches; of freely floating sects without geographical bounds.[6] To this Joseph Campbell added: "Membership [in these churches] is not a matter of either time or place, but of the knowledge and execution of the statutes, which are at once secular and religious; revealed, not invented by man; and categorical, not subject to review."[7] Islam is the prime example to this day.

The lasting legacy of the religious complexion of the universal state has been the pernicious tension in the relationship between the territorial state's religion and that of its parochial groups and communities, a tension with serious political undertones of constitutional contradictions and divisive national identities for the modern territorial state as will be brought out in more detail in Chapter Five.

The dissatisfaction of Syrian monophysites with Byzantine orthodoxy in the 7th century prompted the negotiated surrender of Damascus in 635 AD to the besieging Arab Muslim armies by Mansur ibn Sarjun, a high Syrian official in the Byzantine administration and the grandfather of St. John the Damascene, one of the early saints of the Christian Church.[8] A similar church-state drama would play itself out in the Sassanid Empire to the East. The Christian minority in this theocratic Zoroastrian state, where law and justice were also a clerical preserve, survived periods of oppression in between periods of self-rule in the management of their domestic affairs. But the Byzantine-Sassanid conflict for supremacy over the Near East would drive them to secede from the Byzantine Church and form their own Nestorian church as an expression of loyalty to the Sassanid throne[9]

In return for the surrender of Damascus, the Syrian Christians were promised by Khalid Ibn al-Walid, the conquering Arab commander, security for their lives, property, and churches, so long as they paid the poll tax.[10] Al-Walid's promise would amount in practice to a pact granting both Christians and Jews whom Islam considers believers, like Muslims, in a heavenly Scripture, to regulate their own religious and domestic affairs:

> To you We have sent down the Book with truth, confirming the Scripture already in possession and determining its meaning. Accordingly judge between them by what God has sent down and do not follow what they lust after, diverting you from the truth that has come to you... For each of you We have assigned a divine law and a rule of life. Had God so willed He could have made you a single nation...[11]

This was the basis for the intractable legal institution of personal status and domestic relations which has survived to this day as is more fully explained in Chapter Two. And although Islam has, historically speaking, shown greater tolerance and respect for its non-Muslim subjects than did Christian sects towards one another before the peace of Westphalia in 1648 ended the thirty years war and established the principle, *cujus regio, ejus religio,* the institution of personal status is the cause for social and legal differentiation between Muslim and non-Muslim citizens even under today's radically altered conditions of the nation state and its proclamations of freedom and equality.

The appearance of Islamic law on the world scene coincided with the demise of Roman law as a living force in Europe in the 6th century following the break up of the Roman Empire in the West under the impact of the invasions by the Germanic tribes. But Islamic law was yet to be developed from the rudiments of the revealed text as it expanded into territories endowed with their own laws and institutions. And although the emergent Islamic state would in the end fail to identify with the "earlier lettered traditions of its region," it was nevertheless the direct heir to the Babylonian, Byzantine, and Sassanid states it had displaced. In time the new universal state was able to work out the "relative weighting" of, and the "balance" among, the different elements in the emergent culture, thanks to the flexibility of Islam.[12]

The formative period of Islamic law is associated with the first regime of the Islamic state, that of the Omayyad Caliphate (661-750 AD) whose seat of power was Damascus, Syria. It was a period of institution building directed towards worldly ends to manage an expanding empire, rather than the well-being of the new religion. While the conquering Arabian rulers wielded the power, the administration of the newly acquired territories was run by the same local functionaries who had served the previous rulers of these territories,[13] a situation sometimes compared to the Germanic invasion of the Roman Empire in the West. The difference however was that the Arab rulers brought with them a new religion and a new law which necessitated a great deal of innovation and adaptation to local custom and practice far different from what they were familiar with in Arabia.

Through the free use of opinion (*ra'y*) as well as analytical analogy (*qiyas*), Muslim jurisconsults succeeded in their separate ways and disparate locations to evolve the law from the sparse precepts of the Qoranic text,[14] away from the direct influence of the sayings of the Prophet (*sunna*), whose oral sources were yet to be authenticated and recorded. They would eventually become known as the protagonists of legal opinion (*ahl al-ra'y*) as distinct from their later compatriots who held to the letter of the revealed text and the sayings of the Prophet, known as the protagonists of tradition (*ahl al-hadith*).

But if the Omayyad Caliphate in Syria represented the effervescent era of Islamic law, its golden age came during the Abbasid Caliphate in Baghdad (750-950 AD). It marked a new point of departure for Islamic jurisprudence.[15] Instead of the Omayyad tradition of legal pragmatism and free use of opinion to reconcile local custom and usage with the revealed text, the Abbasid era saw a more academic and speculative development of jurisprudence at the hands of religious scholars, the *ulema*, who identified more closely with the Qoran and the sayings of the Prophet. Their work would crystalize into a number of doctrinaire schools of jurisprudence, or more literally rites (*madhahib)*, which formed around, and named after, their founders. The most prominent among the Sunni schools were those of Shafi'i, Hanafi, Maliki, Hanbali; and the Imamiya, Yazidiya, and Isma'iliya, among the Shiite schools. It was the crowning era of Islamic law which coincided with the period of intellectual ferment in the Islamic Empire as the literary and scientific heritage of Hellenism was being transmitted from Greek into Syriac and then into

Arabic, only to be reworked and enriched by Muslim philosophers and return in time to fuel the Enlightenment of Europe.

The formation of these schools of jurisprudence, however, gave greater impetus to speculative controversies over imaginary rather than real legal issues, until they became entangled with the wider controversies of scholastic theology in Islam (*kalam*) between such strains of thought as the *Mu'tazila*, the rationalists who believed the Qoran was created and its comprehension was subject to human reason, and that of the *Ash'ari* followers who held to the limitations of rational knowledge in relation to religious truth and the metaphysical concept of God's sovereignty and omnipotence.[16] The *Ash'aris* were associated with the Shafi'i school of jursprudence who adhered more closely to the traditions of the Prophet (*sunna*), and the *Mu'tazila* with the Hanafi school which identified more closely with the exponents of opinion (*ra'y*).[17]

These scholastic controversies are blamed by modern Arab jurists for the arrest which set in shortly thereafter in the development of Islamic law. By coopting the theories about the roots of Islamic law (*usul al-fiqh*), scholastic theology forced jurisprudence to abandon the world of reality and changing conditions of society in favor of sterile speculative arguments about imaginary situations, something Muslim scholars have not completely abandoned to this day.[18] One is reminded in this connection of "scholastic rational theology" in medieval Europe. It too allowed natural reason a wide range of speculation, provided the limits set by supernatural revelation were respected. But European scholasticism moved on to bridge the chasm which separated reason from revelation at the hands of such men as Marsilius of Padua who succeeded in reconciling the natural with the metaphysical in order to arrive at the conclusion that the validity of the law is derived from the person who participates in its creation. The irony in all this is that Marsilius built his argument upon "the naturalist interpretation of Aristotle in the sense of Averroes," the 12th century Andalusian Muslim philosopher Ibn Rushd.[19]

The creative phase of Islamic law came to an end with the political upheavals which also eclipsed the Abbasid Caliphate beginning with the 10th century. Mongol, Kurdish, and Seljuk invadors and aspirants for power, whom Brockelmann described as continuously "at swords' point with each other,"[20] had little concern for the legal order they appropriated from their Arab predecessors. Not only did the Mongols, for example, reel physical havoc on the calipheal seat of power in Baghdad and depose its occupant, they introduced their own edicts and customary codes. Under the circumstances, the *ulema* continued to hold themselves the legitimate guardians of the true law and the ecumenical unity of the Islamic Community, or *Umma*, its political dismemberment notwithstanding. But the spirit of *ijtihad*, the ability to evolve the law by reasoned deduction and analogy (*qiyas*) had dissipated. "All they could do from then on was to associate themselves with the opinions of the old sages of the law."[21] The age of stagnation or *taqlid* (imitation), as it became known, had set in.

This happened at a historic juncture for world law. While the creative epoch of Islamic law was coming to an end, the renaissance of European law was about to take off with the rediscovery in 1050 AD of the Corpus Juris of Justinian which made possible the formation of the Civil Law system as we know it today. Some modern researchers have argued against the atrophy of Islamic law, that the "gates of *ijtihad*" were never closed,[22] to say nothing of the claim often proffered by Islamists that the revealed text is good for all times and climes. The fact remains however that Islamic law had failed to regain its position as a living force, and instead fell into a condition of stasis which ultimately invited the 19th century influx of European law to displace it, as is more fully explained in Chapter One. Where it not for its rich written legacy, one could safely say that Islamic law has, for all intents and purposes, been reduced to something akin to customary law to be integrated into the borrowed European law which actually happened in the creation of the modern Arab civil codes described in Chapter Three. It is a development which is not unlike what took place in Europe from post-Roman times until the codifications of the 18th century, when Roman law and legal custom coexisted as two elements of European law[23]

The parting of ways between Islamic and European legal systems in the 11th century represented also the beginning of the end to the ideological symmetry between Islamic and Christian notions of law and society which prevailed throughout the Middle Ages. Both accentuated the spiritual and the supernatural, the moral dimension over the material; the measure being conformity with the commands of God. The Qoranic tenet, "*al-amr bil ma'ruf wal nahiy 'an al-munkar*" (command that which is acceptable to God and admonish against that which is unacceptable and reprehensible to Him) which presaged much of Islamic jurisprudence in its formative years, had its equivalent expressions in Christian Europe's view of the nature and purpose of law. In Fortescue's (England) words, law is a sacred sanction commanding those things that are right and forbidding their opposite (*iubens honesta et prohibens contraria*); and according to Juan Mariana (Spain) law derives from the mind of God laying down those things that are upright and salutary, and forbidding their opposite (*honesta et salutaria prescribens, prohibensqua contraria)*.[24] Law in their view, Muslims and Christians, dispensed duties and obligations, not rights; and being morally valid, it was just.

Such a concept of law was of course a reflection of the divine notion of society. The *Societas Christiana*, as with the *Muslim Umma*, was made up of the universal *Congregatiu Fidelium*, or the Community of the Faithful in which the temporal and the spiritual overlapped. Not until the 13th century was the hierocratic idea in Europe of a universal unitary Christian society questioned, and the separation between *imperium* and *sacerdotium* get under way. It got under way at the hands of those scholastics and publicists, such as William of Occam and Marsilius of Padua, who propounded naturalist social and legal ideas based on the thoughts of Aristotle as interpreted by the great Muslim philosophers Averroes and Avicenna.[25] But these same Muslim philosophers would fail to have any lasting effect on Islamic thought. Instead, the proponents of orthodoxy will, such as Ghazali, whose influence as a theologian and jurist in Islam is comparable to that of St. Augustine in Christianity. For the future of Islam however, it would be as if the patristic doctrines of law and society in Europe did not transcend the views of St. Augustine.

The first attempt in Arab Muslim thought to challenge the conception that Islam was as much a precept for governance as it was a doctrine of faith, did not come until the 20th century. In a treatise on the caliphate,[26] Ali Abdel-Raziq, Egyptian jurist and cleric at the famous Al-Azhar Islamic University, shed doubt on the temporal aspects of the Qoranic message and negated the assumption that the institution of the caliphate had any basis in Islamic law. Surveying the Qoranic text and the Traditions of the Prophet, he found nothing which would support the conclusion that Muslims are duty bound to appoint an imam or caliph to attend to their temporal affairs, nor did the Prophet's religious message have anything to do with running a government. These he concluded were purely political institutions to be determined by society on the basis of reason, the experience of nations, and the laws of statecraft. In his own way and milieu, Abdel-Raziq was in effect retracing the path taken in the 13th century by Christian scholastics and would suffer the same fate as that of William of Occam, when he was tried and convicted by a religious tribunal of his peers at Al-Azhar.[27]

What Abdel-Raziq did achieve was to pose for the first time the troubling question for a Muslim that has yet to be answered convincingly: Is it not conceivable for vibrant Islam to exist without Islamic dominion? Count Ostrorog who witnessed the "reformation" which transformed Turkey from the Ottoman to the republican regime early this century, put the question in another way, the way in which it was posed in Europe on the occasion of the Reformation: "Is this new conception heresy, or is it not rather a return to the pure, primitive, liberal conception of Islam as it stood when unaffected by the subtlety of scholastic logicians?"[28]

Abdel-Raziq's quest for some form of separation between religion and state coincided with the turn of the century reform movement in Islam which was led by Muhammad Abdu and Rashid Rida. They sought to liberalize Islam and revitalize it into a "mobilizing ideology" in order to meet the challenge they perceived of 20th century modernization, that is, Westernization, secularization and nationalism. However by merely fashioning the old religious concepts and institutions into a modern garb, they remained essentially within the confines of theology, and overlooked the essential question of the legitimation of power in the modern state, whose elements - legality, justifiability of rules and expressed consent of the citizenry - depends as much on the relationship of these underlying principles as on the nature of the institutions that embody or give effect to them.[30]

This question remains to this day inconclusive in most of the Arab states as the discussion on constitutionalism in Chapter Five shows. By providing for an elected legislature to express the will of the people, but declaring at the same time that Islamic law is the source of legislation, Arab constitutions have left the field fallow for fundamentalists to demand compliance with various notions of Islamic law, a demand to which Arab governments from time to time are forced to concede in order to bolster their legitimacy.

How realistic is this demand by Muslim fundamentalists to reinstate Islamic law? To put the question differently, are there in fact intrinsic impediments in Islamic legal methodology which hinder its revival today under greatly changed social and economic conditions?

The first of these impediments was and still is the self-imposed limitations on *ijtihad*, the ability to reason and deduce new interpretation from the revealed text to suit new facts. That which began as a tool for evolving the law became its impregnable dam once the old masters were done with it. There is no room for *ijtihad* where a definitive text exists, and where the text is vague, *ijtihad* can do no more than explain it along the lines of the underlying principles of the revealed law or elicit a ruling by analogy to another ruling based on a text or an underlying principle.[31]

This is the view even of contemporary legal scholars seeking ways and means to revitalize Islamic law and make it responsive to today's changed conditions. Abdel-Wahhab Khallaf, taking his cue from Muhammad Abdu and Rashid Rida, considers the revealed text sufficiently flexible to admit re-interpretation of the text on the basis of human interest (*maslaha*) or judicial preference (*istislah*), provided no explicit ruling or consensus exists to preempt *ijtihad* in the matter.[32]

Consensus is another of these impediments. In the absence of a formal legislative process in the Islamic legal order, a judicial opinion or ruling acquired the force of law by the express or tacit approval of fellow jurisconsults (*'ulema*), a process known as *ijma'*. As such it is considered the third primary source of Islamic law after the Qoran and the Traditions of the Prophet or *sunna*. Despite serious doubts cast by Muslim scholars in modern times that it had ever functioned as such in the past,[33] *ijma'* is, in the absence of any definitive restatement, the authoritative key to the binding rules of Islamic law as far as Muslim fundamentalists are concerned.

Not only is it impractical for all the *ulema* in all the dominions of Islam to have agreed on the same thing at the same time, what dominates the realm of consensus are the opinions of the early companions of the Prophet and the first caliphs, which traditionalists insist what they ratified in the past cannot be contradicted in the present. This restrictive application of the concept of *ijma'* disregards its wider sense and historic origins which were largely cultural and pre-Islamic. As Hodgson pointed out, it was the principle of adherence to tradition well established among the culturally homogenous communities of Arabia which later on crystallized into the doctrine of *ijma'*, that "whatever had been accepted generally by the Community was to be regarded as sanctioned by God,"[34] which leads us to the probative (*hujjiya*) value of *ijma'*.

According to Khallaf, this *hujjiya* lies in the Qoranic injunction "Obey God and obey the Prophet and those of you in authority," as well as the Prophetic saying "My Community will not agree upon an error,"[35] confusing thereby the juristic function of *ijma'* with the political concept of *shura* or consultation. Neither *shura* nor *ijma'* is however clearly mandated in the Qoran, not in the political and legal sense imparted to them here. The former appears among the ethical exhortations urging Muslims to avoid conflict and to counsel and reconcile with one another.[36] The latter, as a juridical function, is a matter of deduction from the Prophetic saying about the infallibility of the Muslim Community, a deduction to which a modern scholar took exception as leading to a *petitio principii* or vicious circle comparable to the Catholic Church's attempt in seeking the truth by declaring itself infallible.[37]

Shafi'i, one of the founders of the four major Islamic Sunni schools of jurisprudence, is said to have subscribed at first to the relationship between the juridical function of *ijma'* and the ordained infallibility of the Muslim Community until he was convinced of his error by the fact that seldom were the *ulema* everywhere able to agree on the same ruling at the same time.[38]

These built-in methodological brakes on the evolution of Islamic law under modern conditions, are compounded today by the isolationist attitude of Islamist legal scholars. Like their Orientalist colleagues in the West, they tend to pigeonhole and separate Islamic law from all other legal systems, and if compelled to view it in a comparative context, as is often the case now, given the inroads made by Western law into the Arab legal systems, they invariably accentuate the differences instead of exploring the possible avenues of conciliation, in order to safeguard the purity and authenticity of its revealed sources.

The glaring contrast between this self-centered attitude of Islamic law revivalists today and the openness displayed by European jurists upon their rediscovery of Justinian's Cropus Juris in the 11th century, cannot be overlooked. A process of assimilation of the Germanic customary codices, canon rules and the principles of Roman Law preceded the formation of the Civil Law we know today. The extent to which European law became receptive of diversity was immediately evident in the first European codification, the Assizes of Ariano, by the Norman King Roger II of Sicily. The code drew on customary law, natural law, and divine law, fusing in the process diverse features of Byzantine, Muslim, Lombard, Norman, and Romano-canonical legal traditions.[39]

The most striking thing about this isolationist attitude is the refusal of Islamic thought even today to entertain a role in the reform process for natural law, which was perhaps the most important factor in the European transition from the medieval to the modern notion of law. Allal al-Fasi, Moroccan scholar and lawyer, after noting that the Greeks developed the ideas of natural law, the Romans the *jus gentium*, the English equity, to make up for the "deficiencies" in their positive laws for equality and fairness, he dismisses the need of Islamic law for such "extraneous sources," since the concepts of equality and fairness were already comprehended in its own principles and purposes. By simply equating natural law with the idea of justice, which he says positive law lacked together with all the other attributes of divine law, that is, compassion, fairness, and permanence,[40] Al-Fasi overlooks the link which natural law provided between the "eternal law of God" and the "moral law of man,"[41] a linkage which any reform of Islamic law would need in order to break the deadlock between revelation and reason.

Thomas Aquinas, whom Finnis called a "paradim natural law theorist,"[42] brought about the break-through in modern legal thought by arguing that man-made law consists of rules derived from natural law, just as in every other field of human activity where particular forms are deduced from general principles and ideas, positive law derives its validity from natural law. While natural law figured significantly in Christian scholastic thought, it remained alien to its Islamic counterpart, *kalam.* Instead, Muslim theologians indulged in protracted controversies over the good *(hassan)* and the bad (*qabih*), which in the divinely ordained Islamic *weltanschauung* translated to "right" and "wrong" in man's relations to God and His laws.[43]

In one of the rare Arabic books in modern times devoted to the study of natural law,[44] the author concludes that despite the controversy which separated the rationalists (*Mu'tazila*) from the Orthodox (*Ash'ari*) over the role of reason in the doing good (*tahsin*) and the doing bad (*taqbih*), neither conceptualized its view in a structured manner. Nevertheless, the controversy left its mark in the form of new discretionary criteria in the interpretation of the revealed text, such as *istihsan* and *masalih mursala,* criteria which the author says approximate the role played by natural law in the evolution of Christian scholastic thought. But the ideas of *Ibn Rushd* the Muslim philosopher Avirroes, on which, the author says, Aquinas based his theory of the hierarchy of laws, did not leave their mark on Islamic jurisprudence, the way Aquinas' theories succeeded in transforming the criterion for the validity of the law in Christendom from revealed to positive.

Not as antagonistic however is the attitude of Muslim scholars towards imputations that Islamic law benefited from local custom. Indeed, custom (*'urf*) and usage (*ma'ruf*) are common terms in the Qoran, the Prophet's Traditions, and the commentaries of the jurisconsults. But the classical exegists tended to impart a religious sense to the terms, thereby restricting their use to that which God enjoins or that which is in conformity with revelation[45] Under this category implicitly fall many of the pre-Islamic customary practices in Arabia which are more readily acknowledged by Islamists today, having received at the time the Prophet's approval by word or deed. Many of what we now know as Islamic contracts of sale were in existence in pre-Islamic Arabia. On the other hand, Islam put an end to certain customary practices common in pre-Islamic Arabia, such as adoption, aleatory transactions, and the use of certain weights and measures in assessing non-usurious exchanges and barter deals which were judged contrary to the welfare of the Community at large.

It will be in the former Byzantine territories of Syria, Iraq and Egypt, where the new Islamic rulers would encounter more highly developed legal institutions than those they knew in Arabia, that the main controversy over foreign influences, whether customary or Roman law, on Islamic law would center.

Not yet a legal system, or a body of general principles, when it first ventured into these territories, what constituted Islamic law then were *ad hoc* rulings on specific situations typical of classical law generally,[46] making it undoubtedly receptive to customary practices. But Egyptian legal historian, Sufi Hassan Abu Talib, says that custom played a major role in the evolution of Islamic law only in its early formative period. By the time Islamic law came to the Byzantine territories where Roman law applied, custom had lost its allure and the purity of Islamic law from foreign influences was maintained.[47]

In support of this view, Abu Talib distinguishes between the imposition of Islamic law in the former Byzantine provinces and the earlier extension of Roman law to the Roman provinces in the Near East in 212 AD in the wake of Caracalla's *constitutio Antoniniana* which granted Roman citizenship to all the peoples of the Empire. While he realizes how difficult it was for Roman law to be accepted by the inhabitants of these provinces who not only held fast to their own customary practices, but in the end left their mark on Roman law,[48] he speaks of Islamic law displacing Roman law in the Byzantine provinces as if by a simple and sudden exchange, rejecting any suggestion that Islamic law was influenced in the process by either Roman or Provincial law.

It does not matter for our purposes here whether or not Islamic law borrowed from Roman law. As has already been mentioned, the subject was exhaustively researched by the 19th century European legal historians with differing conclusions, and refuted by Muslim scholars. What matters for the continued modernization of Arab law, even for the revival of Islamic law on modern scientific bases, were it to be seriously contemplated, is that the legal culture expounded today by jurists, lawyers, and scholars not be a culture removed from the realities of Arab society and the cumulative achievement of modern legal systems.

In a short but highly incisive article,[49] Alan Watson examines the influence of subordinate law makers, lawyers, jurists, scholars, in developing their legal culture detached from social reality. He takes the examples of the Pentateuch in the Christian Scripture, the Roman Twelve Tables, and the rabbinical law in the Mishnah and Talmud. Although Watson did not examine the role of the *ulema*, the learned men of the law in Islam, the conclusions he arrived at in the three examples he chose apply equally well to Islamic law. Here is a summary of his findings and their relevance to our subject:

(1) Law and narrative are intertwined in the Pentateuch which continually stresses the first occurrence of a transgression, and when a legal rule is developed, it is developed by men "reflecting on ancient traditions and legends." This is indeed what one finds today in the numerous treatises and articles by Muslim authors expounding the rules of Islamic law. There is no analysis of the justification for the rules or their validity in the light of modern conditions. Instead, the reader is treated

to a historic narrative of what the Prophet and the first four caliphs had said or done. An oft repeated example is that of the Caliph 'Umar who exonerated a thief from the punishment of severing his hand on the ground that he was driven to steal by the incidence of famine. His decision became the basis for validity of otherwise reprehensible acts on the ground of public interest or welfare, which became known in Islamic law as *al-masalih al-mursala.*

(2) No matter that the plebians thought that the Roman Twelve Tables was an egalitarian document and therefore a victory for them. What mattered was that its interpretation was given to the College of Pontiffs, a patrician group, who had a monopoly of interpreting the law. There is practically no survey of Islamic law put out today which does not give the reader the impression that the law was hostage to what *ijma'*, the consensus of the *ulema*, decreed on this or that issue. They too had a monopoly of interpreting the law. And as in the case of the Pontiffs, the concern of the *ulema* was to safeguard the revealed law not to systematize or reform it.

(3) Rabbinic law, being religious law, differs from secular law in so far as it is a guide to conduct; "religious law is law as truth." Surveys of Islamic law bring out the same consequences which Watson saw in Rabbinic law. The revealed text forbade this or that, but the determination of what counted as this or that became the subject of protracted arguments among the *ulema*. Only in a limited number of instances did the text prescribe worldly punishment, but generally speaking it did not foresee a legal process if one acted contrary to its admonitions. Nevertheless, for the *ulema* as for the rabbis it was an intellectual challenge to indulge in meticulous interpretations and formulate ideal rules of conduct.

The *ulema* have been a nebulous category of people in Islam. Ideally, anyone learned in the law would fit that category. And although they were never formally recognized as such, they did in practice become the custodians of the law and hence an authority to be reckoned with in the Islamic hierarchy. Today, with the politicization of Islam through the fundamentalist movement, the rise of a secular elite to man the government and the need to give the revealed law and its rulings a modern expression, legal scholars and jurists are more and more assuming the role previously played by the *ulema*, the subordinate law makers Watson described in his enlightening article.

This introduction began with the statement that the roots of the law in the Near East go back to antiquity, to the transcendental, the customary and the codified rules of behavior by which people there lived since recorded time. It will end by saying that the future of Arab law, or any other law for that matter, depends on its ability to comprehend and to adapt to the social and economic realities whose symmetry world wide has become increasingly evident. Any movement, legal or otherwise, which seeks to undo what has been achieved instead of building upon it, is a backward movement contrary to the very notion of Progress which derives its value and power from its bearings on the future. Here I am quoting from J.B. Bury:[50]

The idea of human Progress is a theory which involves a synthesis of the past and a prophecy of the future. It is based on an interpretation of history which regards men as slowly advancing - *pedetemtim progredientes* - in a definite and desirable direction, and infers that this progress will continue indefinitely... [But] the process must be the necessary outcome of the psychical and social nature of man; it must not be at the mercy of any external will; otherwise there would be no guarantee of its continuance and its issue, and the idea of Progress would lapse into the idea of Providence.

ENDNOTES

1. Hans Julius Wolff, *Roman Law: An Historical Introduction*, Norman Oklahoma/London (1951/1987) p.50f.
2. Philip Hitti, *History of Syria: Including Lebanon and Palestine*, New York (1951) p. 326. For a history of the Beirut law school, see P. Callinet, *Histoire de l'ecole de droit de Beyrouth*, Paris (1925).
3. See Patricia Crone, *Roman Provincial and Islamic Law: The Origin of the Islamic Patronate,* Cambridge (1987).
4. See Sufi Hassan Abu Talib, *Bayn al-Shari'a al-Islamiya wal-Qanun al-Rumani* [Between Islamic Law and Roman Law], Cairo (195?)
5. Arnold J. Toynbee, *A Study of History*, [Abridgement of vols. VII-X by D.C. Somervell] Oxford (1957), p. 50f.
6. Oswald Spengler, *The Decline of the West*, [English transl. by Charles Atkinson] New York (1926), vol. II, p. 235.
7. Joseph Campbell, *The Masks of God: Occidental Mythology*, New York (1964/1976) p. 221-222.
8. Hitti, *History of Syria*, op.cit. p.414-417.
9. Toynbee saw in the Nestorian and Monophysite "heresies" failed attempts to de-Hellenize Christianity and feeble reactions against the intrusion of Hellenism in the Syriac World. It would be left for Islam to complete the eviction, reintegrate in the Arab Caliphate the Syriac Society and endow it with an indigenous universal church--the Islamic Church which became the chrysalis out of which the Arabic and Iranic civilizations emerged. Toynbee, *A Study of History*, op.cit. p.144-145.
10. Hitti, *History of Syria*, op.cit. p.415.
11. Sura v:48, Kenneth Cragg, *Readings in the Qoran*, London (1988), p.268.

12. Marshall G.S. Hodgson, *The Venture of Islam*, vol. I, *The Classical Age*, Chicago (1958/1977) p.103-104.
13. Albert Hourani, *A History of the Arab Peoples*, Cambridge (1991) p.26-27.
14. Of the 6000 odd *ayas* (verses) in its 114 *suras* (chapters), only some 200 verses are in the nature of legal norms. These pertain to the rites and duties of a Muslim--prayer, pilgrimage, dietary rules, decent attire, marriage, divorce, paternity, succession, *zakat* (alms tax), *waqf* (charitable trusts), commercial transactions and contractual obligations, loans, usury, major crimes, adjudication and evidence.
15. See N.J. Coulson, *A History of Islamic Law*, Edinburgh (1964/ 1990) p.37.
16. For greater detail about scholastic theology in Islam, see Majid Fakhri, *A History of Islamic Philosophy*, New York (2nd. ed. 1983) p.203f. Paraphrasing al-Farabi, Fakhri explains the enduring entanglement between jurisprudence and theology as follows: "Jurisprudence is the art of determining the right religious beliefs and practices, on which the lawgiver (God) was silent, by analogy to the express provisions of Scripture. Theology, on the other hand, is described as the art of defending those beliefs and practices, as well as rebutting the arguments disputing their truth." (p.115-116).
17. Hodgson, *The Venture of Islam*, op.cit. vol. I, p.440.
18. Ahmad al-Khamlishi, Manhaj al-Fikr al-Qanuni fil Fiqh al-Islami [The Legal System of Thought in Islamic Jurisprudence], *Al-Majalla al-Maghribiya lil-Qanun wal-Siyasa wal-Iqtisad* [The Moroccan Journal of Law, Politics and Economy] No.16 (Dec. 1984) 11 at p.31.
19. Carl Joachim Friedrich, *The Philosophy of Law in Historical Perspective*, Chicago (1958/1963) p.44-45.
20. Carl Brockelmann, *History of the Islamic People*, New York (1939/1960), p.221.
21. Muhammad al-Khudari, *Tarikh al-Tashri' al-Islami* [History of Islamic Law] Cairo, 1925/1985, p.266-267.

22. W.B. Hallaq, "Was the Gate of Ijtihad Closed?" 16 *Int'l. J. of Middle East Studies 1* (1984) 3-41.
23. Alan Watson, *The Evolution of Law*, Baltimore (1985) p.43f. "In large measure, the main task of lawyers of that long stretch of time was the unification or harmonization of the two strands of Roman law and custom [He cites *French droit coutumier* (Coutume de Paris, e.g.) the German *Sachsenspiegel*, and the Catalan law]."
24. Cited in J.M. Kelley, *A Short History of Western Legal Theory*, Oxford (1992) p.183-184.
25. See Michael Wilks, *The Problem of Sovereignty in the Later Middle Ages*, Cambridge (1963).
26. *Al-Khilafa was Usul al-Hukm* [The Caliphate and the Bases of Government] by Ali Abdel-Rziq, Cairo (1923).
27. Three categories of accusations were levelled against Abdel-Raziq by his peers: (a) Those in which he claimed that the message of Islam was spiritual in nature, not intended to be the basis for government or the conduct of wordly affairs; (b) Those in which he denied the long-standing consensus of the Muslim Community's need for a caliph to guide its spiritual and temporal affairs and to safeguard its unity; (c) Those in which he denied that the administration of justice was a function of the Sharia. The text appeared in *al-Siyasa Newspaper*, Cairo, issue of 13 August, 1925.
28. Count Leon Ostrorog, *The Angora Reform*, London (1927), p.98.
29. Albert Hourani, *Arabic Thought in the Liberal Age 1898-1939*, Cambridge (1962) is the best study in English of the Islamic reformers in the Arab World.
30. David Beetham, *The Legitimation of Power*, Atlantic Highlands, New Jersey (1991) p.158.
31. Abdel-Wahhab Khallaf, *'Ilm Usul al-Fiqh* [The Science of Islamic Jurisprudence], Cairo (10th printing 1972), p.216-221
32. See generally Abdel-Wahhab Khallaf, *Masadir al-Tashri' al-Islami fi ma la Nassa Fih* [Source of Islamic Legislation Where no Text Exists], Cairo 1955.

33. Khallaf, *`Ilm Usal al-Figh*, op.cit. p49.
34. Hodgson, *The Venture of Islam*, op.cit., vol.I p.324. "The mind of God and the mind of the Community are the same," is the way Spengler has put it, adding that *ijma'* is the key of all Early Christian, Jewish and Persian Councils. Spengler, *Decline of the West*, op.cit., p.
35. Khallaf, *'Ilm Usul al-Fiqh*, op.cit. p.47.
36. *Qoran*, verse xlii:38 "And those who answer the call of the Lord...and whose affairs are a matter of counsel..." and verse iii:159 "It was by the mercy of Allah that thou wast lenient with them...Pardon them and ask forgiveness for them and consult with them upon the conduct of affairs..."
37. George Hourani, "Authority of Consensus," *Studia Islamica*, vol. XXI (1964), p.13-60.
38. Al-Khudari, *Tarikh al-Tashri'*, op.cit. p.151-153.
39. Harold J. Berman, *Law & Revolution: The Formation of the Western Legal Tradition,* Cambridge (1983), p.419.
40. Allal al-Fasi, *Maqasid al-Shari'a al-Islamiya* [The Objectives of Islamic law], Casablanca (1963), p.34-52.
41. Lloyd Weinraub, *Natural Law and Justice*, Cambridge (1987) p.59.
42. John Finnis, *Natural Law and Natural Rights*, Oxford (1980/1992) p.28 and 284-285.
43. Wilfred Cantwell Smith, "The Concept of Shari'a Among Some Mutakallimun," in.60-67. *Arabic and Islamic Studies in Honor of Hamilton A.R. Gibb,* ed. George Makdisi, Leiden (1965) 581, at p.595-596.
44. Muhammad Sharif Ahmad, *Fikrat al-Qanun al-Tabi'i 'ind al-Muslimin* [The Notion of Natural Law Among the Muslims], Baghdad (1980).
45. Farhat J. Ziadeh, "'Urf and Law in Islam," in *The World of Islam: Studies in Honor of Philip K. Hitti,* ed. J. Kritzeck and R.B. Winder, London (1960) p 60-67, "The term begins to acquire a social value when 'the known' becomes 'the familiar,' 'the customary,' 'the good,' as distinguished from 'the unknown,' which becomes 'the strange' (*munkar*) 'the bad.'"

46. Spengler, *Decline of the West*, op.cit p.63, described "classical law" as law "not deliberately invested with validity for the future, but more or less recreated again and again as empirical rulings ad hoc."
47. Sufi Hassan Abu Talib, *Tatbiq al-Shari'a al-Islamiya fil-Bilad al-'Arabiya* [Application of Islamic Law in the Arab Countries], Cairo (3rd. ed. 1986) p.182.
48. Abu Talib, *Bayn al-Shari'a al-Islamiya wal-Qanun al-Rumani*, op.cit. p.15-16.
49. 43 *Amer. J. of Comparative Law* (1995) 469-476.
50. *The Idea of Progress: An Inquiry into its Origin and Growth*, (Dover, N.J. ed. 1987) p.5.

CHAPTER ONE

The Beginnings of Modernization

When legal modernization began in the 19th century, the Arab states were for the most part, in one form or another, territories of the Ottoman Empire. Those situated in North Africa were, however, poised to come under the direct influence of the European powers, while those lying to the East would remain under Ottoman suzerainty until the end of world war I in 1918. Although in either case the result would be the same, that is, the displacement of a major segment of the traditional Islamic legal order by European type codes and courts, the motivation and the means were different. In North Africa direct imposition by the European powers of their laws was motivated by the desire to enhance their trade and dominion; in the Eastern provinces, borrowing of European laws by the Ottoman authorities was meant to meet the growing challenge of Europe to the survival of the Empire.

Because of this varied approach in the process of modernization, it will be necessary to trace its course individually in selected states. To begin with, the Ottoman reforms were part and parcel of state reorganization or *tanzimat*, as it became known. In the face of growing challenge from the European powers, the Sultan sought by a series of *faramans* or charters (the *Hatti Gulhane* of 1839 and the *Hatti Humayun* of 1856) to modernize Ottoman society by putting into practice European standards of law and administration with civil equality and liberty for all citizens.[1] But it took world war I (1914-1918) to bring about the actual break up of the politico-religious Islamic legal order, which had dominated the Middle East and North Africa since the 7th century, and the abolition of its core institution, the Caliphate. In the meantime, the gradual introduction of European laws side by side with the existing Islamic, tribal, and customary laws and tribunals, would bring about a dichotomy in the legal system and an extended period of adjustment with its expected conflicts and dislocations.

The demise of the Ottoman Empire in 1918, would leave its former Arab territories to continue the process of adjustment, both complemented and complicated by the presence of the British and French rule in these territories who proceed in imposing some of their own laws. Only in the present Turkish Republic, the successor regime to the Ottoman Sultanate, will the process achieve a clear and complete break with the past as early as the 1920's.

The newly elected Turkish National Assembly sought at first to divest the calipheal office of its temporal powers alone, leaving it with its spiritual functions which are the vicarship of the Prophet and the guardianship of the faith. In a detailed opinion or *fetwa,* a group of Muslim religious scholars, or ulema, sympathetic to the aims of the Turkish reformers, stated that the Caliphate had become a convenient tool in the hands of the office holder for the exercise of "arbitrary power." Digressing for the first time from the conventional Islamic view that sovereignty resided with God, the fetwa decreed that political power belonged with the people who were after all its "rightful owners."[2]

To the founder of modern Turkey, Kemal Ataturk, however, divesting the office of its temporal powers alone would not deprive it of its tremendous spiritual symbolism as the head of a pan-Islamic *umma* or community, a notion which stood contrary to the concept of the nation-state which Ataturk espoused.[3] In the end the National Assembly had no alternative but to adopt the decree of March 3, 1924, which categorically declared: "The Caliph is deposed." It went on to rationalize its action by stating that the office had become redundant, displaced by the institutions of the new state. "The Caliphate is essentially comprised in the meaning and significance of the terms government (*hukumiyet*) and republic (*jumhuriyet*)[4]

Two other decrees adopted simultaneously by the National Assembly signified modern Turkey's resolve to achieve a radical break with the past. These were law No. 429 abolishing the Commissariat for the Sharia or religious Tribunals and transferring their jurisdiction to the civil courts, and law No. 430 placing all scientific and educational establishments within the purview of the civil authorities, including the traditional medreseh, the schools and seminaries run by the clergy. To complete what had become in effect a process of secularization, the new Turkish regime adopted on February 17, 1926, the Swiss Civil Code which replaced the Islamic rules of domestic relations as well as the rules of contracts and obligations.

The Arab States of the Fertile Crescent

No such decisive break with the traditional Islamic legal order would develop in the successor Arab states of the former Eastern Ottoman territories. Here the reform of the law would continue along the same course taken by the Ottoman sultans: rationalization and codification of the Islamic law rules still considered viable, and the gradual borrowing of European law where Islamic law was deficient. On the one hand, the post World War I concept of the territorial state as a legal order was yet to be reconciled with the notion of Arab nationalism and its Islamic overtones. On the other, the attractiveness of European law was understandable given its rational formality and accechpater fourssibility when compared with Islamic law whose arrested development had left it with a motley of diverse and scattered rulings and outdated commentaries. The free use of opinion (ra'y) and reasoned deduction (*ijtihad*) which made possible the evolution of Islamic law from the scant rulings of the Qoran and the Sunna, the traditions of the Prophet, to the state of high accomplishment it had achieved, lost much of its impetus by the 10th century. What followed since has been a jurisprudence of imitation (*taqlid*), of earlier scholars and legal schools or madhahib,[5] much of it obscure and incomprehensible under modern conditions. When the need to modernize arose in the 19th century, the condition of Islamic law was not much different from that in which Roman law found itself when Justinian ordered the preparation of the Corpus Juris: a mass of authoritative and quasi authoritative commentaries and treatises written by legal scholars with many different points of view much of it dated, repetitive and obscure.[6]

The European laws which the Ottomans introduced in the 19th century would remain applicable in the former Eastern provinces to become French and British League of Nations mandated states of Syria, Lebanon, Iraq, Jordan and Palestine, long after the dismemberment of the Ottoman Empire. The first of these laws was the Ottoman Penal Code which was modeled after the French code of 1810 and subsequently updated by two new versions in 1851 and 1858. It was complemented in 1861 by a code of criminal procedure also based on its French counterpart. These codes constituted a radical departure from Islamic law by abolishing the medieval bodily punishments of stoning and severing of limbs. More significantly, they introduced the juridical principle of the Enlightenment, *nulllum crimen sine lege*, which had gained recognition in 18th century Europe and found expression in its penal laws. They represented a radical departure from the Islamic penal rules which subscribe to a limited number of crimes whose compulsory punishments are specified in the revealed law, and anything else is left to the discretion of the judge, as is more fully explained in a subsequent part of this book.

The other field which benefited from this borrowing was commerce and trade, where the French Code du Commerce of 1807 became the Ottoman Commercial Code of 1850, amended in 1860. The code validated for the first time in an Islamic country interest payments which Islamic law prohibits as a form of usury. This was followed in 1863 with the Ottoman Maritime Law, and in 1880 with the Ottoman Law of Civil Procedure, both of which were based on their French counterparts. The latter became necessary when civil courts displaced for the most part the Islamic Sharia tribunals whose jurisdiction became restricted to matters of family law, inheritence, charitable endowments, customary transactions and proprietary rights.

What the Ottoman reforms retained from Islamic law were the rules of personal status and domestic relations, codified in 1917 as the Ottoman Law of Family Rights, and the rules of transactions and obligations, known as mu'amalat, codified in 1876 as Majallat-i Ahkami Adliye. Another codification which drew partly on Islamic law and customary usage was the Ottoman Land Law of 1858. The codification of Islamic law was in itself an act of modernization. Past attempts at codification failed, not only because of the differences in the schools of Islamic jurisprudence and their identification with particular reigning caliphs, but more so because the entire notion of legislation was repugnant to Muslim opinion. Legislation was considered the divine prerogative of God, whose law was already revealed for all time in the Holy Qoran. All that the imam or caliph has in the Islamic order are "organizational" powers (tanzimat) in matters not dealt with in the revealed law. To this day Saudi Arabian legislation is designated *nizam* (ordinance) and not *qanun* (law) in deference to the Sharia revealed law.

Being the first major codification of Islamic law, the Majallat deserves some comment. It restated the rules of transactions or mu'amalat according to the Hanafi school of Islamic jurisprudence, roughly corresponding to a civil code with its combined rules of contracts and torts. Following an introductory part made up of one hundred Islamic legal maxims of general application, the substantive rules of the Majallat were arranged in sixteen books each dealing with a separate segment of the rules of transactions: sales, hire/lease, suretyship, transfer of debt, pledge, safekeeping, gift, wrongful taking and destruction, interdiction compulsion and preemption, joint ownership partnership and servitudes, agency, compromise and release in bankruptcy, admission, adjudication, evidence and oath, judges.

But the Majallat was not so much a reform of the rules of transactions as their reformulation, to make them more intelligible and accessible. In their report to the High Porte,[7] the members of the committee charged with the task of compiling the Majallat, cited the deficient state of Islamic law and the difficulty of reconciling the obscure and scattered Islamic rules of transactions with the modern provisions of the commercial code as justification for the Majallat. The expansion of trade had necessitated the adoption of the French inspired commercial code. But it remained incomplete without a modern civil code to deal with matters not covered by the commercial code, such as transfer of debt, agency, pledge, guarantee, bankruptcy. Without a civil code these matters would have had to be governed by the unorganized and inaccessible Islamic law rules of transactions. The difficulty was compounded by the judicial duality between the commercial courts and the Sharia tribunals. The former were not qualified to delve into Islamic law and the latter had no jurisdiction over commercial code matters. You could imagine the conflict and confusion which would ensue if the commercial courts had to deal with the commercial law elements and the Sharia tribunals with the Islamic law aspects of the same case.

Thus the Majallat would suffer from some of the same defects which generally afflicted Islamic law in the view of those Arab reformers who in later years would decide to discard both the Majallat and the rules of Islamic law in favor of modern European civil codes. It lacked the general principles on the basis of which the specific rules of contracts, torts and other obligations would be construed. It perpetuated the concept of the divine source of the law and its immutability by defining its contents as the "record of the practical issues found in (Islamic) Sharia," a definition which made it practically impossible for man-made laws to alter or amend any of its provisions. Instead, specific statutes would be enacted to supplement or improve upon the Majallat, implicitly abrogating or contradicting in the process many of its provisions.[8]

The Majallat continued to constitute the law of transactions in Lebanon until 1934, when the Code of Contracts and Obligations, a replica of the Code Napoleon replaced it, and in Syria until 1949, in Iraq until 1951 and in Jordan until 1976 when it was replaced by civil codes patterned after the Egyptian code of 1949, itself an improved version of the earlier code based on the French code Napoleon.

The Arab States of the Nile Valley

The Ottoman reforms were not unknown to the Arab states in Africa which were also part of the Ottoman Empire until the European powers began to carve out a presence for themselves there about the time the Ottoman reforms began to be introduced. But the existence historically of indigenous, autonomous ruling authority in some of these states, coupled with direct European influence on the ground, in the form both of political representation and legal institutiions, brought about new and distinguishing elements in the reform of their legal systems.

Egypt.

If there is a name and an event which stand out as creator and catalyst of Egypt's 19th century legal reforms, it is Muhammad Ali who became governor in 1805, and the Mixed Courts which were establish in 1876.

A Macedonian Turk who was sent at the head of Ottoman forces to defend Egypt against the French, Muhammad Ali (1805-1848) succeeded in becoming governor of Egypt with considerable autonomy from his bosses in Constantinople. He lost no time in building a strong local army and an effective administration which practically brought Egypt out from under Ottoman influence.

Following classical Islamic practice, the Ottoman government used to delegate a judicial official to the territories who in turn appointed assistants as local qadis in the different provinces. Besides displacing Egypt's Shafi'i school of Islamic jurisprudence by the Hanafi school, the Ottoman judicial appointments in Egypt became no different from most other government positions--an office offered in return for money or favor to the detriment of the prestige of the judiciary[9]

Muhammad Ali reversed this trend by an extensive program of administrative, judicial and legislative reforms. He divided the country into seven diwans or councils charged with administrative and judicial tasks, and proceeded to legislate laws and regulations to modernize and vitalize the various social and economic sectors, such as the long neglected peasantry who constituted the backbone of the country. He established the judicial councils, a sort of administrative tribunals and commercial courts applying the French inspired Ottoman Commercial Code. But their competence would soon extend to civil and criminal matters side by side with Sharia courts whose jurisdiction would begin to diminish correspondingly.[10]

The other legacy of Ottoman rule which needed to be overcome before a modern Egyptian legal system would emerge, was the regime of the Capitulations: the concessions granted by the High Porte to the European powers to protect and adjudicate among their own nationals in the Ottoman Empire by applying the extra-territorial jurisdiction of consular tribunals. The origin of the Capitulations dates back to the 16th century and the treaty of 1535 between King Francis the First and Sultan Suleiman the Magnificent. Other treaties followed with the other European powers granting them similar concessions as those obtained by France. By the 19th century, no less than fifteen foreign consular tribunals existed in Egypt with competence in all matters pertaining to their own nationals and in cases involving foreigners and Egyptians.

Taking into account the different local courts with their often overlapping competencies, the existence of these consular tribunals only added to the multiplicity and confusion which characterized the administration of justice in Egypt at the beginning of the last quarter of the 19th century. At this point Nubar Pasha, the grand vezier of the Khedive Ismail (1862-79) convinced the European Powers to settle for a single judicial institution with mixed Egyptian and European judges, and with competence over foreigners in civil and criminal matters and over civil matters between foreigners and Egyptians. From their founding in 1876, the Mixed Courts became the dominating judicial institution of the country.[12]

The founding of the Mixed Courts, which will have a significant impact on the legal reforms in Egypt, came at a time when Egypt was riding the wave of economic and literary revival which began with Muhammad Ali and continued under his successors. The Suez Canal was opened, trade flourished, education expanded, but with it came direct British intervention in 1882 till 1936.

Britain's occupation of Egypt was ostensibly motivated by the need to protect its route to India and safeguard its investments in the Suez Canal and the cotton trade. More important however was Britain's desire to keep France, which had already installed itself in Algeria, from extending its hegemony to the rest of North Africa. Ironically however it will not be British but French influence which would leave its indelible mark on the Egyptian legal system.

The establishment of the Mixed Courts called for a set of corresponding legislation which Egypt was required by the Courts' charter to provide:

> "The new Courts, in the exercise of their jurisdiction in civil and commercial causes, and within the limits of the jurisdiction conferred upon them in criminal matters, shall apply the codes presented by Egypt to the Powers, and in case of silence, insufficiency and obscurity of the law, the judge shall follow the principles of natural law and equity."[13]

That is how Egypt became the recipient of the first civil code based on its French counterpart. Very little is known about the circumstances in which the code was prepared and promulgated, except that it was drafted by a French attorney in Alexandria by the name of Manoury. Maitre Manoury was first recruited by Nubar Pasha as his aide and then as Secretary General of the international commission which studied and approved Nubar Pasha's proposal for the Mixed Courts. Manoury succeeded in putting together a code made up mostly of provisions taken from the code Napoleon with some entries from the 1866 Italian code and Islamic law. The original text was in French and then translated into Arabic by a committee of Egyptian jurists. Other codes were adopted between 1876 and 1883 in the commercial, maritime, penal and procedural fields, most of them patterned after the Ottoman codes which in turn drew mostly on their French counterparts.

A similar set of codes as those presented to the Mixed Courts would be adopted for application in the Egyptian national courts established in 1883.

Modeled after the Mixed Courts, with similar set of initial and appeal jurisdictions, these national courts were dubbed *nizamiyah* or *ahliya*, to distinguish them from the *Shar'iyah* or Islamic religious courts, whose competence was considerably reduced and restricted to matters of personal status and domestic relations of Muslims only. Other religious communities, specifically the various Christian denominations and the Jewish sects, would maintain their own ecclesiastical tribunals with similar competence over their own members.

Notwithstanding this emergent duality in the private law field between domestic relations and civil transactions, which would remain intact to this day both in Egypt and the other Arab states,[14] the legal system of Egypt assumed in 1883 some of the basic characteristics and modern concepts of legality and due process found in the European civil law system at the time. While the Capitulations provided the direct catalyst for the introduction of these changes, their survival to this day provides yet another example in history, from the reception of Roman law by the Germanic tribes in Europe to the reception of European law by Japan, of the successful borrowing of foreign law even where the social and economic circumstances of the recipient are different from those of the donor.[15]

Two things however remained to be done to bring the modernization process in Egypt to where it stands today: the abolition of the Mixed Courts and the reformulation of the old codes to render them more compatible with the situation in independent Egypt.

The abolition of the Mixed Courts became bound up with the Egyptian movement for independence from Britain in the 1930's. As Egypt's quest for independence began to bear fruit in 1936, the treaty of Montreaux was concluded the following year between it and the European and other Powers,[16] to regulate the demise of the regime of Capitulations which, according to the treaty, was "no longer in harmony with the new situation" in Egypt. Consequently, the treaty provided for the abolition of the Mixed Courts on October 14, 1949. After that, all cases pending before the Mixed Court were to be remitted at the stage which they had then reached to the National Courts.[17]

The post-independence period following the end of world war II would witness a second, more meaningful phase in legal reform to deepen and expand what had been achieved until then. Particular effort would be directed towards the revision of the civil code, whose deficiencies and defects were detailed by the author of the revised code, Egyptian jurist al-Sanhuri, in justifying the revisions he introduced to the old code,[18] as will be detailed in a later Part of this book. The other code which received special attention was the penal code, whose early Ottoman version tried unsuccessfully to combine French and Islamic criminal law principles. It was superseded by a new code drawing on Italian, Belgian, Anglo-Indian, as well as French criminal law and procedure.

But the mould of modernization had been cast by the 19th century reforms and there will be no turning back. What will follow would simply be the domestication or Egyptianization of the borrowed law through almost a century of interpretation and application by the Egyptian courts under local social and economic circumstances. As the codification movement in Europe has shown, the nationalization of law and the promulgation of national codes were essential components of the new legal order of the territorial states and were relentlessly carried along by the economic, social and intellectual currents generated by the Enlightenment.[19]

Sudan.

While the French civil law system entrenched itself in Egypt, the Sudan became the recipient of the common law system. Not unlike the situation in Egypt at the dawn of the modern period, Sudan's legal tapestry under the joint Ottoman-Egyptian administration (1820-1884) was a mosaic of Islamic, Turkish, Egyptian and customary laws. But the reforms this administration began to introduce along Egyptian lines brought about a reaction from the Mahdiya Islamic reform movement, which like the Wahhabi movement of Arabia and the Sanussi in Libya at about the same time, sought a revival of the Islamic Community on puritanical lines. Without understanding the cultural and economic processes involved, points out Islamic historian Hodgson, these movements rejected violently the Muslim upper-class accommodation with the imperial West as a betrayal of Islam.[20]

But the Mahdiya movement's bid to revert to Islamic rule, which would recur time and again in Sudan's modern history, would prove largely ineffective and short-lived. Since the rules of the Qoran and the Sunna, the two main sources of Islamic law, did not comprehend all the problems and issues faced by a highly diverse Sudanese society, the law became increasingly the Mahdi's word. He became also the supreme head of the judicial structure with the appointment of local judges delegated to the governors of provinces and districts.[21]

But the Mahdi's rule succeeded in bringing about an end to the Ottoman-Egyptian administration of the country and precipitated Britain's direct involvement in the affairs of Sudan when it moved in 1899 to suppress the Mahdiya movement. From that point on, the law in Sudan would come increasingly under British influence. The Anglo-Egyptian condominium which replaced the former Ottoman-Egyptian administration set up a new system of government headed by a British Governor-General whose policy was to bring the administration of law in Sudan into harmony with the generally recognized principles of civil justice.[22]

In doing this he would rely on the provisions of the Condominium Agreement which not only gave him the power to make, alter or abrogate existing laws and ordinances, but more significantly for the course of legal reform, to deny any Egyptian law or Ministerial decree enacted by Egypt after 1884, the year Egyptian administration of Sudan ceased following the Mahdiya uprising, from applying to Sudan, except where he by Proclamation decided otherwise. This meant that not only Egyptian legislation but the regime of the Capitulations and its Mixed Courts as well would be kept out.

The way was now open for the application of English common law principles and procedures. And as in the case of Maitre Manoury in Egypt, the first Governor-General of Sudan, Lord Kitchener, would appoint an Englishman by the name of Edgar Bonham-Carter as his Legal Secretary to draft new statutes and organize the courts. In setting the procedure for settling civil disputes in the Civil Justice Ordinance of 1900,[23] he would also lay down a principle of jurisprudence which would become the vehicle for the introduction of English common law.

As the Ordinance would have it, any question in a civil action regarding succession, inheritance, wills, legacies, gifts, marriage, divorce, family relations or the establishment of *waqfs*, shall be decided by:

(a) any custom applicable to the parties which is not contrary to justice, equity and good conscience, and has not been altered or abolished by law,

(b) Islamic law where the parties are of the Muslim faith, and the law or custom of the parties who are of the non-Muslim faith.

(c) in cases not provided for in the above section or in any other law, "the Court shall act according to justice, equity and good conscience."

In the absence of any civil laws to speak of, this last phrase was tantamount to opening the way for English legal principles. What facilitated this development even further was the fact that the Sudanese courts were manned by British and British-trained Sudanese judges who would have anyway invoked justice, equity and good conscience, in the common law tradition.[24] It was nevertheless still necessary for the emergent legal system to reorganize the courts and the administration of justice and to enact new codes where English statutes did not apply.

In addition to the Civil Justice Ordinance which set up the procedure for settling civil disputes, a Mohammedan Law Courts Ordinance (1902) defined the structure and jurisdiction of Islamic Sharia courts. In the substantive law field, the most prominent legislation about that time were the Penal Code and the Code of Penal Procedure of 1899, which drew on existing Indian, other British colonial ordinances.

As was the case with most of the newly emergent states in the 19th and 20th centuries, the choice for Sudan was not between developing its own indigenous law or borrowing foreign law. The former simply did not exist except as scattered tenets of Islamic law mixed with local customary and tribal practices. And by the time it achieved its independence in 1956, Sudan's legal system was dominated by three strains of law: the common law in the civil and criminal fields, Islamic law in domestic relations and customary practices in the outlying areas of the country.[25]

The Maghreb States of North Africa

In Algeria, Morocco and Tunisia, the French connection was very real. As the colonial power in Algeria, and the protectorate power in Morocco and Tunisia, France determined the direction of law reform there in the 19th and 20th centuries. Once the exclusive preserve of Islamic law according to the Maliki school as well as the local tribal and customary law, these North African countries were shepherded or coerced as the case may have been to adopt much of the legal system and laws of the dominant power.

As was the case with the Arab countries to the East, the reception of French law by these North African states was preceded since the 17th century by a motley of European jurisdictions under the Capitualtions regime. It will therefore be left for France to negotiate an end to these jurisdictions in return for its commitment to admit before the French courts it would establish in the North African states the laws of the Powers concerned.[26]

But the legal reform emanating from French intervention would take a greatly different course in Algeria from that in Morocco and Tunisia. In the latter, the Moroccan sultan and the Tunisian bey survived as symbols of national unity and sovereignty, and, in dealing only with them through a Resident General, the French helped in perpetuating this symbol. In the case of Algeria, whose Northern districts became part of Metropolitan France, French rule was more direct and more radical; assisted as it were by the presence of a large number of settlers, the colons, with their unswerving allegiance to France.

It was only a matter of time when the French would begin to assert control over Islamic authorities and courts by integrating them as much as possible within the French administration. Their first attempt was to institute appeals, where none existed before, from the *Sharia* courts to the higher council or *majlis* of Islamic scholars or *ulema*, only to discard this procedure in the 1860's and direct the appeals instead to the French courts of first instance. In the *Kabyle* regions where Berber customary law applied, French *juges de paix* were installed and their decisions were appealed to the same courts of first instance.

The French judicial reforms in Algeria were driven by both a policy of assimilation and a passion for systematization and rationalization. Integrating the Islamic courts and the tribal councils into the French judicial system, gave the French courts at the appellate stage considerable powers to review questions of Islamic law and apply as they saw fit extraneous principles of equity, justice and natural law. This gave rise, according to Schacht, to an Islamic case law particular to Algeria, known as *droit musulman algerien*, reminiscent of the Anglo-Muhammedan law in British India.[27]

The imposition of French law was naturally more direct and pronounced in those areas of legal relations and transactions which were outside the jurisdiction of Islamic courts. All French legislation existing at the time the Algerian provinces were annexed in the 1830's became automatically applicable there. The case for local law was not helped at all by the lack of any clear comprehensive codification of Islamic law rules readily ascertainable and applicable by the courts. Ironically, it would be the French who would initiate such a codification, and without much enthusiasm from Muslim qadis who saw in it a French design to tamper with the divine law.[28] The code was nevertheless drafted by Marcel Morand, a professor of law at the University of Algiers Law School, and a specialist in the Maliki school of Islamic law. But the *avant-projet de code du droit musulman algerien* which was for years in the making was never enacted into law.

Except for matters of personal status and domestic relations which remained within the purview of traditional Islamic law, French legal influence in Tunisia and Morocco was no less pervasive for being more politic. The 1883 and 1912 treaties establishing the French protectorate over the two states gave France the right to introduce the necessary judicial reforms while preserving the traditional status of the Muslim religious authorities. This is how the mandate given to France by the Moroccan treaty read:

> The Government of the French Republic has agreed with His Majesty the Sultan on the establishment in Morocco of a new order which would bring about the administrative, judicial, educational, economic, fiscal and military reforms the French Government considers useful to introduce in Morocco.
>
> This order shall however preserve the religious status quo, the respect for, and the traditional position of, the sultan, the exercise of the Muslim faith and Islamic institutions.[29]

But although France had the lion's share of influence in Morocco, parts of the country were under Spanish control. This meant that a parallel agreement to the above mentioned treaty would be concluded in 1912 between France and Spain in which France sees to it that Spain is granted concessions similar to those it obtained from the sultan of Morocco and ensures at the same time that Spain respects the treaties France concluded with the other Powers concerning the rights of foreigners in Morocco.

For instance, article 24 of this French-Spanish agreement gave either party the right to set up in their respective zones of influence such judicial institutions as their own laws provide. Thereupon both parties undertake to subject their nationals and persons under their protection residing in their respective zones to the courts of either party in those zones.

In a series of decrees (*dhahir*) the sultan of Morocco would formally enact the various laws which put into effect what these treaties with France and Spain and between them provided. This included the organization of the courts in the French and Spanish zones and the laws applicable in each. As a result a dichotomy would emerge not only between the judicial systems of the two zones, but also between the French and Spanish courts and laws on the one hand and Islamic and tribal jurisdictions on the other.

The traditional Islamic courts and tribal and administrative tribunals continued to have jurisdiction in matters of personal status and domestic relations, inheritance, civil disputes, and unrecorded real property governed by Islamic Maliki rules and customary usage. In Morocco, Islamic courts which applied a 17th century compilation of Islamic and customary rulings on a wide variety of issues known as *'amal* (short for *bi ma yajri bihi al-'amal*, that is, according to practice), helped them to hold on much longer to their competence beyond the area of personal status and domestic relations.

But the competence of the local courts would begin to recede when the introduction of modern French law, such as the 1912 Commercial Code, would dispel much of the uncertainty caused by the uncodified Islamic rules and customary usage, and render civil and commercial disputes more readily justifiable before French courts. In time therefore these courts would coopt a growing segment of civil suits, commercial activity and recorded property rights, as well as the affairs of foreign nationals.

In Tunisia this development was speeded up by the resort to administrative tribunals and the early adoption of a modern code of contracts and obligations. Work on this code began as early as 1899 when Italian jurist and specialist in Islamic law, David Santillana, produced the first draft of a civil and commercial code for a French-Tunisian Law Commission. This draft would eventually become the Tunisian Code of Contracts and Obligations of 1906, and in 1913 would be adopted by Morocco.

Following the protocol called for in the Moroccan-French protectorate agreement, the code had to be first enacted by the sultan of Morocco, after which the French Resident General would present it to the French Government for its promulgation as well. In their submission of the code to the French President, the French Ministers of Justice and Foreign Affairs advised the President that the code should be acceptable to both the Europeans and the Muslims. The former would find that its provisions were to a great extent adapted from their national laws, while the Muslims would find nothing in it which would hurt their religious feelings since it contained nothing which was contrary to Islamic *Sharia.*

In fact the code combined certain elements of Islamic law with provisions from the code Napoleon and other European codes, particularly the German code. Before its enactment it received the approval of a number of Sharia court judges and scholars from the Zaytuna University, the leading Islamic university of Tunisia. In the view of a French observer of the North African legal scene, the matrix of the Santillana code is more European than French. It contains a scholarly amalgam of diverse European systems and the Malikite rules of Islamic jurisprudence with a dash of Hanifite rules; an exceptional procedure which led to a rare phenomenon in the reception of foreign law.[30]

But the order issued by the Bey of Tunisia on December 15, 1906, enacting the code into law, would not allude in any way to its ideological make-up:

> "From the servant of the Almighty God, on whom we depend and whose lead we follow in all our affairs, Abdu Mohammad al-Nasir, Pasha Bey of the Tunisian Kingdom, may the Almighty God guide his handiwork and grant him his wishes;
>
> To all those private and public persons who are responsible to this our Order;
> Having regard to the need to codify the rules and practices pertaining to obligations and contracts; and having regard to what our Grand Minister has submitted to us; We have issued our Order as follows:
>
> Article 1. The texts presented hereafter and pertaining to obligations and contracts have been compiled in one collection under the title the Tunisian Code of Obligations and Contracts.
>
> Article 2. The Code is made up of two books, the first covers articles 1 to 717 dealing with obligations, and the second covers articles 718 to 1632 dealing with contracts and quasi contracts.
>
> Article 3. This Code shall take effect and its rules become applicable in our Tunisian courts as of the first of June 1907 with no retroactive effect."

[Non-retroactivity is of particular significance here because of the shift in the law from the old Islamic rules to the provisions of the new code.]

So long as the French Court of Cassation had the final say on the interpretation of the new code by the local Tunisian and Moroccan courts, the code was seen as a mere reflection of its French counterpart. Even with the independence of the local judiciary after the end of the French protectorate, the code continued to rely in its application on French opinion and scholarly writings. As will be discussed more fully in a subsequent part of the book, this has prompted legal scholars in recent times to call for a "new reading" of the code in the light of changing local needs and circumstances after more than seventy years since its enactment.[31]

In the case of Morocco, where a Spanish zone coexisted with the French, a second code of obligations and contracts would be enacted along the Spanish civil code. Like the French inspired code, it would exclude any matters dealing with domestic relations, inheritance, and property rights, matters which were left to the personal law of both Europeans and Muslims. But the Spanish inspired code introduced certain rules which jurists had espoused in more recent European codes, particularly those of Germany and Switzerland. It incorporated also certain rules of Islamic law, such as those pertaining to sales, loan of non-fungible things, lease, and the prohibition of interest payments considered usury in Islam.[32]

Several other codes would be enacted, in both the French and Spanish zones, including the law of judicial organization--the structure and competence of the French and Spanish courts in civil, commercial and criminal matters. Upon independence the judiciary was unified and brought under Moroccan aegis by decree of January 26, 1965. Some of the substantive laws introduced during the French protectorate have either been replaced by new legislation or are slated for revision. Both the Commercial Code and the Civil Code have survived as originally adopted during the French protectorate. But as we shall see in a subsequent part of the book, there are active considerations for revising these two major pieces of borrowed law even though their basic principles would in all probability be maintained.

A similar transition from French to national courts took place in Tunisia following its independence from France in 1957. New substantive laws were also introduced including a penal and a commercial code. In Algeria which obtained its independence later than Morocco and Tunisia, the judicial system was unified in 1965, and new substantive and procedural laws were also introduced. In all three North African countries domestic relations of their Muslim citizens are today regulated by new Codes of Personal Status adopted since their independence as will be discussed in more detail in the part of the book dealing with Family Law.

The Arabian Peninsula (Saudi Arabia, Yemen & the Gulf States)

The Ottoman reforms which initiated the legal modernization in other Arab provinces of the Ottoman Empire had only a foot hold in the Hijaz, the Western part of present day Saudi Arabia. It was therefore inevitable for the founder of the Saudi state, King Abdul-Aziz, who was determined to create a modern society to find himself in conflict with the *ulem*a, the religious scholars of the puritanical Wahhabi sect with whom he was affiliated. This came about early in his reign over their attempt to ban the few Ottoman inspired regulations which Abdel-Aziz espoused.

Among these regulations was the 1927/1931 Commercial Court Regulation, which besides providing for the establishment of a commercial tribunal outside the purview of the Sharia courts, regulated land and maritime commerce, bills of exchange and bankruptcy as well as elements of a company, agency and arbitration law. Fearing however that the civil tribunal would only reduce their traditional jurisdiction, the Sharia judges blocked the establishment of the tribunal and left the Commercial Court Regulation in abeyance.

Meanwhile Abdel-Aziz turned to the reform of the judiciary whose diversity extended from the rudimentary tribal trials in parts of *Najd* to the fairly advanced administration of justice in *Hijaz* and the ubiquitous Sharia courts in between. He sought also to liberalize and codify the sources of Sharia law by recognizing as equally valid the four main schools of Islamic jurisprudence, rather than the Hanbali alone, the school of the dominant Wahhabi sect. In one of his earliest decrees, Abdel-Aziz ordered Sharia judges "not to be bound by the rules of one school of jurisprudence to the exclusion of all others, even where this would constitute a violation of the rights of a party who expects the decision to be made in accordance with the school of his affiliation," provided that this did not result in one school's ruling abrogating another's. And where the majority opinion does not prevail in the court, the case will be referred to the Judicial Supervisory Commission whose decision "shall bind the Commission itself and all other courts in future (similar) cases."[33]

The *ulema*, religious scholars, however would not countenance the admissibility of other schools of jurisprudence, let alone the introduction of the concept of precedent novel to Islamic law nor the codification of Sharia. They prevailed on the Judicial Commission to issue its directive to all Sharia judges in the Kingdom to adhere to the Hanbali school except where in the judge's opinion the application of the Hanbali rules would result in undue hardship to the party concerned or would be detrimental to the public interest.

By the 1960's however it became abundantly clear that the traditional Sharia law and courts were utterly inadequate for conducting the massive development of the country which was totally dependent on foreign know-how and technology. It required modern regulations and adjudication of business enterprises and commercial relations; a fact realized by every development plan since 1970. They provided for legal reform and improvement of the administration of justice, but not at the cost of the Sharia which would continue to be observed and safeguarded.

The result was that a great deal of legislative adroitness, resort to gaps, exemption clauses and manipulation of terminology went into the adoption of modern statutes in order that the Sharia rules remain inviolable. An example of this doctoring of the law came in 1963 with the adoption of the 1930 Geneva Uniform Law of Bills of Exchange as the Saudi Commercial Paper Regulation.

Provisions in the Geneva text dealing with interest, which Islamic law prohibits as usury, was either left out of the Saudi text or ordered to be disregarded if it appeared in a bill. A similar problem arose when the authorities sought to impose a modern graduated tax system. It met with opposition and was discarded at least for Saudi nationals for being incompatible with the rudimentary Islamic fiscal system of *zakat*, which corresponds to the medieval Christian tithe, except that *zakat* is assessed at 2.5 percent rather than a tenth which is the case with the tithe.

Nevertheless Saudi Arabia proceeded to expand its statutory enactments in practically every business and commercial field, from agency to banking to company regulations, labor and social security, combat of commercial fraud, customs, trade marks and maritime regulations. This necessitated the creation at the same time of civil tribunals to deal with infractions under these regulations which the Sharia courts applying Islamic law were ill-equipped to handle. Some of these tribunals were no more than ministerial committees of an administrative nature for reconciling differences, others such as the Commission for the Resolution of Commercial Disputes and most recently the Board of Grievance are more judicious in their handling of claims against the government.

This is not to say that the Sharia courts were neglected; far from it since these courts are the courts of general jurisdiction dealing with anything from personal status and domestic relations to crime and commerce, except where specifically excluded by regulation granting a civil tribunal competence in the matter in dispute. Following on Abdel-Aziz's initial reforms, the Saudi authorities introduced important administrative and procedural changes in the Sharia court system culminating in the 1975 Judicature Act, which compares favorably with its counterpart in the more advanced of the Arab states.

But the dichotomy in the law and in the administration of justice in Saudi Arabia between Islamic and civil is far greater than anything found in the other Arab states, a situation made even more legitimate and lasting by the provisions of the recent Basic Law, the first constitution of the Kingdom, as is more fully explained in the part of the book dealing with constitutionalism.

Having missed much of the 19th century Ottoman reforms and escaped the post world war I British influence in the rest of the Gulf region, Saudi Arabia's approach to law reform has been cautious and piecemeal, the product of conflicting priorities. On the one hand there is the oil revenue fueled drive for modernization and development, and, on the other, the perceived need to preserve traditional social values and religious mores. It is a situation fraught with both present instability and future uncertainty as far as the law is concerned so long as the immutable revealed text of the Sharia holds veto power over man's right to legislate.[34]

Yemen

Legal development in Yemen had a more checkered history than most other Arab states. Already in the heyday of the Islamic Empire in the reign of the Abbasid Caliph al-Ma'mun, Yemen was able in 821 AD to secede and declared its political independence, assisted as it were by its forbidding topography and strong tribal allegiances. Jurisdictionally, the country would fall into a diversity of conflicting Islamic, customary and tribal rules. The coming in the 16th century of Ottoman rule with its own official Hanifite school of jurisprudence would only add to the complexity of the situation. But this first Ottoman occupation which lasted for only 70 years was triggered by the Portuguese naval expansion into the Red and Arabian seas and took place long before the inception of the tanzimat, the 19th century Ottoman administrative reforms. It will therefore not be until the second occupation of Yemen in 1879 that the Ottomans would introduce their legal and administrative reforms which only added to the diversity and dichotomy in the already fractured legal system of Yemen.

Some contemporary students of the modernization process in Yemen consider this period the start of the on again off again conflict in Yemen between modern legislation and Islamic law, when many Yemenis felt that the Ottoman laws were an affront to the sanctity of Islamic Sharia, a feeling promoted in no small measure by the verbal opposition mounted against the Ottoman reforms by the ulema, the religious scholars, for their own political purposes.[35]

It was only natural therefore that the end of Ottoman rule in 1918 would see the return to the Islamic juridical order. This came about at the heels of the departing Ottomans when Imam Yahya succeeded in subduing the various contending tribes and extending his authority throughout the land. He lost no time in abolishing all Ottoman legislation and judicial administration and in directing the courts to abide instead by the Zaydi, Shiite jurisprudence.[36] In order to bolster his return to Islamic law, the Imam then turned to codifying the rules of Zaydi jurisprudence which, like the jurisprudence of other Islamic schools, was until then the subject of scattered and uncomprehensive commentaries. These efforts remained however inconclusive. While the commission charged with compiling these rules completed its work in 1952, the compilation was never formally published or adopted.[37] By then the country was already seething with discontent against the rule of the successor to Imam Yahya, Imam Ahmad, whose regime would be toppled in 1962 by the incipient forces of modernization and reform.

It took ten more years for the republican regime to consolidate its power and begin to institute the desired changes in the legal order. These changes, which would ultimately mean reconstituting the entire state structure, included the adoption of a modern constitution declaring the autonomy and independence of the judiciary, the establishment of a ministry of justice, and the appointment of a commission for the codification of Islamic law. The latter which would materialize in 1979 in the adoption of what was labeled the civil code of Yemen, a far cry from a modern Arab civil code, showed however that the forces of tradition were still alive and well entrenched.

These forces put up their strongest opposition to the changes the new regime introduced in the administration of justice. First came the Judicature Act of 1976 organizing the judiciary. Then came the 1977 Attorney General law separating for the first time the office of prosecutor from that of the judge, and the enactment in 1976 and 1978 of civil and criminal procedure codes drawing in the main on Egyptian law. The purpose of all this legislation was to deal with the endemic weaknesses of the judiciary in Yemen, a left over from the Islamic administration of justice in the age of decadence which lacked not only guarantees of autonomy and fairness but precise, written and uniform rules of procedure as well. Objections of traditionalist jurists forced the government to rewrite these laws.

As is the case in Saudi Arabia, the challenge to legal reform in Yemen has been the need to assimilate the old and the new into a vibrant legal system which would take cognizance of the economic and social development of Yemeni society. Once again we see a piecemeal approach to law reform, introducing the new without abrogating the old and creating in the process a dichotomy in the legal order which retrenches rather than resolves social conflicts and economic uncertainties.

Kuwait, Bahrain, Oman, Qatar, United Arab Emirates

These former territories of the Ottoman Empire were for 150 years prior to their independence under British control. Although "protected" territories of the British Crown, Britain enjoyed considerable extra-territorial jurisdiction over them exercised by virtue of Orders-in-Council. Consequently there were two systems of jurisdictions running in parallel with a certain amount of overlap between them: the jurisdiction of the British Crown, and the jurisdiction of the local ruler whose courts whether the traditional Sharia applying Islamic law, including the Ottoman Mejella, or the civil applying Indian colonial and English common law statutes.[39]

Kuwait was the first and so far the most advanced in the reforms these Gulf states rushed to introduce upon the demise of British rule. In anticipation of its independence in 1961, it invited the renowned Egyptian jurist and author of the Egyptian civil code, Abdel-Razzaq al-Sanhuri, to draft a series of codes, including a civil and a commercial code. A kind of commercial code was first enacted in 1961 to take up some of the rules of obligations regulated until then by the Ottoman Mejella. This was replaced by a true Commercial Code when the

Civil Code based on the Egyptian and Iraqi codes was adopted in 1980. The explanatory memorandum of the Code described the relationship between the new Commercial Code and the Civil Code as the relationship between a special law and a general law which must be referred to for the general principles of obligations when needed to complement the specific Commercial Code.

Kuwait also set up with the help of al-Sanhuri a national court system complete with a court of cassation and a constitutional one at the top of the judicial ladder with modern civil and criminal procedure laws. The traditional Sharia tribunals are today a matter of the past, even in matters of personal status and domestic relations. Both the burgeoning oil industry and the influx of Egyptian lawyers and jurists helped advance the process of reform. But it was the commitment of the Kuwaitis to the cause of modernization which guaranteed its success.

In Bahrain, Oman, Qatar, United Arab Emirates, reforms were neither as speedy nor as comprehensive. With the British legal legacy more deeply entrenched, the wholesale introduction of continental type codes and civil law judicial system into these Gulf states, proved more tedious and tardy. In Bahrain for example the situation resembled that of Palestine during the British mandate from 1918 to 1948 with a mix of local and British common law statutes such as Commercial Companies, Agencies, Labor, Patents and Trademarks, Civil Wrongs and Maritime laws.

Oman, on the other hand, remained closed to legal reform, relying more on traditional Islamic law and Sharia Courts, until 1970 when new legislation was enacted in the commerce and investment fields. A major codification in the continental tradition came in 1991 with the adoption of the Commercial Code patterned after its Kuwaiti counterpart. It encompasses a great many activities governed by earlier piecemeal legislation. But both Oman and Qatar remain very much a mix of Sharia and civil jurisdictions, resembling Saudi Arabia. A major codification in Qatar is the Civil and Commercial Code patterned after the 1961 Kuwaiti Commercial Code to compliment the Ottoman Mejella which was never formally abrogated. A modern court system, however, has been set up with new civil and criminal procedure, but the traditional Sharia courts continue to function with an indefinite jurisdiction which in addition to domestic relations sometimes hear criminal and morality cases subject to Islamic law.

The United Arab Emirates, formerly known as the Trucial Coast, have since their independence in 1971 been constituted as a federated state of seven sheikhdoms with considerable local autonomy. Despite the novelty of their state structure in the Arab World, the Emirates have developed an impressive record of legal modernization--constitutional, commercial, criminal, as well as judicial. A Commercial and a Civil Code were adopted in 1984 and 1985 modeled after the Kuwaiti codes. As far as the administration of justice is concerned, coordination between the local and federal courts was enhanced by the 1978 Federal Union Courts Law which transferred to the federal courts the local jurisdictions of most sheikhdom courts, and in 1992 federal criminal and civil procedural laws became applicable. At the top of the judicial establishment is a Union Supreme Court which acts both as a Court of Cassation and a Constitutional Court with competence to decide disputes between the sheikhdoms and between them and the Emirates state, interpret the Constitution and rule on the constitutionality of legislation at the sheikhdom and the Emirates levels.

While the more developed Arab states of the Mediterranean littoral have been nurturing a new legal tradition since the mid 19th century, the Gulf states have belatedly become virtual laboratories for the evolution of their laws. The reception of Roman law went on in Europe from the 11th to the 18th century during which time considerable adjustment had to be made to account for legal borrowing from a society with different social and economic conditions. Legal institutions are after all societal institutions.[40] The reform of the law in the Gulf states came rather suddenly and in response to the discovery and exploitation of petroleum resources which brought about an influx of foreign enterprises, expansion of economic activity internally and the countries' thrust into the world of trade and finance externally.

Guided by expatriate Arab jurists trained in the civil law systems of their own countries, the direction of legal modernization in the Gulf states is decidedly towards codification and administrative regulation, rather than the more flexible, case by case, approach of the common law system. The latter, one would like to think, is closer to the informal, conciliatory approach of tribal and Sharia adjudication both of which are very much in the tradition of the Gulf societies.

This is not to say that the borrowed legal institutions have displaced the old societal values. The lack of genuine synthesis between Islamic law rules and modern legislation constitutes an actual source of conflict no matter how much the Governments justify the legislation as being in conformity with the Sharia or declare their adherence to the old values. Notwithstanding their conformity with the new laws, controversy abounds over Western forms of banking and investments, interest payments and dividends, life and other forms of insurance, future contracts and risk taking, taxation, on the ground that they are prohibited by the revealed text.

In the face of such challenges, the Gulf states, including Saudi Arabia, formed in 1981 the Gulf Cooperation Council (GCC). "Aware of their mutual bonds of special relations, common characteristics and similar systems founded on the Creed of Islam, and the common destiny that links their peoples," they declared in their charter their desire "to effect coordination, integration and interconnection between them in all fields." Among these fields is legislation and administrative affairs, including the formulation of "similar regulations," according to article 4 of the Charter.[41] Attempts to unify their laws are still in the preparatory stage at the Secretariat of the GCC.

ENDNOTES

1. Marshall G.S. Hodgson, *The Venture of Islam*, Chicago (1958/1977) vol.3, p.231-232.
2. Abdel Ghani Sani, *Al-Khilafa wa Sultat al-Umma* [Arabic translation of the 1923 fetwa issued by the Muslim ulema in Turkey] Cairo (1924)
3. See Niyazi Berkes, *The Development of Secularism in Turkey*, Montreal (1964).
4. Article 1, Law No.431. Text in Arnold Toynbee, ed., *Survey of International Relations,* vol.I (1925), *The Islamic World*, p.525
5. Muhammad al-Khudari, *Tarikh al-Tashri' al-Islami* [History of Islamic Law] Cairo (1925/1985) p.266-267
6. John Henry Merryman, *The Civil Law Tradition*, Stanford (1969/ 1985) p.7
7. Introductory Report, *Al-Majallat* [Arabic version] Constantinople, (1297 AH. 1879 AD), p.1
8. See Tariq Ziyadeh, *Dirasat fil fiqh wal Qanun* [Arabic] Studies in Law and Jurisprudence, Beirut (1990). See also Subhi al-Mahmasani, *Falsafat al-Tashri' fil Islam* [The Philosophy of Islamic Law], Beirut.
9. Muhammad Nur Farhat, *Al-Qada' al-Misri Qabl Insha' al-Mahakim al-Ahliya* [Egyptian Administration of Justice Prior to the Establishment of National Courts], Cairo, p.85
10. See Farhat J. Ziadeh, *Lawyers the Rule of Law & Liberalism in Modern Egypt*, Stanford (1968) at p.10-15
11. Nouradounghian, *Actes Internationaux de L'Empire Ottoman* vol.I
12. See Jasper Yeates Brinton, *The Mixed Courts of Egypt*, New Haven & London, rev. ed. (1968). In the appendices to his book, judge Brinton has the texts of the 1875 charter of the Mixed Courts as well as the convention which

formed part of the 1937 Montreaux Treaty on the end of the capitulations and the dismantling of the Mixed Courts of Egypt with effect from October 14, 1949.

13. Charter, Title I, Article 34.
14. Although Egypt abolished in 1956 the religious tribunals of both the Muslim and non-Muslim communities, their jurisdiction in matters of personal status and domestic relations was simply transferred to the national civil courts which will apply the same religious laws previously applied by the religious tribunals. See George N. Sfeir, "The Abolition of Confessional Jurisdiction in Egypt: The Non-Muslim Courts," *Middle East J.* vol.10, No.3 (Summer 1956), p.248-256.
15. Alan Watson, "Legal Transplants and Law Reform," 92 *Law Q. Rev.* (Jan. 1976) p.79-84.
16. Text of Montreaux treaty in Brinton, *Mixed Courts*, op.cit.
17. See Anton Sfeir, *Majmu'at al-Qawanin wal Lawa'ih al-Tashri'iya* [Compendium of New Laws and Regulations] 1940/41, vol.I p.198, vol.2 p.183, for the series of laws extending the jurisdiction of the Egyptian courts to all matters previously handled by the Mixed Courts.
18. Abdel-Razzaq al-Sanhuri, *Al-Wasit fi Sharh al-Qanun al Madani al-Jadid* [The Intermediate in Explaining the New Civil Code] Cairo (1952)
19. See R.C. Van Caenegem, *An Historical Introduction to Private Law*, Cambridge (1992) p.125f. As an example, he points out that the promulgation of the national code in France was at the expense both of the cosmopolitan ius commune and of particular local customs.
20. Hodgson, *Venture of Islam*, op.cit. vol.3 p.247-248
21. Zaki Mustafa, *The Common Law in the Sudan*, Oxford (1971) p.38-41
22. Egon Guttmann, "The Reception of the Common Law in the Sudan," 6 *Int'l & Comp. L.Q.* (July 1957) 401 at 403, citing Cromer's Memorandum accompanying the draft Anglo-Egyptian treaty.
23. Text in *Laws of Sudan*, vol. 10, Title xxvi, sub title 1.

24. Mustafa, *The Common Law in Sudan*, op.cit. p.55.
25. Abdalla Ahmad al-Na'im, *Al-Qanun al-Jina'i al-Sudani* [The Criminal Law of Sudan], Umm Durman 1986, p. 11-13.
26. For example, the German-French Treaty of 1911.
27. Joseph Schacht, *An Introduction to Islamic law*, Oxford (1964/ 1984) p.97-99.
28. Allan Christelow, *Muslim Law Courts and the French Colonial State in* a, Princeton (1985) p.254.
29. Article 1, French-Moroccan Protectorate Treaty of 1912.
30. Joel Moneger, "Biographie du code des obligations et contracts: De la reception a l'assimilation d'un code etranger dans l'ordre juridique marocain," *Al-Majallat al-Maghribiya Li Qanun wa Iqtisad al-Tanmiya* [Revue Marocaine de Droit et D'Economie du Development] No.7 (1984) 16 at p.29.
31. See Ahmad Khasmlishi, "Kayf Taqra' Dhahir al-Iltizamat wal 'Uqud," [How to Read the Code of Obligations and Contracts], *al-Majallat al-Maghribiya li Qanun wa Iqtisad al-Tanmiya*, No. 7 (1984) p.7-40.
32. E. Mora Regil and Rodriquez Aguilar, *Report to the Spanish Foreign Minister on the Proposed Moroccan Laws, vol.1 Basic Laws,* [Arabic translation, Maitre Musa Abboud], p.42-67.
33. *Umm al-Qura* [Saudi Arabia's official gazette] No.141 dated 28 Safar 1346/26 August 1927.
34. See George N. Sfeir, "The Saudi Approach to Law Reform," 36 *Am. J. of Comp. Law* (Fall, 1988) 729.
35. Rashad Muhammad 'Ulaymi, *Al-Taqlid wal Hadatha: Al-Nizam al-Qanuni al-Yamani* [Tradition and Modernity: The Yemeni Legal Order], Cairo & Beirut (1988).
36. Unlike the Orthodox Sunni schools of law, the Zaydi Shiite jurisprudence draws on the doctrines of the Mu'tazilites, an Islamic theological school of the 8th century which espoused reason in theological controversies and have been compared to the medieval Christian scholastics in Europe. See 'Isam Muhammad Abdul Ghanem, "The Development of the Hidawi Doctrine: The

Neo-Rationalists of the Zaydi school since 1948 and the Current Role of 'Ilm al-Kalam (or Scholasticism) in Yemeni Courts, Part I," 3 *Arab Law Q.* (November 1988) 329.

37. 'Ulaymi, *Al-Taqlid wal-Hadatha*, op.cit. p.129.
38. Unlike other Arab civil codes which declare the supremacy of the legislative text, the Yemeni code subjects the purport of its provisions to the Sharia. Article 1 states: "This law which is derived from the rules of the Islamic Sharia shall apply to all transactions and issues which are expressly or intently dealt with in its provisions. In the absence of an applicable text, reference shall be made to the principles of Islamic Sharia which is the source of this code; and if none are applicable, the judge shall rule according to custom consistent with Sharia; and if none are applicable then in accordance with the principles of justice which conform to the entire sources of Islamic Sharia."
39. For a series of articles and reports on the state of the law in the Gulf states concurrent with the end of British rule and the beginning of independence, see W.M. Ballantyne, *Legal Development in Arabia*, London (1980).
40. "Legal institutions are societal institutions; the detailed rules derive from societal values; even the elements of the trial process and the ways of creating law will stem from societal facts," Alan Watson, *The Evolution of Law*, Baltimore (1985), p.69.
41. English text of the GCC Charter in John A. Sandwick, ed. *The Gulf Cooperation Council: Modernization and Stability in an Interdependent World*, Boulder (1987) p.217.

CHAPTER TWO

Personal Status and Domestic Relations

This is an area of the law in which the process of modernization has had the least effect. Known as the Institution of Personal Status, or *Ahwal Shakhsiya*, it comprises all matters dealing with the consummation, birth, paternity, custody, age, and support of the child, as well as marital relations--marriage, divorce, alimony, marital property and inheritance. Furthermore, being essentially religious in its conception, it is an area of the law where Islamic law applies to Muslims and canon law applies to Christians and Talmudic law applies to Jews, the social consequence of which is a communitarianism of a divisive nature in the legal system.

The Institution of Personal Status has its roots in the ascendancy of Islam in the Middle East and North Africa. In a universal, historical sense, however, communal exclusivity has also been a function of the geographical spread of a new dominant state with its own institutions. Toynbee points to the striking similarity in this regard between the spread of Roman and Islamic laws. Roman law was a privilege of Roman citizenship, until the edict of Caracalla conferred citizenship on all the Empire and with it the privilege of being the subject of Roman law. Likewise, the spread of Islamic law with its principle of personal law went in tandem with the conversion of the non-Muslim subjects of the conquered territories.[1] Those who did not convert were left to their own personal laws.

Considered at first *dhimmis*, that is people protected by covenant granted by the early Caliphs, Christian and Jewish communities would later assume, in the multi-racial and confessional Ottoman state the status of autonomous administrative units known as *millet*. Left to administer their own internal affairs, no less than fifteen *millets* gained formal recognition from the High Porte, including Orthodox, Monophysite, Catholic, Eastern Catholic or Uniate churches, the Jewish community, and from 1850, the Protestant church. The logical outcome of this policy would lead in time to the recognition of the Sunni Muslim majority as a separate *millet* with the establishment of the Office of *Shaykh-al-Islam* in Constantinople as head of the Islamic *millet*, just as the Patriarchs or the Chief Rabbi were the heads of the non-Muslim *millets*.

Today, the rights and privileges of these religious communities are guaranteed by the constitutions and the pertinent laws of the various territorial states in which they exist, their legislative and judicial autonomy however somewhat curtailed. While the non-Muslim communities continue to enjoy independence in legislating their own family laws and need only notify the state of any new legislation, the laws of the Muslim community, to which the overwhelming majority of Arabs belong, were caught up in the codification drive of the Ottoman and subsequently of the independent Arab states.

It all began in 1917 when the Islamic rules of personal status and domestic relations were first codified in the Ottoman Law of Family Rights and continued to apply in a number of Arab states until the 1950's long after the break up of the Ottoman Empire. Today almost every Arab state has its own code: the Jordanian Law of Family Rights 1951, the Personal Status Law of Syria 1953, of Tunisia 1956, of Morocco 1958, of Iraq 1959, the Yemeni Family Law 1978, the Kuwaiti and Algerian Personal Status Laws of 1984 and the Sudanese of 1992.

Egypt which began as early as 1920 to introduce legislation in this field and updated it subsequently, an attempt in 1980 by the government to introduce a comprehensive new code of Family law more favorable to women was short lived. No sooner was the law adopted however than it was abrogated under pressure from clerical circles. But it was in Egypt, a country with a diversity of religious communities, Christian and Jewish, that the traditional autonomy of ecclesiastical tribunals was first challenged. A 1956 law abolished outright all these tribunals,

Muslim and non-Muslim, and had their jurisdiction transferred to the national civil courts which continue however to apply the same religious laws their predecessors applied.[2]

It was a development not dissimilar from that which took place in Europe following the Reformation when canon law was gradually brought under state regulation, depriving the Church of its monopoly over matrimonial causes, without however introducing much change in the substance of the law. Unlike the situation in the Arab states however, in recognizing the civil nature of the contract of marriage, European law laid the ground for the incorporation of marriage, divorce, and the entire spectrum of marital relations into the civil code.[3] In the Arab states, on the other hand, marriage which in Islam is ironically a civil contract devoid of the sacramental element it enjoys in Christianity, the institution failed to find a place for it in the civil code as is more fully explained in Chapter III.

Still, the movement for codification in the Arab states did achieve the consolidation and systematization of the disparate traditional rules of domestic relations found scattered in the works of the classical sources of Islamic law, particularly those belonging to the *Hanafi, Shafi'i* and *Maliki* schools of jurisprudence, and the *Zayidi* in Yemen. Two early compilations helped in this effort, that of the 1917 Ottoman Law of Family Rights already mentioned, and the earlier codification by Egyptian jurist Muhammad Qadri, *Al-Ahkam Al-Shar'iya.* Being of divine origin however, family law reform was by necessity limited and eclectic with legislators forced to resort to certain expediencies to bring about even the limited changes they introduced, or hide behind procedural and administrative devices to frustrate an undesirable rule, such as child-marriage and limit the husband's unilateral repudiation of marriage.[4]

The Christian Communities

The ancient canon laws of the Eastern Christian communities have also become available in modern compilations, albeit without great change in the traditional rules or the historic diversity between the churches. With the exception of the Protestant (Evangelical) Church, a recent transplant from the West, and the Maronite Church which has maintained its autonomy and unity since its founding in the sixth century, the present split in the Christian community of the East into various churches goes back to the Council of Chalcedon in the fifth century and its controversial decisions on the monophysite nature of Christ and the canonical rules it adopted. Today these Churches comprise the Antioch Patriarchate of the Syrian Orthodox Church, the Jerusalem Patriarchate of the Greek Orthodox Church, the Armenian Orthodox (Gregorian) Church, the Alexandria Patriarchate of the Coptic Church, the Chaldean Orthodox Church, an offshoot of the Assyrian (Nestorian) Church, and the Melkite community, so nicknamed with the Syriac word *malki* for royalists because of their support for the Byzantine Emperors. A further split in the Eastern Churches took place more recently, beginning in the 16th century when groups of their adherents decided for doctrinal and security reasons to unite with Rome and recognize the spiritual authority of the Roman Pontiff. Those left behind constitute today the Orthodox branch of the same Churches, while those in communion with Rome became known as the Uniate Eastern (Catholic) Churches.

The canons of the Eastern Churches follow to this day their separate historic codes which evolved in the first centuries of the Christian era and codified in the twelfth and thirteenth centuries. The code of the Syriac Church, for example, is based on the work of the 13th century Catholicus *Ibn al-'Ibri* or Bar-Hebraeus, as he is known in the West, now in a 1929 edition; that of the Antioch Orthodox Patriarchate in a 1952 edition; that of the Coptic Orthodox Church in a 1938 edition; and that of the Protestant (Evangelical) Church in a 1949 edition.

In the case of the Eastern Catholic communities, while the Roman Curia has exercised the same firm spiritual and disciplinary authority over them as it exercises over the Latin or Western Catholic Churches, the *Codex Iuris Canonici* which was promulgated by the Vatican in 1917, did not apply to the Eastern (Uniate) Churches. Each of these Churches continued to apply its own historic canon law as that of their Orthodox counterparts, until 1929 when Pope Pius XI established a Pontifical Commission for drafting a common Code of Eastern Canon Law applicable to all the Uniate Churches in the East. Following several texts and revisions, the final draft of the Code was submitted to the Pope and was promulgated on October 18, 1990.[5]

While the Code is based on Eastern legal sources and tradition and recognizes the Eastern Churches as *sui juris* and self-governing, it emphasizes the ecumenical unity of the Catholic Church and those Churches in communion with it under the primacy of the Roman Pontiff. Thus the encroachment on the autonomy of the Christian communities in communion with Rome, came not from the state, as was the case with the Muslim communities, but from the Vatican. It was a reversal of fortunes for the Maronite, Melkite, Syriac, Coptic, and Armenian Eastern Catholic churches whose traditional canons were formulated in the past individually by their own synods of bishops. Furthermore, it was a development which gave credence to the objections of the proponents of a civil law of domestic relations and the apprehensions of the non-Catholic and Muslim communities that the Uniate Churches are beholden to foreign ecclesiastical authorities. The Vatican's reasoning for assuming the power of legislator and judge of last resort over these Churches, a power traditionally exercised by their synods, is purely pragmatic: "The centralization and usurpation of exclusive legislative power by the popes was generally beneficial," the argument goes, adding that when the Code in future will require additions and corrections, "[it] can be [more] easily carried out when everything is in the sole hand of the pope or his curial officials."[6]

The Islamic Codes of Personal Status

In the case of the Muslim communities who constitute the overwhelming majority in all Arab states, with the exception of Lebanon, the secular legislators did no better in relating the new codes to the modern conditions of their societies or in addressing the core issues of nuptial relations which needed to be addressed;

in particular the freedom of marriage, mixed (inter-faith) marriages, polygamy, and the repudiation of the marriage (*talaq*) by the husband. Even where some reforms purported to deal with one or the other of these issues, they were either couched in vague language or contrived religious arguments which emptied them of their desired intent.

Thus, the Tunisian prohibition of polygamy was justified not on the ground of modern social values or the constitutional equality of men and women, rather on a new reading, attributed to the *ulema*, the religious scholars, of the Qoranic text, whose "misreading" in the past is made responsible for the practice of polygamy. Here's what the Explanatory Memorandum of the 1956 Tunisian Code of Personal Status said at the time:

> "We obtained the opinion of certain Islamic *ulema* on the subject of polygamy and its prohibition which they had reached in their interpretation of the Qoranic verse on the subject, and the impossibility for [men] to be just in the full sense [of the term] exactly as God had intended it [when He said] 'Ye shall be unable to be just among women even if ye wanted to be."

Still, the Tunisian legislator had the courage to prohibit polygamy outright under penalty of law. The most that other Arab legislators were able to do was to introduce procedural hurdles to polygamy. In Iraq and Syria a judge has the power to withhold permission for more than one wife unless the man can show legitimate cause and financial ability, while in Jordan and Morocco the wife may stipulate against it in the marriage contract, and in Egypt it is incumbent upon the man to declare in the marriage document what his social status is and whether he is already married to another woman.

With regard to the woman's freedom to marry, the Moroccan Government, responding to protestations from women groups, introduced in 1993 amendments to the Code of Personal Status which purported to do away with the power of the guardian, who is usually the closest or eldest male member of the family, to interfere with the right of the woman to marry whom she pleased. The new language of the code describes guardianship as "the woman's right" and that marriage will not be concluded "without her consent." But it still maintains in article 12 that "the woman may not [herself] initiate the [marriage] contract, but shall delegate to her guardian [the right] to conclude the contract for her."

In the Eastern Arab states, a formerly married woman and one who has attained the age of 25 is allowed to enter into a marriage contract on her own, or as the Kuwaiti code states in article 30, has "freedom of choice in her marriage." A woman who has not been formerly married and one who is under the age of 25, on the other hand, cannot marry on her own, but must be betrothed by her guardian.

Thus, the guardian or *waliy* as he is known in Arabic, a symbol of the traditional inferiority of the woman to man, and a product of a bygone era, remains very much present and alive in the Arab codes, the use in the Moroccan and other Arab codes of such phrases as "the guardian may not force the woman to marry," and "the guardian may not contract the woman's marriage except by delegation from her," notwithstanding. Even those codes which expressly provide against compulsion in marriage, whether from kin or stranger, or categorically state that compulsion will vitiate the marriage, as the Iraqi code does, the guardian continues to figure in the marriage ceremony.

In other respects the failure of the modern codifications to address the core issues of nuptial relations was due to the blind adherence to traditional rules without any rational reason for maintaining them under changed social conditions. A striking example of that is the continued role given to the mahr or *sadaq*, which is the dower paid by the husband. Whether its value is nominate, *musamma*, or indeterminate and considered reasonable in the particular situation of the spouses, *al-mithl*, and whether payable immediately or subsequently, its effect on the validity of the marriage contract is not that clear. Neither the Syrian (article 12), nor the Jordanian (article 16) codes include dower among the "conditions" of a valid marriage; while the Algerian (article 9), the Moroccan (article 5), and the Tunisian (article 12) do. In one way or another, dower figures in all the Arab codes, more as a carry over from earlier times than a reasoned expression of its purpose.

With its origin lost in antiquity, the dower was still common in medieval times among the Arabian tribes as it was among the Germanic tribes in Europe. That which began as "purchase price" for the woman, given to her guardian in marriage, took the form of a "bridal gift" or *sadaq* after the coming of Islam: "And give them, whom ye have enjoyed, their reward as a wedding gift." Still, the prevailing opinion among classical scholars was that dower is an element in the conclusion of the marriage contract, no matter how trifle its value may be.[7]

But this seemingly innocuous "bridal gift" has become in practice the subject of complex, often contradictory, regulations, not all of which are complementary to the woman. The dower is said to become due and payable to the wife only after "*dukhul*" or copulation with her husband, as the Algerian (article 16) and the Moroccan (article 20) codes provide; or the husband may not require his wife to have sex with him until he had paid her the dower as the Tunisian (article 13) code provides. Other codes make the payment of the dower due and payable upon divorce only if copulation had taken place and the divorce was not the fault of the wife.

Dower is a good example of the carry over of traditional rules prevalent under different social conditions without first subjecting them to a reasoned analysis of their function or purpose: Is the dower a consideration for the marriage contract and hence an element in its validity, or a mere bridal gift voluntarily given in anticipation of the marriage? In a modern codification should not the more appropriate rule of Islamic jurisprudence for today's social conditions govern?

The Hanafi school of jurisprudence considers a contract of marriage valid whether it stipulates a dower or not. The Maliki school, on the other hand, takes the contrary view and regards the marriage contract which does not stipulate a dower or stipulates that there will be no dower, as invalid. But then the Moroccan code which is based on the Maliki school describes the dower in article 16 as "the amount of money a husband proffers as an indication of his desideratum to get married..."

The imprecise language in the codes led one Algerian scholar to observe that the phrase "paid to the wife" in article 14 of the Algerian code may be interpreted to mean to the woman whom the man plans to marry, that is his betrothed (which he believes to be what the Algerian legislator had in mind), or to the woman who had actually become his wife, in which case the dower is a consequence of, and not a condition for, the marriage contract.[8]

These uncertainties about the dower are symptomatic of a greater confusion in the Arab codes about the nature of the institution of marriage itself: what constitutes wedlock, what is the object of conjugal relations, and what role, if any, does the presence of a cleric during, or the subsequent certification or recording of, the marriage play? As far as the bond of wedlock is concerned, Islamic law conceives of marriage as nothing more than a contract between a man and a woman, a conception not different from that in Christianity prior to its elevation in the 16th century by the Council of Trent from a revocable contract under Roman law to a sacrament of the Church, requiring for its celebration the presence of a priest.

The classical definition of marriage as contract in Islam can still be found in the Algerian (article 4), the Jordanian (article 2), and the Syrian (article 1) codes: "Marriage is a contract concluded legitimately between a man and a woman." The Tunisian code, on the other hand, does not define marriage, while the Moroccan goes far beyond the act of bonding to describe its purpose. Stripped of its modern administrative requirements of recording and certification by a cleric, marriage in the Arab laws is still a contract whose elements are variously listed as an offer and acceptance of a clear and present expression of marriage, made by the husband or his proxy, to an eligible woman, and the presence of witnesses, guardian, dower, certification by a cleric, and recordation in civil status register. But it is highly doubtful that failure to abide by the administrative requirements of recording or certification, or the presence of the guardian, or even mention of the dower, would constitute ground for invalidating an otherwise legitimate, publicized, marriage contract.

As a matter of fact the Arab codes provide for various stages of validity in a marriage with varying legal consequences for each. This is clearly described in the Kuwaiti code (articles 46-51). The *sahih nafidh* marriage is valid and legally effective in respect of all its consequences. The *sahih ghayr-nafidh* marriage is one that is valid but not legally effective until such time as it is approved and consummated. However while approval renders it legally effective *ab initio*, from the date of marriage, consummation will only bring it to the same status as a consummated voidable or *fasid* marriage. The *fasid* or voidable marriage has no legal consequences to it unless it has been consummated. And finally, *batil* is an invalid marriage, lacking in any legal consequences. What makes marriage invalid? One which is defective in form or in the capacity of the parties, such as the wife belonging to one of the categories of prohibited relations, or is a divorcee who has not completed her waiting period, or is not a member of the heavenly faiths, Islam, Christianity and Judaism, and the marriage of a Muslim person to an apostate from Islam, or one between a Muslim woman and a non-Muslim man.

It is however in the nature of the spousal relationship, the true measure of modernization in the institution of marriage, that the Arab codes have lagged. This is not to say that the European family law was more forthcoming in this regard; but when it did finally come in the 1970's it created a clear ground for comparison with Arab laws. The French and German codes now speak, for example, of a "community of life" to which the spouses are mutually bound in order that they may together assure the "moral and material direction of the family." This finally moved the law away from the old assumptions about marriage and introduced in its place the notions of autonomy and equality to marital relations; a culmination to a historic movement towards "individualistic, egalitarian, and secularizing trend" that has been gaining strength since the 18th century.[9]

The closest that an Arab legislation has come to this notion of marital relation is the Tunisian code whose amended article 23 introduced for the first time to the Arab legal terminology of domestic relations the concepts of mutuality and cooperation in spousal relations and obligations: "Spouses shall cooperate in the running of the affairs of the family and the upbringing of the children," and while the cost of maintaining the family falls primarily on the husband, "in his capacity as the head of the family," the wife is also required to contribute to this cost "if she has the means to do so." Still, this mutuality and cooperation in spousal obligations introduced into the Tunisian code in 1990, is not absolute, but "shall be undertaken in accordance with custom and tradition."

And yet it is this custom and tradition which has safeguarded until quite recently in Arab and European society, the unchallenged male dominance as an aspect of the *patria potestas* which goes back to antiquity.[10] When it came to marriage, the husband's dominance was symbolized by the proprietary transfer in the wedding ceremony; either the payment of the dower to the wife's *paterfamilias* as compensation for her loss as was the case with the Arab and Germanic tribes, or the transference of her property to the husband as was the case in Italy as late as the Middle Ages, and by the concurrent removal of the woman from the legal control of her father, from his *patria postestas* and placing her under the legal control of her husband.[11] The oft quoted Prophetic saying in Islam, *"Al-Rijal qawwamun 'ala nisa'ihim"* [The men are the custodians or guardians of their women] reflected therefore the tradition of the times and was by no means particular to Islam.

These uncertainties in the state of the law of domestic relations are further aggravated by two other failures of the process of codification and modernization in this area of the law. The first is that the positive legislation constituting the code of personal status in any one particular Arab state falls far short of being the comprehensive body of rules of Islamic family law. The latter remain ensconced in the body of the Sharia developed by the various schools of jurisprudence in the classical era of Islamic law. It is therefore imperative upon jurists, whether of the Bench or of the Bar, to delve into these antiquated sources to interpret or complement the text of the positive law; a procedure bound to encourage reliance on the past and on rulings made to suit social and economic conditions far removed from conditions prevailing today.

The other is the failure of the new legislation to unify the rules of domestic relations and achieve equality and uniformity before the law. Instead, the traditional communal particularism and diversity is maintained in the codes of personal status, whose application is consequently cause for jurisdictional conflicts among members of the same society belonging to different religious communities or to the various schools of jurisprudence among the Muslim community, as will be more fully discussed later in this chapter..

While practically all Arab constitutions guarantee freedom of belief and the exercise of religious rites for all citizens, as well as their equality before the law, not all constitutions endorse the institutions of personal status, even where it has traditionally continued to exist. There is no reference to it in the Egyptian constitution of 1971, nor Iraq's of 1970, nor Syria's of 1973, nor of course in any of the North African Maghrib states, or in the Saudi Basic Law where no indigenous non-Muslim community actually exists.

It is only in the Lebanese and the Jordanian constitutions that we find a direct reference to separate judicial rights for religious communities. The Lebanese Constitution has the most explicit statement on the subject. Article 9 provides that the State "shall guarantee for all citizens, whatever their religious convictions, respect for the institution of personal status and religious interests."

This constitutional provision is further amplified by Decree 60/LR of 1936, which lists the communities with recognized personal status rights. They include among Christians the following communities: Maronite, Greek Orthodox, Melkite, Armenian Gregorian, Armenian Catholic, Syriac Orthodox, Syriac Catholic, Assyrian Chaldean (Nestorian), Chaldean, Latin or Roman Catholic, Coptic, and Evangelical Protestant. Of the Muslim communities, the decree lists the Sunni, Shi'ite (Ja'fari), Alouite, Ismailite, and Druze; and of the Jewish congregations, those of the Aleppo, Damascus, and Beirut Temples. The absence of other religious faiths is not limited to Lebanon. In all the Arab States, not only does the religiously based institution of personal status not comprise a faith other than Islam, Christianity, and Judaism, it denies validity to civil or any other marriages performed locally outside the prerogative of the ecclesiastical authorities.

In the case of the Jordan, the institution of personal status is dealt with in the part of the Constitution devoted to the judiciary. It provides that Muslim Sharia courts and non-Muslim religious tribunals shall be the competent organs in all matters of domestic relations, and religiously constituted charitable trusts, and succession. As in the case of Lebanon, the Jordanian recognition of the competence of religious communities to handle their own domestic relations is limited to the Muslim community following the Hanafite school of jurisprudence, and to the Greek Orthodox, Greek Catholic, Armenian, Latin or Roman Catholic, and Evangelical or Anglican Christian communities.

A Synopsis of Islamic Family Law

(1)**The Constituent Elements of Marriage**: As has already been pointed out, marriage in Islam is a contract between man and woman concluded by an offer and an acceptance, in the presence of two male witnesses or one man and two women and the promise or payment of a symbolic or significant dower. Basically an informal consensual agreement, something akin to present trends in both civil and common law countries where legal formalities do not exceed the requirements of licensing and registration. While Arab laws do not subscribe to any specific solemnization, or licensing, they do however require registration and in some cases pre-nuptial medical tests.

But this informality in concluding marriage in Islam should in no way be confused with freedom to marry. There has been little recognition in modern Arab legislation of a person's right to marry whom he or she chooses; it perpetuates instead the traditional impediments of Islamic law which go beyond the usual criteria of age and blood relationship found in most other laws. The social and economic changes which in America and Europe have moved the law towards more freedom to marry, have not had the same effect on the Islamic rules of domestic relations.

Before discussing some of the major impediments to the freedom of marriage in Arab law, it is necessary to say a word about the constituent elements of a valid marriage. These comprise the presence of witnesses, role of the guardian (*wali*), of the dower (*mahr* or *sadaq*), and of stipulations in the marriage contract.

The presence of witnesses is an essential condition for the validity of an Islamic marriage; they ensure that the marriage was adequately publicized if it is to avoid the suspicion of an illicit relationship. The number of witnesses required are two competent male men or one man and two women, which is the normal complement of witnesses required to testify in ordinary cases.

The role of the guardian of the bride who traditionally concluded the marriage on her behalf, is retained in a much more restricted fashion in the modern legislation. The woman who has attained the legal age can now obtain the judge's permission to marry against the objections of her guardian, if the judge considers these objections unjustified. Certain laws now require that that the marriage "agent" or guardian act only in accordance with a written mandate. They also distiguish between the roleo the guardian, even if he was the father, in cnsenting to, and between compelling, an of-age woman to marry. The latter is denied him in several states--Algeria, Iraq, Jordan, Syria.

The conflict between the customary and the legal in family law is quite apparent in the anomalous role which continues to be given to the guardian in an Islamic marriage. This is clearly reflected in the Moroccan legislation on the subject. While denying the guardian father the right to force his of-age daughter, even if she were still a virgin to marry, her agreement and consent being required the law goes to say, "save when it is feared that the woman may be corrupted," the judge shall have the right to force her to marry so that she may be placed "in the virtuous custody of a suitable man who would look after her."

The rationale of the Moroccan legislator is well expressed in the

Explanatory Memorandum of the Code of Personal Status: The Moroccan woman, it says, has not yet attained the social standard which would enable her to enjoy such freedom or justify such a radical departure from Islamic custom and propriety.

As has already been alluded to earlier, the role of the dower in the validity of the marriage contract is not quite clear. A gift in money or kind made by the husband to the bride is often justified as proof of the husband's intention to marry and to provide her with security in case of death or divorce. It was a customary practice in pre-Islamic Arabia, which had also found its way into Roman Law in the period from Constantine to Justinian when imperial law came under the influence of Christian and Near Eastern ideas and customs.[12] Its reflection in the Qoran is however ambiguous: "And give unto the women whom you marry, free gift of their marriage portions; but if they of their own accord remit unto you a part thereof, then you are welcome to retrieve it."

It is this type of wording in the revealed law which left some doubt among classical jurists whether the dower was essential for the validity of the marriage contract, or was simply a legal consequence of a valid marriage, subject to intricate rules of what will be due to the woman if the marriage is dissolved before or after it had been consummated and whether the husband has the right to consummate the marriage before paying the dower.

The positive legislation, makes the dower due and payable to the wife upon the conclusion of the marriage contract, whether it was stipulated in the contract or not. Although the legislation does not require the dower to be of any specific amount so long as it is of value, failure to quantify it in the contract would make the husband liable to what is common to the wife's social milieu.

The effect of stipulations in the contract of marriage laying down conditions advantageous to either party is now permissible by law, and will give the aggrieved party the right to sue for divorce if the other spouse fails to live up to the stipulated conditions. But the conditions must not be contrary to the aims of marriage, or contrary to law or jeopardizing the rights of the other party. Under

Jordanian law, for example, such conditions as denying the husband the right to take a second wife or requiring the wife to live where her husband has his place of work, are binding. Even without such stipulations, courts in the more liberal milieus, such as Tunisia and Jordan, have become more inclined to correct the gender imbalance whenever it becomes an issue in marital relations.

(2) **The Impediments to Marriage**: Besides the questions of age and competence, there is considerable literature in Islamic law dealing with the extensive categories of blood, marriage and foster relations which the Qoran has prohibited in marriage. The positive laws of personal status subscribe to these prohibitions without exception.

There are however three impediments to marriage in Islamic law which the positive legislation continues to endorse despite their incongruity in modern times, and their inordinate burden on the woman. These are the waiting period known as *'idda* before a woman, widowed or divorced, may remarry, the limitation on the number of wives a man can have which implies the permissiveness of polygamy, and lastly the issue of mixed marriages between persons of different faiths more restrictive for the woman than for the man.

(a) Both classical Islamic law and modern day statutes require the woman who has been divorced from her husband following the consummation of their marriage, as well as the woman who has been widowed, whether prior or subsequent to the consummation of the marriage, to observe a waiting period, measured by the lapse of three menstrual periods or lunar months in the case of a divorcee, and four months and ten days in the case of a widow, before she could marry again. And if the wife was pregnant at the time of her divorce or the death of her husband, the *'idda* period comes to an end with the termination of her pregnancy.

Ostensibly the purpose for this waiting period is to ascertain whether the wife is pregnant with the child of her former spouse and consequently to determine the paternity of their offspring. It is also said in justifying the *'idda* that it provides an opportunity for the husband to reconsider and take back his divorced wife. However the conjugal relationship cannot be revived after a final divorce before the wife had been through a marriage with another man, and in the case of a revocable divorce, she will have to remain in conjugal limbo until the end of her waiting period when the divorce becomes final. One wonders whether there is need for such a waiting period today when advances in medicine and technology makes it possible to ascertain in no time whether a woman is pregnant or not.

(b) A Muslim man cannot conclude a valid marriage with another woman if he already has four wives, the limit of polygamy in Islam. At variance not only with Christian practice, but with such close faiths to Islam as the Druze and the Alouite, the legal basis of polygamy in Islam is a Qoranic verse which curiously enough begins with the expression of compassion in the treatment of orphans: "And if you fear that you cannot deal fairly with the orphans, marry of the women who please you two or three or four; and if you cannot do justice to all of them, then one..." (Sura 4:3) Reformers say that this verse sought to do away with the multiplicity of wives not to endorse it. They blame the sanction of polygamy and the repudiation of marriage on the formulators of the law in the Abbasid era who deliberately disregarded the emphasis in the Qoran on the need for justice and on the equality of women and men and were instead influenced by the social milieu of the Sassanids whose practices the Abbasid caliphs adopted.[13]

Today polygamy is fast becoming outmoded if not illegal in Muslim society. While both economic conditions and cultural perceptions are lending a hand in its demise, the law as usual has lagged behind. The only Arab legislation which prohibits polygamy outright is the 1956 Tunisian Code of Personal Status; others only try to make its occurrence less facile. The Ottoman Law of Family Rights of 1917 permitted a woman to stipulate in the contract of marriage against her husband taking a co-wife, which would give her the right to divorce him if he did. A similar provision is also found in the Syrian law, which also provides that a judge may not permit the husband to take a second wife if he is not in position to support them both. The Iraqi Law of Personal Status of 1959 gives a judge similar powers under more stringent conditions of support, just treatment and legitimate cause, and a penalty of one year in prison and one hundred dinars fine in the event of default.

Other laws which are not as categorical, such as those of Jordan, Egypt and Morocco, provide nevertheless that the wife may stipulate in the marriage contract against the husband taking a second wife, the husband disclose any marital relationship he may have before concluding a marriage, or the wife seek relief from the courts for any injury the second marriage may have caused her.

(c) Lastly, there is the impediment against certain mixed marriages which is becoming increasingly onerous to Muslims in present day society, where interaction with other peoples of other religious persuasions has become common place, even a necessity.

The Qoran sanctions the marriage of a Muslim man to a woman belonging to one of the two other heavenly religions, that is Judaism and Christianity. "This day all good things are made lawful for you. The food of those who have received the Scripture...and the virtuous women of those who have received the Scripture before you, give them their marriage portion and live with them in honor, not in fornication, nor taking them in secret as concubines." (sura II:5) He is thus prohibited from marrying a woman who is not a believer in Islam or in one of the other scriptural religions, referred to as the People of the Book (*ahl al-kitab*); while a Muslim woman may not marry a non-Muslim man even if he were a member of the scriptural religions, that is a Christian or a Jew. This is attributed to the Qoranic verse which states "Wed not polytheists till they believe... and give not your daughters in marriage to polytheists till they believe..." (sura II:221).

Positive legislation in all the Arab states has perpetuated this prohibition by declaring invalid the marriage of a Muslim woman to a non-Muslim man and denying the wife the benefits which normally accrue to her in a valid marriage, such as dower, alimony, inheritance and paternity for her child from the marriage.

A Muslim is also prohibited from marrying an apostate from Islam (*murtad*) and if the wife in a scriptural couple converts to Islam and her husband refuses to follow suit, their marriage must be terminated, as the Yemeni law unequivocally provides.

The canon laws of Christian communities of the Middle East impose similar impediments to inter-faith marriages on members of their faiths. The Law of the Sacrament of Matrimony of the Eastern Uniate Church "forcefully warns" against the conclusion of a marriage between a Catholic person and another belonging to "a heretical or dissident faction;" and if the marriage poses the risk of loss of faith to either the Catholic party or the children of the marriage, then it should be prohibited "in accordance with the law of God." The law goes on to list a number of conditions under which such a marriage may be permitted: "forced" on the Church for serious cause, the non-Catholic party guaranteed that the spouse remains devout Catholic, and the children baptized and brought up as Catholics.

The canon of the Antioch Patriarchate Orthodox Church which displays greater leniency towards mixed marriages, still requires the non-Orthodox party to abide by the laws and rites to which the Orthodox spouse subscribes.

(3) **Dissolution of Marriage**: Contrary to popular perception, the termination of marriage in Islam is more highly regulated than is its conclusion. This is not to say however that the traditional advantages which men have over women is any less. Positive legislation however has sought to redress the sexual imbalance between them no matter how inadequately and indirectly. The law now requires that divorce even by repudiation must be exercised before a judge who, as in the case of Egypt, is duty bound to try and reconcile between the spouses before pronouncing the marriage dissolved.

From a comparative law perspective then, while Arab law has been seeking recently to restrict the resort to unilateral divorce and encourage reconciliation by the courts, European and American law was in the last two decades been abandoning the restrictive fault divorce in favor of the mutual and unilateral non-fault divorces.

Traditional Islamic law recognizes three main avenues for the dissolution of marriage: the right of the husband to repudiate (*talaq*) the marriage in the privacy of his home or by proxy and even by delegating to his wife the power to divorce herself; divorce by mutual consent (*khul'*), usually initiated by the wife for a consideration she has to pay her husband; and judicial separation (*tafriq*) at the behest of either spouse for cause such as incompatibility, debilitating sickness, desertion, and lack of support.

Positive legislation protects the wife against divorce by repudiation if the husband is mentally deranged, in a state of rage or intoxication, unconscious or terminally ill. It also disallows a contingent pronouncement of repudiation made effective upon the wife doing or refraining from doing something. It also denies the effect of a triple pronouncement of repudiation uttered simultaneously at the same session which traditionally rendered the divorce final and irrevocable (*ba'in*).

Normally, repudiation takes the form of a revocable (*raj'i*) divorce by the pronouncement made once or twice only. Although the rationale given for this form of divorce is to give the man time to reconsider, it leaves the woman in an indeterminate state at the beg and call of her husband. He continues to have the right to cohabit with his wife or to take her back, with or without her consent, provided he does so before she completes her *idda*, or waiting period of three menstrual cycles. In an irrevocable or final repudiation at the end of the waiting period, however, the husband is not permitted to take his wife back unless she married someone else first and is later divorced from him. In either case the woman is not permitted to remarry during this waiting period or *idda.*

The law now requires these unilateral divorces to be formalized before a judge or state official (*ma'zun*) and recorded as all other changes in civil status in the official civil status registers.

The new legislation enables also either spouse to petition the court for judicial divorce on the grounds of physical defect or incurable disease, separation by reason of desertion or imprisonment, and discord in the marital relationship. The Egyptian and Syrian legislation add failure of the husband to provide his wife with proper maintenance, and the Iraqi law permits the wife to petition for divorce if her husband commits adultery or takes a second wife without court permission, while the Arab states of North Africa allow the wife to petition for divorce on the grounds of cruelty and abuse. Before, however, a judge approves the divorce, he must try in person or through arbiters to reconcile between spouses.

The dissolution of the marriage may also be by mutual consent or *khul'*, literally meaning release. It is especially available to the wife to redeem herself from the marriage by making an offer to the husband with consideration which he will accept. The consideration may be anything of value including the deferred amount of the dower or the cost of custody of the marriage child. Unless the offer is withdrawn before the husband had accepted it, the divorce becomes final.

The avenues for the dissolution of marriage available under Arab codes of personal status bear many of the markings which characterized European law in its transition in the last two decades from restrictive fault-based divorce to the liberal mutual consent divorce and divorce sought by one spouse on the ground of irreconcilable differences or breakdown of the marriage whose detractors have described as no more than "divorce by repudiation."[14]

(4) **Establishment of Paternity**: The more intricate rules in Islamic family law are those by which the paternity (*nasab*) of a child are determined. One can only surmise that this is so because of the importance given originally to the subject of lineage in the tribal milieu of Arabia where Islam was born. Its significance in law is that it is the criteria which determines much more than the child's belongingness--his or her legitimacy, upbringing, maintenance, guardianship and inheritance, all of which are associated with the male parent.

There are three ways by which paternity can be established. The first is a valid marriage as prima facie proof of connubial relationship, or in Islamic paternity parlance, *al-firash*, that is, the marriage bed, which Schacht reminds us correspondence to the Roman rule "pater est quem nuptiae demonstrant."[15] This manner of proving paternity entails of course inquiry into the possibility of actual cohabitation, the minimum and maximum periods of possible pregnancy, and the length of time a woman has been divorced or widowed from her husband, in order to ascertain that the child was conceived in a valid or even a voidable marriage contract within the natural limits of pregnancy which according to the Syrian law is a minimum of 180 days and a maximum of 365 or as the law describes it, "solar year," in contra distinction to the lunar year on which the Islamic calendar is based.

Still the law gives the husband the possibility of denying his paternity to a child if he does so immediately upon learning of the child's birth, or accuses his wife of infidelity, before a judge. The latter is a procedure known as *li'an* or imprecation, leading to annulment of the marriage by the court.

Proof of paternity of a child of unknown parentage is also established by acknowledgment on the part of a person whose age and circumstances (such as possibility of having children) makes the claim of paternity credible; whereas a married woman's acknowledgment would require the husband's confirmation or other evidence. Under some of the codes of personal status the acknowledgment may be initiated by the child, provided the child is of unknown parentage and is not born out of wedlock.

The condition that a child be of unknown parents and not the issue of illicit intercourse if he or she is to qualify for an acknowledgment of paternity, stems from the harsh view Islamic law takes of the crime of *zina* that is adultery or any type of sexual relationship a woman has had out of wedlock.

(5) The Problem of Adoption: What makes matters worse for children born out of wedlock is the prohibition of adoption in Islam. Although widespread in Arabia at the coming of Islam, a subsequent verse in the Qoran implores against adoption: "...Nor has He made those whom you claim (to be your sons) your sons...This is but a saying of your mouth. But Allah says the truth..." (sura 33:4) There are those who associate this change of attitude to the Prophet's desire to marry the wife of his adopted son which would not have been possible if adoption were to stand, as alluded to in sura 33, verse 37. Tunisia is the only Arab country which has legalized adoption.

The world's legal systems have been slow to recognize adoption. It was not known to American law before 1850 for fear that it would threaten the security of title to land, violate the rules of inheritance and undermine the Christian canon of marriage and legitimacy. and it came about only as an innovation in family property law. It was left to legislation to overcome these Common Law suspicions, with the first statute coming in 1851 in Massachusetts. In England, the mother of the Common Law it would be much later that the Adoption Act of 1926 would be adopted. In either case, this development would not have been possible without the larger and more fundamental changes which in the meantime had taken place in the status of husbands and wives and of parents and children.[16]

Islamist jurists justify their opposition to adoption on grounds not dissimilar to those which kept the Common Law from accommodating the institution in the past. They describe adoption as a distortion of reality in nature and an affront to the divine order of things. But it is the highly regulated inheritance rules in Islam, rules judged immutable for being divinely revealed, which give opponents of adoption their strongest argument. They consider a person who adopts a child to have "invaded" the proprietary rights of his family and relatives and denied them their rightful share in the inheritance by allowing an adopted child to share in the estate.[17]

Faced by the increasing attention the international community is giving to the problems of orphans and their adoption, the Arab states felt compelled in recent years to promote the concept of *kafala* as the Islamic counterpart to adoption. When the United Nations Convention on the Rights of the Child (1989) sought to have states parties to it uphold the right of a child who is temporarily or permanently deprived of a family environment to foster placement or adoption, the Arab and Muslim states objected to the proposed text and at their insistence the drafting committee added the notion that an abandoned or orphaned child may be taken care of by a person or institution on the strength of a pledge or guarantee, that is *kafala*, given by that person or institution. In its final version the relevant article of the Convention read: "Such care could include, *inter alia*, foster placement, *kafala* of Islamic law, adoption or if necessary placement in suitable institutions for the care of children."[18]

But *kafala*, originates in the law of obligations, both Islamic and civil. Known in French law as *stipulation pour autrui*, it found its way into the Arab civil codes. It permits a person to enter into a contract in which he commits himself to certain undertakings in favor of a third party if he has a material or moral interest in such undertakings. But it does not exactly conform with the Western concept of adoption which conveys on the foster child all rights accruing to a natural child, including family name and inheritance Nor has it been formally endorsed in Arab positive legislation on domestic relations except in the case of Tunisia which also recognizes adoption and Algeria which does not.

The Tunisian code of Personal Status defines *kafala* as a "contract" by which an adult person or a charitable institution "guarantee" a minor child the care and attention it needs. The parties to a *kafala* contract are the prospective guarantor and the parents of the child, if they exist, or the public or charitable institution in whose charge the child happens to be. But the code goes on to provide that child of *kafala* would retain its right to the name and the inheritance of its natural parents, and that the arrangement would terminate upon his attaining the age of maturity.

The prohibition of adoption in Islam is further aggravated in the case of illegitimate children by Islam's denial of legal status for such children or their legitimation by the subsequent marriage of the mother and the putative father. Because of the indelible delict of *zina* (illicit sexual relationship) in Islam, children born out of wedlock are *filius nullius*. Nor did Islam accept the principle of *legitimation per subsequens matrimonium*, a principle of Roman law which has now found its way into the law of most modern states. It remains to this day alien to Arab legal culture.

(6) **Custody and Guardianship**: The protection of a child and its upbringing is extensively covered in Islamic law and modern legislation. The mother has priority for the custody (*hadana*) of her children in the majority of

Arab legislation (Algeria, Jordan, Morocco, Syria, Yemen), whereas the Tunisian code grants the "parents" the custody of their children while the marital relationship persists. In the event the mother is incapacitated or is unavailable, a list of preferred female relatives beginning with the mother's side and moving on to the father's are designated custodians by law. The duration of the custody of a child is not uniform in all the Arab codes of Personal Status. But it is usually later for girls than for boys: 7 and 9 in Syria and Tunisia, 9 and 11 in Jordan, 10 and 12 in Egypt,10 and marrying age in Algeria, 10 in Iraq, and 7 in Yemen for both boys and girls, with the possibility for extending the duration by court order if it is in the interest of the child to do so.

All the codes grant visitation rights to the other parent and place restriction on the right of the mother to remove the child from the matrimonial home to a distant place (other than her own hometown) without the consent of the father. Likewise modern legislation prohibits the father from taking the child away from its guardian mother's hometown without her permission, as the Syrian and Tunisian codes provide.

In principle, the cost of a child's custody is defrayed from its own assets if it has any, such as gifts or inheritance; otherwise it is the father's responsibility. Modern legislation however is sometimes more inclusive, such as the Iraqi and Syrian laws, which hold "whoever is responsible for the support (nafaqa) of the child" is responsible for its custody costs.

Conflicts and Inconsistencies:

Those familiar with the developments in European family law in the past two decades will undoubtedly realize that these developments would not have been possible without the social and economic changes which transformed the traditional patterns of family organization and marital relations. Such changes have obviously not coalesced sufficiently enough in Arab society to bring about similar developments in the Arab law of domestic relations. As societies more experienced with legal reform in this field have learnt, before a country could have the desired reform, attitudes to the institution of marriage and the family must first change.[19]

Beyond this social condition however, Arab legislators face a greater obstacle in the reform of family law which their European counterparts did not face, not in recent history anyway. One could even speak of a dilemma. Arab family law is practically immutable in some of its essential elements being a direct expression of revelation, when in reality it ought to constitute an instrument of social policy and change. By keeping domestic relations outside the purview of the Civil Code, the organic law for all branches of Private Law, Arab legislators simply perpetuated this dilemma. They vested family law with the special, sacral, status it now occupies in the legal system, subject for its reform to the whims and wishes of the clerical interests in society.

When it came to incorporating the rules of personal status and domestic relations in the Civil Code in the 1940's, its author, Egyptian jurist Abdel-Razzaq Al-Sahuri, simply demurred. His explanation at the time was indicative of the emotions which are still associated with religion in the highly sectarian Arab society To try and include in the code a part dealing with family law, as is the case with its European prototypes, he explained, would have saddled the code's drafting committee with "obvious difficulties." Not only were these rules totally based on religious Islamic tenets as were the family laws of the non-Muslim communities based on the tenets of their own religions, there had been no attempt in the past to unify, let alone secularize, these rules. To try and do so in conjunction with the drafting of the Civil Code, Sanhuri went on to say, would have thrown "insurmountable obstacles and confusion into the [drafting] of the code."[20]

The positive legislation of domestic relations we have been reviewing so far is essentially a restatement of the Qoranic rules as formulated by the classical schools of jurisprudence in the 8th and 9th centuries. The result has been the creation of an irreconcilable dichotomy between the medieval, religious rules of family law and the rest of the modern, secular rules of the legal system.

There are to begin with inconsistencies with the constitutional provisions pertaining to the basic freedoms of belief, expression and association. Practically all the Arab states' constitutions uphold these freedoms and declare all citizens equal before the law in their rights and obligations, irrespective of their race, sex, social status or language. Several of them even include religion, as the constitutions of Jordan and Iraq do; while others underscore the social, economic and political rights of women and their equality with men, as is the case with the constitutions of Egypt and Algeria.

These contradictions in the same legal system are due to the fact that the secular and the religious laws do not draw for their legitimacy on the same enabling source; a fact well demonstrated recently by the case of Professor Nasr Hamid Abu Zaid of Egypt. In 1993, a group of fundamentalist lawyers, who thought that Professor Abu Zaid's lectures and writings on the interpretation of the Qoran were so out of line with the traditional Islamic view that they amounted to heresy, petitioned the court to divorce him from his wife, who as a Muslim was prohibited from being married to an apostate from Islam. The court of first instance dismissed the case, citing civil procedure rule that the petitioners had no cause of action, not being a party to the dispute in the case. But the appellate court applying an ancient, little used, Sharia rule, that of *hisba*, whereby any person may take it upon himself to do the work of the State whenever a violation of God's law has occurred, allowed the petition. Furthermore, the appellate court took it upon itself to pass judgment on Abu Zaid's writings and declare them heretical, thereby justifying the ruling that he must be divorced from his wife as the law of personal status clearly provides.

Because of the dichotomy in the legal system, the court was not constrained by the constitutional provisions on freedom of belief, of expression, of association, so long as matters of personal status and domestic relations are the preserve of the religious law. In a unified, secular, legal system things would have certainly been different, given that the Constitution is supreme.

The effect that constitutional provisions could have on the state of family law was well demonstrated in post-war Germany. The 1949 grundgesetz, the Basic Law of the German Federal Republic declares, as does the Egyptian constitution, that "all persons shall be equal before the law; men and women shall have equal rights; and no one may be disadvantaged or favored because of his sex, his parentage, his race, his language, his homeland and origin, his faith, or his religious or political opinions." The 1976 changes in the provisions of the German civil code dealing with marital relations came about when the courts found that these provisions were in conflict with the letter and spirit of the Basic Law. To comply with the court decision, the legislature enacted the Marriage and Divorce Reform Law of that year, to replace the traditional model of "housewife and maintenance" marital relationship by that of marriage as a "partnership of spouses pursuing their chosen occupations and arranging their home life by common accord."[21]

A step away from the traditional communitarian regime was taken in Egypt in 1955 by the abolition of the religious tribunals and the transfer of their jurisdiction to the national civil courts. But law No. 462 of 1955 which brought about the unification of the court system did not unify the rules of domestic relations and comply with the constitutional requirement that all citizens be treated equally before the law. The transfer of the jurisdiction of the religious tribunals to the civil courts changed the venue but not the substantive law in the adjudication of marital controversies. Without a civil law of marriage and divorce available to them, the civil courts were bound, as the 1955 law actually requires to do, to apply the same religious laws previously applied by the religious tribunals, thereby perpetuating the discriminatory treatment of Egyptian citizens in their domestic relations.

This is quite obvious in the law's treatment of change of religion among the parties to the dispute ostensibly to avoid the rigors of their own faith. It states unequivocally that the confessional law of non-Muslim litigants would apply only where both parties belonged to the same recognized religious creed and community. In other words, if the litigants belonged to two different Christian communities or to a non-recognized community, then Islamic law would apply. If in the course of the proceedings one of the parties in the case changes his/her denomination, the choice of law rule in the 1955 law requires the courts to continue to apply the same religious law to the case if the conversion was from one non-Muslim sect to another, whereas the conversion from a non-Muslim sect to Islam would bring about the application of Islamic law, whether the conversion was by one or both litigants in the case.

The Explanatory Memorandum of the law justifies the change of religion provisions by asserting that they only follow the general choice of law rule that change of religion, like change of nationality, "should give the party concerned the right to enjoy all the privileges available to it in the new religion." In saying that the Egyptian legislator was apparently oblivious of the Constitutional provisions on equal treatment and more concerned that the principles of Egypt's ordre public with its Islamic values and morality predominant.

Legal scholar Ahmad Salamah dismisses the reasoning given in the Explanatory Memorandum as unconvincing to the extent that it does not provide the same treatment to change of religion from and to any other faith besides Islam. He believes that the only explanation lies in the legislators' intent to see to it that the law to apply where the parties belong to different faiths would be Islamic law on the ground that it is the general law of domestic relations, whereas the canon laws of non-Muslim communities are particular laws, and that a Muslim in an Islamic state must not be made subjected to a law other than Islamic law.[22]

Professor Salamah goes on to show how the rules on change of religion in the 1955 law contradict also the principles of contractual relations in the Civil Code. Not only because they sanction the detrimental effects visited upon the other party which remained faithful to its religious faith, but also because the law of contracts does not permit a unilateral change in the rights and obligations of the contracting parties originally arrived at by their own free will. He points out however that the courts have rejected these arguments when applied to marital causes, opting instead to apply the provisions of the law even where the change of religion happens to be fraudulent [23]

It ought to be noted here that the 1955 law does not specifically mention change of religion from Islam to another faith. Such a conversion is inconceivable under present conditions in which Islamic law, the law applicable to Muslims in matters of personal status and domestic relations, considers such a change apostasy, notwithstanding the freedom of belief and association provisions of the Constitution.

These constitutional provisions are also controverted by the concept of "recognized religious communities" for purposes of matters of domestic relations and confessional jurisdictions of non-Muslims. This recognition is limited in all the Arab states to the main Christian and Jewish sects, or what became known in Islam as *Ahl al-Kitab*, or Peoples of the Book, that is the scriptural heavenly religions. In the case of Egypt, for example, the 1955 law restricts the application of non-Muslim religious law to litigants who are "united in their denominations" and belonged to a community with "recognized status" at the time the law was adopted. These are the Coptic, Protestant, Catholic, Armenian and Jewish communities.

In Lebanon, where the institution of personal status is more highly developed and the recognized religious communities enjoy greater equality than their counterparts in Egypt, the law does not make the jurisdiction of the religious tribunals conditional upon parity of confessional affiliation between litigants. Instead, Decree LR/60 of 1936 makes the conclusion of the marriage rather than the religious denomination of the litigants the basis for determining jurisdiction. In the words of the decree, "the religious authority competent to consider the validity of the marriage and its effects is the authority before which the marriage was concluded." The decree does not make it clear however whether this rule would still apply if both spouses convert to the same new faith, for example if a Christian couple convert to Islam. But it does provide that in the case of two or more valid marriages, the authority before which the first of these marriages took place will be the competent authority.

Many of these provisions are undoubtedly intended to block prospective litigants from seeking more liberal rules of divorce by converting from a religion strict on divorce, such as Catholicism, to one more lenient, such as Orthodoxy, or to one even more so, such as Islam.

No matter how precise and comprehensive the legislator may be, when applied to actual cases, the laws of personal status and domestic relations could hardly be devoid of awkward consequences, considering the multiple scenarios that are possible among spouses of various faiths. Add to this the element of foreign nationality in matrimonial causes, which in most Arab jurisdictions falls between what the Civil Code provides and what the religious law demands, and the result is a conflict of laws nightmare for which the judiciary is ill prepared. As British jurist F.M. Goadby, who dealt with inter-religious jurisdictions in the 1920's during the British mandate in Palestine has observed, "a court that only administers the lex fori is not suited to deal with cases involving a conflict of law."[24]

The situation is of course aggravated by the absence in the Arab jurisdictions of civil marriage, that is marriage performed outside the authority of one of the recognized religious communities. In Lebanon, for example, a civil marriage performed in Lebanon between Lebanese nationals is invalid; while a civil marriage between Lebanese or between a Lebanese and a foreign national is valid if performed abroad in accordance with the lex loci celebrationis. It is not clear however which court in Lebanon and what law, if any, is applicable to the effects of such a marriage and its dissolution. To say, on the other hand, that issues arising out of a civil marriage are subject to the civil law, would only beg the question. Whatever the provisions dealing with marriage and divorce in the Arab civil codes, they are meant to answer conflict of law questions only. Indeed, Egyptian courts have maintained that the Civil Code is not a law of domestic relations to be applied by either the Islamic Sharia courts or the Christian ecclesiastical tribunals, and that Islamic law is the basic law of Egyptian nationals in matters of personal status and domestic relations where no other law is applicable.

It must be obvious by now that the system of confessional jurisdictions in matters of personal status and domestic relations suffers from serious shortcomings. It had evolved historically under circumstances far removed from those of the modern territorial state; its claim to legitimacy being the divine origin of the law and the traditional autonomy granted to religious communities in the past.

Reformist legal scholars fault the legislative process in the Arab states today which permits clerical interests to impose their will in the enactment of domestic relations laws. In a review of the state of the Moroccan Code of Personal Status on the occasion of the 15th anniversary of its adoption,[25] legal scholars Ahmad al-Khamlishi and Abdel Razzaq Mawlai Irshid, attributed the failure of the code to deal with the three preeminent problems in Muslim matrimonial relations--consent of the woman, polygamy and divorce--to this clerical influence. The legislative process, they pointed out, was dominated by *ulema*, the religious scholars, whose training at the religious university of al-Qairawan was based on curricula dating back to hundreds of years. As such they were not only unaware or unconcerned with the tremendous social changes which had taken place in Moroccan society by the late 1950's when the Code of Personal Status was promulgated, but were also unable or unwilling to entertain the rules of other Islamic schools of jurisprudence which may be more appropriate to modern times than the Maliki school in which they had been immersed all their lives. This focus on rules of family relations which evolved under completely different circumstances brought about the discrepancies that exist today not only between the personal status code and social conditions, but between the code and other legislation which follow modern law principles.

The only serious attempt at doing away completely with the institution of personal status and its concomitant, confessional jurisdictions, took place in Lebanon in 1951. It took the form of a protracted strike by the Beirut Bar Association whose aim was to unify and secularize the laws of domestic relations in Lebanon.

The action by the Beirut Bar, which lasted for more than six months and brought the entire administration of justice in the country to a halt, was not totally devoid of self-serving interest on the part of the lawyers. The system of confessional jurisdictions denied the civil courts and the rest of the administration of justice system of a great number of causes and actions, leaving them in the recesses of the ecclesiastical courts and their clerical coterie. But the strike came to naught because of the fierce opposition put up by the clerical establishment to any change in the status quo. The ecclesiastical authorities of the Christian, Muslim and Druze communities, the three major denominations in the country, held fast to their claim that their traditional judicial privileges and powers were not owed to any lay legislation and cannot therefore be diminished or denied by any civil authority.[26]

This was exactly what the Bar Association objected to. In the words of its Secretary General, Michel 'Aqel, the powers and privileges of the ecclesiastical authorities "contradicted the national sovereignty, independence and the provisions of the constitution of the country." As quasi sovereign bodies whose laws and courts were outside the supervision of the national authorities and in some cases subject to foreign ecclesiastical authorities, the recognized religious communities "perpetuated the segregation and diversity of the courts and laws (of domestic relations), when the need of the country was for a unified law applicable to all Lebanese without any distinction.[27]

The continuing adherence of the Arab states to the institution of personal status is a consequence of their inconsummate constitutional transformation. The dependence of communities on their distinctive, sacred laws and their clerical leadership is an anachronism in today's liberal territorial state where citizenship is presumed to convey a sense of equivalent identity and individual capacity for free choice. But this is another issue which will be taken up in the part of the book dealing with constitutionalism.

ENDNOTES

1. Arnold Toynbee J., *A Study of History* [Abridgt vii-x], (London 1957), p. 51.
2. George N. Sfeir, "The Abolition of Confessional Jurisdictions in Egypt," *The Middle East Journal*, Washington (1956) 4
3. Mary Ann Glendon, *The Transformation of Family Law: State, Law and Family in the United States and Western Europe,* (Chicago 1989) p. 32f
4. J.N.D. Anderson, "Codification in the Muslim World", 30 *Rebels Zeitschrift fur Auslandisches und internationales Privatrecht*, (Tubingen 1966).
5. For an English language text, see Victor J. Pospishil, *Eastern Catholic Church Law,* (Saint Maron Publications, Staten Island, N.Y. 1996).
6. Ibid. Popishil, *Eastern Catholic Church Law*, p. 80-81. Despite its more progressive approach to the institution of marriage than its 1917 predecessor, the Code was criticized by both the Catholic and Orthodox authorities in the Eastern Churches for the onerous conditions it places in articles 813 and 814 on mixed marriages between Catholic and non-Catholic Christians. With only Church marriages possible for Christians in the Middle East, the Synod of the Melkite Church urged the removal from the Code of any provisions or practices which impede the good relations between Catholic and Orthodox Christians. The Orthodox Patriarchate, on its part, called on the Catholic Church in Syria, Lebanon, and Palestine, where the Institution of Personal Status applies, to do away with the provisions in articles 813 and 814. Responding to these criticisms, the Catholic-Orthodox Patriarchal Colloqium adopted in October 1996 the following guiding principles for mixed Christian marriages: (a) the right of the wife to remain in her own Church, (b) the wedding to be performed in the bride groom's Church with the priest of the bride's Church invited to participate in the ceremony, (c) the children to be

baptized in their father's Church, and (d) these guiding principles to be adopted by the synods of the two Churches. Ibrahim Tarabulsi, "Majmu'at Qawanin al-Kana'is al-Sharqiya" [The Code of the Eastern Churches]. *Al-Nahar*, (Beirut 5 May, 1997) p. 15.

7. *Encyclopaedia of Islam*, new ed. (Leyden 1986) MAHR p. 78-80.
8. Fadel Sa'id, *Sharh Qanun al-Usra al-Jaza'iri* [Interpretation of the Algerian Family Law], (Algiers 1985) p. 83.
9. Glendon, *The Transformation of Family Law*, op.cit. p. 292.
10. See Henry Sumner Maine, *Ancient Law*, (London, 1861/Dorset Press 1986).
11. Thomas Kuehn, *Law, Family & Women: Toward a Legal Anthropology of Renaissance* Italy (Chicago, 1991) p. 198.
12. Hans Julius Wolff, *Roman Law: An Historical Introduction*, (Norman 1951/1987) p. 151.
13. Leila Ahmad, *Women and Gender in Islam: Historical Roots of a Modern Debate* (New Haven 1992) p. 88.
14. Glendon, *The Transformation of Family Law*, op.cit. p. 167.
15. Joseph Schacht, *An Introduction to Islamic Law* (Oxford, 1964/1984) p. 21.
16. Jamil Zainaldin, "The Emergence of a Modern American Family Law: Child Custody, Adoption, and the Courts 1796-1851" 73 *Northwestern Univ. L.R.* 6 (1979) 1038 at p. 1045-1046.
17. Fadil, *Interpretation of the Algerian Family Law*, op.cit. p. 224-227.
18. Article 20(3), 28 *ILM* (1989) p. 1448.
19. S.M. Cretney, The Codification of Family Law, 44 *The Modern Law Rev.* (London) 1 (1981) p. 20.
20. Abdel-Razzaq al-Sanhuri, *Al-Wasit fi Sharh al-Qanun al-Madani al-Jadid* [The Intermediary Work on the Interpretation of the New Civil Code] (Cairo 1952) vol. I, p. 26-27.
21. Glendon, *The Transformation of Family Law*, op.cit. p. 93.
22. Ahmad Salama, *Al-Ahwal al-Shakhsiya lil-Muwatinin Ghayr al-Muslimin wal-Ajanib* [The Personal Status for Non-Muslim Nationals and Foreigners]

(Cairo 1962) p. 260f.

23. Ibid. p. 281f.

24. F.M. Goadby, *International and Interreligious Private Law in Palestine* (Jerusalem 1926) p. 118.

25. *Al-Majalla al-Maghribiya Lil-Qanun, wal-Siyasa, wal-Iqtisad* [Moroccan Rev. of Law, Politics & Economy] vol. 10, p. 31

26. The Congress of Christian Communities meeting at Bkerky, the seat of the Maronite Patriarchate, issued a statement on January 24, 1952, rejecting "any retreat from the rights and traditions which had been acquired from earliest times and recognized by succeeding government of the country." *[An-Nahar* (Beirut 26 January 1952)] The Muslim Congress, presided over by the mufti of Lebanon, declared on January 7, 1952, "the Sharia courts have applied the precepts of the everlasting Sharia, the law of our fathers and forefathers for hundreds of years, so that it has become our natural right." [*Bayrut* newspaper (Beirut 8 January 1952)] In a memorandum presented to the Lebanese authorities, the head of the Druze Community, Shaykh al-'Aql, stated that "the Druze believe that their personal status matters form an indivisible part of their religion which no one has the authority to add to or detract from them, except the Druze Community itself." *[An-Nahar* (Beirut 5 January 1952)]

27. *Al-Zaman* (Beirut 2 June 1991); also a report by Michel 'Aql on the Beirut Bar Association's action (unpublished) made available at the time to the author.

CHAPTER THREE

Civil Code

For all their drawbacks, the rules of domestic relations proved the most stable and predictable rules of Islamic law. In the other area of Private Law, the rules of commercial transactions or *mu'amalat*, ironically the most developed, will prove inadequate to the needs of modern times, making the resort to foreign law in the 19th century inevitable. Their sources remained diverse and dispersed until the Ottoman Majalla was composed in 1876. Even then, reflecting the state of Islamic law in the 9th century, the Majalla lacked a general theory of obligations, the mainstay of a civil code, was sparing in its rules relating to torts, and so restrictive in its conditions for the validity of contracts, that the Ottoman authorities had to resort to a procedural ploy, that of article 64 of the Code of Civil Procedure, to get around the Majalla's immutable rules to remedy its shortcomings.[1]

The reception by the Arab states of foreign law of contracts and obligations in the post world war I period had therefore all the elements of receptivity working for it: the inadequacy of the existing law, the changed social and economic conditions, and the presence of a catalyst for reform. Lebanon provides a typical example in this regard.

As part of the Ottoman Empire, Lebanon was subject to Ottoman laws, including the Majalla. With a new statehood in the 1920's following the break up of the Ottoman Empire, and with a long history of commerce and trade behind it, Lebanon was ready for a new law of contracts and obligations. The presence of the French Mandatory Power provided the needed catalyst. A French jurist was asked to prepare a draft code, which was then given to a committee of Lebanese jurists who introduced their revisions to render it more compatible with customary practices in the country, some of which had their roots in Islamic and Ottoman law. The new code was enacted by the Legislature in 1932, and a year later was complemented by a Code of Civil Procedure

It will be recalled that the Tunisian/Moroccan codes, which preceded the Lebanese code came about in a similar manner, as has already been described in Chapter I. These earlier attempts at a civil code in the Arab states, including the first Egyptian code, had as their model the old French code of 1804.

In a review of the Moroccan code on its seventieth anniversary,[2] Ahmad al-Khamlishi, a Professor at the University of Rabat Law School, and a believer in the revival of Islamic law on scientific basis and comparative law principles, says that there is no escaping the reality of the organic connection with the French code on which the Moroccan code has relied for juridical and academic interpretation. On the other hand, he says, there are factors at work which are distancing the two codes from one another. Among these are the differences between Moroccan and French society which have caused French law to part ways with the Moroccan code. In such areas as domestic relations, social security, insurance, and others, French jurisprudence based as it is on positive legislation, has not failed to reflect changing social relations in France. In Morocco, because of the duality in the legal system, these areas continue to depend on the traditional rules of Islamic law.

Despite its many shortcomings, al-Khamlishi continues to uphold the code as an essential source of Moroccan law. And while he does not consider Islamic law should necessarily be a source of law where legislation is wanting, he does believe that judges, in evolving the law, ought to have a free reign in resorting to the rules of Islamic law, to the general principles of the code, and to whatever they think is fair and equitable in the social circumstances.

The post world war II generation of Arab civil codes sought to bridge this duality and create a synthesis between the Islamic and European rules of contract, delict and property. In their various versions, the new codes represent the most ambitious pieces of Arab legislation so far. Their architect was Egyptian jurist Abdel-Razzaq al-Sanhuri (1895-1971), a passionate believer in the revival of Islamic law on scientific bases, detached from its religious moorings and recast in accordance with modern comparative law principles, much like Roman law was revived in Europe.

But the Egyptian *al-Qanun al-Madani*, which became a model for the civil codes of other Arab states from Algeria to Syria, is decidedly French in its orientation. More specifically it is said to draw on the French-Italian draft code of obligations of 1928 and other European codes, such as the German and the Swiss, with certain rules clearly of Islamic origin. However Sanhuri's first attempt at a new codification of the rules of obligations came in 1936 during his tenure at the newly established law faculty of the Iraqi University in Baghdad. There he outlined his ideas for a new civil code to replace the Ottoman Majalla which he said lacked the basic ingredient of a general theory of obligations.

Unlike the situation in Egypt where a code of French origin had existed since 1883 with a record of court decisions based on it going back to over sixty years, Iraq continued to follow the Islamic rules of obligations of the Hanafi school whose 8th century founder was a native of Iraq. As a result, the Iraqi code would contain more than its Egyptian counterpart of Islamic law rules, a hold over from the Ottoman Majalla it replaced. Nevertheless, the Iraqi code is patterned after the Egyptian code which was already enacted by the time the Iraqi code was adopted in 1951.

Neither the Iraqi civil code nor the other Arab codes however would live up fully to Sanhuri's expectations of a comprehensive code of private law and include, as is the case with their European counterpart, the rules governing domestic relations and inheritance for citizens of all religious denominations. These remain to this day outside the purview of the civil code, directly governed by traditional Islamic jurisprudence, or canon law in the case of non-Muslims. It is a situation reminiscent of the Japanese experience in the modernization of their private law. When the first civil code of 1890 was drafted, the parts dealing with property and obligations followed French law, while the parts dealing with persons and inheritance were radically changed to preserve traditional Japanese family rules.[3]

When it came to drafting the Egyptian civil code, Sanhuri was faced with a completely different situation from that in Iraq. Foreign legal influences in Egypt date back to the early 19th century and the French-based Egyptian civil code had become an integral part of the country's legal system since its adoption in 1883. Any radical departure from its basic tenets would have created confusion in the administration of justice. He therefore opted for a revision of the old code rather than its replacement by a new one. But the revision will be quite extensive, given the defects, both in substance and in form, Sanhuri found in the old code.[4]

The code had become antiquated, having remained a mere reproduction of the old French code. It lacked many of the developments in French jurisprudence which had taken place since, such as the abuse of rights and exploitation, rules regarding associations, public utility contracts, insurance, assignment of debt, community property, and others. But more importantly, the revision gave Sanhuri the opportunity to incorporate those provisions taken from Islamic law which he considered to be still viable and were not in the old code or even in the new French text, such as the rules pertaining to the contractual session *(khiyar al-majlis)*, unilateral remission of debt, product inspection and liability, agricultural/rural leases (*muzara'a* and *musaqat*), among others. To achieve all this, Sanhuri drew on three sources of change: the decisions of the Egyptian courts, the comparative advantages of other European codes, and the principles of Islamic law and customary practices particular to Egyptian society.

It was a long and arduous process from the time the first draft code was circulated in 1942 until it came into force on October 15, 1949. The adoption of the code coincided with the abolition of the regime of mixed courts and special laws which catered to foreigners in Egypt since 1875, and a time of heightened national feeling which became apparent in the debates which raged over the adoption of the code. On the one side were the jurists trained in European legal science committed to modernization, and on the other were the conservatives identifying with Islamic law and bent upon resisting Western influence; the same patriotic sentiment and reaction against overrapid westernization which succeeded in delaying the approval of the European civil code of Japan from 1890 to 1898.[5]

It was more important for Sanhuri however that the new code continue the legal tradition established by its predecessor. The new code could therefore do no more than improve on the old one which through decades of application and interpretation by the Egyptian courts had become domesticated and detached from its French origin. It all goes to prove Alan Watson's assertion that successful borrowing could be made from a very different legal system as the law reformer looks for an idea in the foreign system which could be transformed into part of the law of his country.[6]

But Sanhuri was compelled to defend the code against its critics even after it was adopted: that he utilized all the viable Islamic law principles, that he opted for those rules which were more compatible with Islamic law, such as his choice of the objective approach of the German code to obligations over the subjective French approach. Nevertheless a window on Islamic law was left open in the code in article 1 which identified the four main sources of law a judge may draw on in making his decisions. These sources are: the text of the code itself, customary practice (*'urf*), the principles of the Sharia, and the principles of natural law and equity, in this descending order of priority.

The order in which these sources were listed is significant in view of Sanhuri's intention to create an autonomous, self-contained code, answerable only to its own milieu. "Whatever was adopted from other rules, legislation or codes, has been integrated with the rest of the provisions of the code to find expression in the text as a whole and the jurisprudence of the Egyptian courts. This synthesis in the text should also be the most important factor in its interpretation."[7]

Not all the Arab codes however follow the same order in listing the sources of law in the absence of text. The Syrian code of 1949 gives priority to the "principles of Islamic Sharia" over "custom" and "natural law and equity" in the absence of an applicable provision; while the Iraqi code of 1951 limits these sources to "custom" (*'urf*) and "principles of Islamic Sharia," and in this order. The Jordanian code of 1976, on the other hand, which maintains that it is closer to Islamic law than other Arab codes, lists "Islamic *fiqh*," that is empirical rulings, as the source of priority in the absence of an applicable provision before proceeding to the principles (*mabadi'*) of Islamic law, custom, and justice. The Kuwaiti code of 1981 takes a decidedly more practical view by providing that in applying the rulings of Islamic fiqh (in the absence of a legislative text or custom) the judge ought to be guided by those rulings which are "more compatible with the conditions of the country and its interests."

Sanhuri's choice of principles over rulings was dictated by his concern that resort to Islamic jurisprudence in the interpretation of the code might adversely affect its unity and its integrity. Only the use of the more general and ethical Sharia principles would guard against that.[8] One senses here an attempt on the part of Sanhuri to equate Sharia with a higher source of law, something similar to natural law in the Western legal tradition.

It was the Christian scholastics who, in the 13th century, succeeded in reconciling the divine law with the law of nature and human reason to lay down the ground for the intellectual movement away from the medieval sacral concepts of law and society. The European codifications are a product of that newly emerging legal culture which went on to leave its mark equally on the Decretum of Gratian, the canon law of the Church and on the civil law of the chacelleries.[9] No such movement took place in Islamic law. It was no wonder then that when Egyptian legal historian Chafik Chehata came to defend the new code against its critics, he could only draw on recent history to say that the code reflected the country's "legal maturity." He was referring to the movement for modernization which began in the late 19th century with the adoption of Ottoman and French codes to fill the gaps in the country's antiquated legal system. The Sharia, he said, failed to develop the kind of general principles one finds in modern codes to apply in the search for specific solutions, particularly in the field of obligations; a failure he attributed to excessively loose rules of contractual relations and the arrested development of Islamic law generally.[10]

This dearth of a modern legal tradition of any consequence in the Arab states, explains the central role which the precedent established by the Egyptian courts in their application and interpretation of a civil code since 1883 has played in the successful application of the code in those Arab states which have more recently adhered to the Egyptian style code.

The Iraqi code made it a condition in the first article, that "the courts shall be guided by the rulings of the Iraqi courts and the courts of other countries with laws analogous to the Iraqi code," while the Explanatory Memorandum of the Syrian civil code attributed the decision of the legislator to reproduce much of the Egyptian code to the "benefits that can be derived from the decisions of the Egyptian courts and the works of Egyptian jurists," among others. In the case of the more recent code, that of Jordan, an annotated version of the code is replete with references to Egyptian court decisions.

Notwithstanding this practical approach forced as it were on lawyers and jurists by their daily handling of cases, the search for legitimacy by association with Islamic Sharia has continued to agitate legislators and jurists alike since the adoption of the new codes. The Explanatory Memorandum of the 1981 Kuwaiti code goes into great lengths to justify the priority given to custom *('urf)* over Islamic law in the absence of an applicable provision in the code, as both the Egyptian and Iraqi codes had done. Advancing Islamic law over custom, according to the Memorandum, would contradict the accepted logic of the sources of law. Islamic Sharia itself acknowledges the need to resort to custom as one of the most important sources of law. Applying the principles of Sharia would therefore lead one back to custom which was a basic consideration in the formulation of the Islamic rules themselves. The Memorandum goes on to cite sayings of the Prophet in support of its contention that when it comes to civil transactions what matters is what people have voluntarily agreed upon or what customary usage has made acceptable: "You are more knowledgeable about your world," and "What concerns your religion is up to me; what concerns your world is a matter with which you are more knowledgeable."

By way of comparison, the pre-eminent source of law in the European civil law system is the text of the law followed by custom and sometimes the general principles of law. Court decisions and writings of legal scholars are secondary, non-binding, sources. To the extent that codes are comprehensive and homogenous in their structure, judges assume the delicate task of interpretation without alteration. Thus when a judge encounters an ambiguity, gap, or silence in the text, he is bound to indulge in judicial development but always within the general principles or the spirit of the code itself.

Two important considerations underlie this attitude towards the code. One is that the code represents a break with the past inasmuch as it had displaced the old sources of law, whether Roman, divine, or jus commune. The second is that the code is its own authority; any principles of the old law incorporated in the code "received their validity not from their previous existence, but from their incorporation and reenactment in the codified form."[11]

A similar transition from morality to legality can be seen in the common law. In tracing the evolution of rules from their ethical sources to their legal state, Roscoe Pound, points out:

> Moral principles, having acquired the character of legal rules, are carried out to logical consequences until the original principle is lost among the derived rules, or are developed as mere abstractions and thus are deprived of their purely moral character. In this way transition takes place to the next stage, which may be called the maturity of the law.[12]

Comparative law experts link the codification of private law in Europe to the particular historical situation of each country. But the codes were in general founded on the ideas of the Enlightenment and the law of reason and on the assumption that the reconstructed rules of law can bring about or consolidate social change in society.[13]

In their own way too, the Arab codes broke new ground and consolidated changes which had already taken place in the legal culture of Arab society. They benefited from a century of Arab liberal thought since the 18th century when such men as Muhammad Abduh and his disciples sought to modernize Islam,[14] and from a new class of jurists and lawyers trained in European legal science who upon their return to their countries championed the establishment of modern legal doctrines and institutions.[15]

The Arab codes are based on the dichotomy in European law between private and public law which took shape in the 19th century process of codification. The civil code comprised the core of private law; while constitutional law, administrative law and criminal law made up public law.

Also in format and content, the Arab codes follow the European codes, including the law of obligations, both contractual and delictual, specific types of contracts, and real rights, ownership and mortgage. An important part of the European civil codes however which failed to find a place for it in the Arab codes is the part dealing with family law. The simultaneous systematization and rationalization of the civil and the canon laws in Europe beginning in the 12th century, facilitated, in the wake of the Protestant Reformation, the merger of family law matters, once the exclusive jurisdiction of ecclesiastical tribunals, into the civil law. This developed eventually into a clear separation of jurisprudence from theology in the Western legal tradition.[16]

In the case of the Arab states, the lag in the evolution of a modern legal culture meant that the reform of the law would be achieved only at the cost of a dualism between the borrowed civil law and those matters of personal status and domestic relations to which the clerical authorities and ecclesiastical jurisdictions had long laid claim as matters traditionally associated with the faith. These matters comprise the entire spectrum of family law, as well as marital property and succession which are also integral parts of the civil code in Europe.

SALIENT FEATURES OF THE CODE*

The Preliminary Part

This part of the code expounds a number of basic rules common to private law matters, including conflict of laws as to time and place, the status and domicile of natural and juristic persons, classification of things and property. In this respect the Arab code takes after the German code rather than the French which has discarded the extensive *livre preliminaire*.

The initial article establishes the code as the law in all matters comprehended by its provisions "in letter and in spirit." And goes on to identify sources of law on which a judge may draw in the absence of a relevant text, as discussed in the preceding section.

Generally speaking the national law of the person, that of the main place of business of the corporation, the location of the property and where the contract was concluded, determine the applicable foreign law. In matters of marriage and divorce, however, it is the law of the husband; while in mixed marriages between say an Egyptian and a foreigner, Egyptian law applies.

The law applicable to succession and wills is the law of the testator or the place where the will was made. Some of these rules overlap and conflict with the religious laws of personal status and domestic relations which have been excluded from the code. Legal capacity, for example, is set at a certain age (21 years in some codes) but that age differs from the age of maturity in the laws of personal status. Then there is the final article of this part which denies the application of a foreign law contrary to public order and morality, a provision found in all systems of law. But where the laws of domestic relations and social values are based on different religious criteria, the effect of this article is wide ranging. A Christian beneficiary, for example, will be denied inheritance from a foreign Muslim testator whose personal status and domestic relations law prohibits it.

OBLIGATIONS

The Arab code gives the doctrine of obligations the prominent place it occupies in the civil law system. According to Sanhuri, obligations are to law what the backbone is to the human body. It is a doctrine rooted in Roman law which first identified the main sources of obligations. They were reformulated in the 19th century by European codifiers and recently adopted by Arab legislators. These sources of obligations are contracts, unlawful acts or torts, unjustified enrichment and the law. Their survival to this day practically unchanged is a tribute to the 5th century Byzantine jurists at the Beirut and the Constantinople law schools who formulated the Justinian code.

The Book of Obligations is a fundamental part of the Arab code. Its rules comprehend the vast field of contractual and delictual reponsibility, a field which in the Common Law comprises both the laws of contracts and of torts. The introduction of general principles of obligations into the Arab code is an innovation insofar as Islamic law of obligations was not formulated on the basis of general principles but grew out of specific rulings particular to their own time and place. Those familiar with the laws of contracts and torts know how intimately related their evolution has been with changing social and economic conditions.[17]

1. Contracts: As part of the law of obligations, Islamic law lacked also a general theory of contract. Instead Islamic law knew a number of specific types of contracts concluded by one simple mechanism, an exchange of prescribed words of offer and acceptance, whose fulfillment was underscored by the Qoranic injunction, "All you who believe fulfill your pledges" (Sura 5:1). It was more akin to the stipulatio in ancient Roman law, around which Praetors built procedural remedies actionable in respect of specific types of contracts. Only in modern legal systems have formal requirements in contracts become exceptions to the general principle of informality, and the law of contract turned its attention to the general principles of enforceability and rules of construction. In this respect the Arab code severed its relations with the Islamic law notions of contract and in the process did away with a number of its nominate contracts and introduced new ones, such as labor and insurance.

The first article in the Book of Obligations endorsed the modern notion of obligations, founded as they are on economic necessity as well as freedom of contract. It provided that a contract is concluded when there is a mutual exchange of "expressions of concordant intentions" by two parties to the contract. The accent is on the declaration of will rather than the will itself, thereby opting for the German rather than the French code's rules of construction. The Arab code enjoins against looking for the intentions of the parties where the terms of the contract are clear, and, where interpretation is necessary, it should be done in accordance with common commercial usage and the mutual good faith of the parties. Citing article 157 of the German civil code, Chehata points to the origin of this purely objective theory in the Arab code.[18]

It is also a theory favored by the Common Law and present day business relations, with their vastly more complex and impersonal nature. Much of the modern law of contracts is the product of the 19th century ideas of liberalism and laissez faire as well as the development of markets which redirected the attention of the law from considerations of equivalence and just value to the "willed transactions" which the parties to the contract believed to be of mutual interest to them.[19]

The Arab code also subscribes to the view that the contract is "the law" of the contracting parties (al-'aqd shari'at al-muta'aqidin) which may not in any way be altered, replaced, or repealed except with the consent of both parties or for reasons of law. Nevertheless, the code does recognize, as do both the Civil Law and the Common Law, certain conditions relating to the conclusion of the contract which might impair the "concordant intentions" or the "meeting of minds" of the contracting parties. These are mistake, fraud or misrepresentation, and duress.

Following the position favored by French law, for mistake to become a ground for rescission the Arab code requires that it be of such substance and motivation that if the mistaken party were aware of it, it would not have concluded the contract. Mere errors of accounting or wording are not grounds for rescission and should be corrected. The Arab states however join other civil law states, including Austria, Switzerland, Italy, Greece and Turkey, in barring rescission if the other party was prepared, once the error was discovered, to perform the contract in the sense intended by the mistaken party.[20]

Similar rules of substance and motivation apply to fraud, and if the deceit originated from a third party, rescission is permitted only if the other party should have been aware of the fraud. Lastly, rescission of a contract is permitted by reason of duress, which the Arab code defines as the "power of fear" (*sultan al-rahba*) which would have led a party to the contract to perceive imminent danger to himself or to others in body, honor or property.

The Arab code also deals separately from duress with abuse or exploitation of a party's personal condition leading to an unfair or unequal commitments and benefits. The code permits a judge to rescind the contract or reduce the prejudiced party's burden in a manner similar to the way the U.S. Restatement of Contracts deals with unconscionable contracts (art.208, second 1981):

> If the contract or term thereof is unconscionable at the time the contract is made, a court may refuse to enforce the contract, or may enforce the remainder of the contract without the unconscionable term, or may so limit the application of any unconscionable term as to avoid any unconscionable result.

Finally, what makes a promise serious and renders the contract enforceable? In Common Law it is the doctrine of consideration which rests on the twin ideas that a promise is given in return for some benefit to the promisor and the promisee incurs a detriment by his reliance upon it.[21] In the civil law system, it is cause which provides the legal justification for, and hence the enforceability of, the contract.

Although this latter concept has been belittled when compared to the construction of the transaction in distinguishing between serious and spurious promises,[22] the Arab code adhered to it: "An obligation without cause (*sabab*) shall be void;" and where no cause is mentioned in the contract, it will be assumed that a valid cause does exist unless proven otherwise.

Islamic law knew neither consideration nor cause. Instead it spoke of object or purpose (*mahall*) in a contract, a concept found in the French code as a component element of contract, has also been adopted by the Arab code. But in neither case does the concept add much to the nature of contract as it simply requires that the contract be about something in existence or capable of existence, identifiable, possible and legal. In this respect however the Arab code departs from Islamic law in that it validates commitments in futuro, something that Islamic law forbade on the ground that commitments about things non-existent is in the nature of contracts of hazard or risk which the Qoran has admonished against.

Adopted from the Islamic law and adapted it into the Arab code however is the concept of *majlis al-'aqd* or the unity of the contractual session, whose purpose was to avoid the risk of uncertainty and deception *(gharar)* prohibited in Islam. It called for the immediacy between offer and acceptance at the same session. The ulema disagreed however whether the contractual session ended once the parties physically separated, or did the term separation in the revealed text mean a break in negotiations allowing still for the offer to be withdrawn or accepted, so long as the contract had not been concluded [23]

Exploiting this division of views, the author of the code gave the meeting of the parties both its real and figurative senses in order to comprehend on the one hand protracted negotiations over an extended period of time and on the other resort to modern communications in the "contractual session," as is the case with European codes.[24] The relevant article in the Arab code provides in part that a contract shall be concluded even if the acceptance were not immediate, provided there was no indication in the interval between offer and acceptance that the offer had been withdrawn or the acceptance was given prior to the conclusion of the contractual session.

2. Torts: As in the case of contracts, Islamic law had no general theory of delictual liability. Instead, the specific rules dealing with criminal and civil liability were extended to apply to unlawful acts or torts causing injury or damage to others directly or indirectly. A person directly causing damage is liable; a person causing damage indirectly is liable only if he acted intentionally. In its last configuration, in the Ottoman Majallat, the Islamic law conception of delictual responsibility was tempered by the rule: "legal permissibility negates liability," also known in early European law as *Damnum sine Injuria.*

It was only when French jurists began to distinguish between criminal and civil responsibility and then between contractual and delictual liability that a theory of unlawful acts was developed and introduced into the 1804 Code civil. However in its first application, the theory rested on the concept of fault alone which did not satisfy the growing demands of the industrial revolution and had to be complemented by the concept of damage whether caused intentionally or as a result of negligence. It is this fully developed theory of delictual liability which the Arab code adopted, albeit with embellishment from Islamic law instances as formulated in the Majalla in certain versions of he code, particularly those of Iraq and Jordan.

According to the initial article on unlawful acts in the Arab code, "Every fault which causes injury to others obligates its perpetrator to make reparation." Fault here is not dissimilar from negligence, that is failure to adhere to the standard of a reasonable person. However causes beyond a person's control, such as unforeseen circumstances, overwhelming force, the fault of the injured party or a third party, would absolve the accused of responsibility in the absence of a law or an agreement to the contrary. Likewise, self-defense, the discharge of official duties by a public official, and the avoidance of greater damage are justifiable under the code. The code did retain the Majalla rule that legal permissibility negates liability, but qualified it by providing that the use of a right would still be unlawful if intended to cause injury to others, the benefits accruing from it are minor compared to the damage it would cause, and what it sets out to achieve is illegal. This made the abuse of a right unlawful in the Arab code as it is in European law.

The second element in a tort action according to the Arab code is impending injury or actual damage suffered. Under Islamic law a wrongful act created liability, but only if it caused material, not moral injury. The code however recognizes moral injury and personal suffering and places them on the same footing as material damage: "Reparation shall cover moral injury as well." But unlike material damage, compensation for moral injury is not trasferrable to third parties except in the case of death it shall include damages for "pain and suffering" payable to the deceased's spouse and relatives to the second degree.

The code also ascribes responsibility for the acts of others to the person required by law or agreement to supervise their actions. A person responsible for "guarding" animals, buildings, or machines, may also be held liable in specific instances for the damage they cause, a notion unknown to Islamic law.

The third element in a tort action according to the code, which is also the case in French law, is that there should be a causal link between the culpable act and the harm suffered by the claimant. In this regard, the code distinguishes between an obligation to achieve a result (e.g. failure to transfer title) and an obligation not to be negligent (e.g. medical malpractice). In the former, fault, and hence culpability, is failure to execute; in the latter fault is failure to show reasonable care. Here the Jordanian code reintroduces the Islamic law rule that an act is culpable for harm caused indirectly on condition it was intentional and offensive.

More than any other field of law, the law of torts can hardly catch up with the enormous range of causes of action let loose by the industrial and technological revolutions. Ironically, however, the number of provisions in the civil codes dealing with unlawful acts remain one of the smallest: 15 in the Arab code, 5 in the French code and 30 in the German code. It was left to the courts and to special statutes to identify a growing number of causes of action on the strength of practically one general provision in the code, S162 in the Egyptian, S1382 in the French and S826 in the German code. Whatever categories of torts developed in the civil law system, the causes of action and the remedies they generated depended ultimately on these same statutory texts and the fulfillment of their requirement.[25]

In the Common Law, tort law was practically unknown on either side of the Atlantic prior to the industrial revolution. Out of the old writs and bricks of the common law--assault and battery, trespass, slander, a new field of law was built to accommodate the age of engines and machines, particularly railroads, which generated an explosion of negligence cases. But each feature of the new law, fault, assumption of risk, contributory negligence, proximate cause, had to struggle to overcome its own hurdles, before it could be launched on its own separate career.[26]

3. Unjustified Enrichment: Here too the case oriented common law lagged in distinguishing claims for restitution of undue benefits conferred on another from contract law. The various procedures for action were based on an imputed promise and dealt with as quasi contracts. Similarly French law viewed such claims as the restoration of payments made pursuant to a supposed debt; claims for restitution of payments in pursuance of a duty of honor or morals were denied. Islamic law also subscribed to the general rule, in the words of the Ottoman Majallat, "No one may appropriate the property of another without lawful cause." A number of classical scholars however considered unauthorized payments made voluntarily by a person to another in the nature of donations, a conclusion which modern authorities believe was the result of conflicting views among these scholars about the actions of unauthorized agents.[27]

The language of the Arab code is unambiguous: "Anyone who received by way of redemption (*wafa'*) what is not due to him is obliged to return it." The rule applies equally whether the redemption was in settlement of a contractual obligation whose "cause" had not been realized, had become extinct, or, unknown to the payer, settlement was not due. The code however treats differently those who acted in good faith and those who acted in bad faith. The former are obliged to return what was unjustly received by them, the latter accrued interest and profit as well.

Included in the section on unjust enrichment is the "voluntary agent" (*al-fuduli*), who knowingly undertakes to manage another person's affairs. Unless asked to cease and desist, must continue what he started until the beneficiary is in a position to carry on the work himself, when he will be compensated for benefits accrued or losses sustained.

But neither the provisions of the civil code nor of the American Restatement of the Law of Restitution ("a person who has been unjustly enriched at the expense of another is required to make restitution") comprehend all the very disparate situations of unjust enrichment, whose only common feature, comparative law authorities say, is a negative one, namely that they are neither contract nor tort. And although civil law lawyers more readily than their common law colleagues accept that claims for restitution are based on the unitary theory of unjust enrichment, both had to proceed, as classical Roman lawyers did before them, "less on the basis of such general formulas than on a practical consideration of the individual cases."[28]

Specific Performance and Compensation: Generally speaking, the remedies of specific performance and compensation are available in all legal systems for failure to perform on a contract. The purpose of the law of contract whether in the common law or the civil law is after all to hold the contracting parties to their promises. There is, however, a difference of emphasis between the two. In principle, a claimant is always entitled under the civil law to a judgment for specific performance, whereas under the common law, except for the sale of goods, it is less common. In practice, however, the difference is on the wane, particularly that businessmen tend to opt for compensation rather than risk time and costs on a claim for performance.[29]

The Arab code recognizes both remedies--specific performance and/or compensation, depending on the circumstances of the case. The way the code has phrased the general rule, specific performance must be feasible, requested by the parties, and does not cause undue hardship or damage to either of them: "Subject to a formal notification or protest to the debtor, the court shall decree specific performance where performance was possible. But if performance were to cause the debtor extreme hardship, he may be permitted to limit himself to the payment of monetary compensation, but only if this would not result in excessive damage to the creditor."

The code distinguishes between an obligation to transfer ownership or proprietary right, and a contract to perform or refrain from performing work. If the property in the former case is identifiable, the transfer will be carried out. In the case of work, the creditor may seek the court's permission to do the work himself at the cost of the debtor; otherwise seek compensation. Likewise, a party may resort to the removal of what was done by the other party and at its cost contrary to an obligation to refrain from doing what it did.

Compensation is meant to cover the financial losses resulting directly from breach of contract. The amount of compensation or liquidated damages may be specified in advance in the contract itself, or by subsequent agreement, without implying a choice between the two. In other words, liquidated damages will only be available to the creditor in the event of a breach caused by the fault of the debtor.

If the amount of compensation is not specified either in the contract or by law, the judge will decide, taking into account the creditor's losses and lost opportunity from the delay or failure to perform, as well as the creditor's own actions which may have contributed to the losses he sustained.

Furthermore, the debtor may avoid paying damages if he proves that the creditor did not suffer any losses. A judge may also reduce the agreed amount of compensation if the debtor shows that the amount specified in the contract was highly exaggerated or that the original obligation was partially fulfilled.

At this point the code introduces the subject of interest, a subject anathema to Islamic law which considers interest at any rate usury, as will be more fully discussed in a later part of the book. According to the code, in an agreement over a sum of money, the amount of which is specified at the time payment becomes due, the debtor is required to pay creditor interest as compensation for failure to pay on time.

A different rate of interest is set by the code for civil (4 percent) and for commercial (5 percent) transactions. However the parties to the contract may agree on a higher rate of interest, whether for investment purposes or as compensation for late payment, provided the agreed rate does not exceed a ceiling specified in the code (7 percent); and at no time should the total interest paid exceed the principal amount, unless commercial practice dictates otherwise.

Assignment: If there was a lasting contribution by Islamic law to European law, it was in the highly important area of today's financial markets. The *Suftaja* and *Hawala* (the French *aval*), the early forms of a bill of exchange and assignment of debt, were adapted by Islamic law from customary practice in the Near East. The creation of traders to make payments in remote places without the risk of loss or theft, these instruments soon found their way during the Middle Ages to the law merchant in Europe.

In its modern application, assignment means the substitution of a new party for the original debtor or creditor, transferring to it a contractual right or obligation. But as was the case with early Roman law, Islamic law took the position that personal rights were not transferable; only obligations were. To Islamic jurists, only debt comprised both material claim and personal obligation (*dhimma*), akin to the German law distinction between *haftung* and *schuld.* Rights, on the other hand, lacked the element of *dhimma* to make them transferrable,[30] except to the extent that they could be attached, according to the Arab code.

The Arab code allows a creditor to assign its right in a contract to another party, provided that neither the law, the original contract, or the nature of the obligation prevent it. In line with French law, the assignment does not require the consent of the debtor to be concluded; but to be effective against the debtor or third parties, the debtor and the public at large must be notified of the assignment, particularly that it will carry with it the associated mortgages and guarantees. The German law which treats the assignment as a disposition independent of the original contract, does not require that the debtor be informed, a position similar to that of American law, where commercial interests are best served by the substantive law, while the protection of the debtor is left to elaborate procedural rules.[31]

The assignment of a debt by the debtor to a third party, on the other hand, requires, according to the Arab code, the agreement of the assignee. Nor will the assignment become effective as far as the creditor is concerned unless he had consented to it. But while the assignment is not effective upon the creditor for not having been accepted or notified of it, the assignee remains responsible vis a vis the original debtor for the timely payment of the debt. Unlike the transfer of rights, however, the guarantor of an assigned debt whether personal or proprietary will not remain committed to the creditor unless he consented to the transfer of the debt.

As a form of contract, assignment is governed by the rules regulating the formation and validity of contracts; while an assignment of rights against monetary payment is considered a sale, without payment a gift, and in the form of security a mortgage.

Impossibility of Performance and Unforeseen Circumstances: The last chapter of Book I deals with the various ways by which an obligation becomes extinct, other than by performance or damages as discussed above.

According to the code, an obligation will become extinct by certain forms of payment which would amount to settlement; by fulfilling an obligation by means other than specific performance, such as giving something in lieu of what was agreed upon, novation or the extinction of the old obligation and the substitution of a new one in its place, setoff or compensation, and merger. Finally there is the extinction of obligation without payment which includes voluntary release of the debtor by his creditor, prescription, and impossibility of performance due to unforeseen circumstances or causes beyond the debtor's control, which we shall consider here in more detail.

The Arab code simply provides that an obligation becomes extinct if its performance has been rendered impossible by circumstances beyond the control of the debtor. After stating earlier that the contract is the law of the parties which cannot be revoked or modified except by their own consent, the code goes on to say that "if by reason of unforeseen, exceptional circumstances of a general nature, the execution of the contractual obligation, though not impossible, has become so onerous to the debtor as to threaten him with exorbitant loss, the judge may, in accordance with circumstances, and after weighing between the interests of both parties, reduce the exorbitant obligations to a reasonable level. Any agreement to the contrary shall be void."

Practically all legal systems give due cognizance to unforeseen circumstances and supervening events which might render the contract difficult or impossible to perform. The doctrine *clausula rebus sic stantibus*, that the validity of a contract depends on the circumstances obtaining at the time of its conclusion continuing, dates back to the Middle Ages. It appears today in the common law as the doctrine of frustration of contract by which performance though not impossible has become largely pointless. French law remained reluctant to go beyond the notion of *force majeure* until the Conseil d'Etat reacting to the public interest in public works contracts and public utility concessions resorted to the *theorie de l'imprevision* in dealing with the changed economic equilibrium in contracts as a result of unforeseen circumstances.

Except for those based on the earlier version of the French code, (Morocco's, Tunisia's, Lebanon's codes), the Arab code adopts the French theory and lays down a number of conditions for its application: The intervening circumstances must be exceptional and of a general nature, not particular to the debtor alone; and while performance may not be completely impossible, it would result in enormous disadvantage or loss to the debtor.

This distinguishes unforeseen circumstances from force majeur which makes performance impossible and leads to the extinction of the obligation. That is why the unforeseen circumstances rule applies normally to contracts of term or those of staggered or delayed implementation which allow time for the circumstances under which they were first concluded to change and their implementation under the changed circumstances cause enormous losses to the contracting party.[32]

None of these modern rules of unforeseen circumstances, supervening events or *force majeure* figured prominently in Islamic law, which restricted contractual obligations to what is known and existing at the time of the contract. What this law recognized was the simple notion of excuse or '*udhr* which gave a party the right, particularly in contracts of hire and lease, to rescind the contract under conditions which render its performance impossible. A land rented for the cultivation of crops which lost its source of water is ground to rescind the contract, so is the lease of premises damaged by fire.

4. Nominate Contracts:

Book II of the civil code covers contracts of various specific transactions or purposes. They are contracts of ownership which include sale, exchange, gifts, partnership, loans and annuities, and compromise; contracts of use which include leases and hire; contracts of service including contracting, concessions and worker contracts, agency, and deposit; aleatory contracts which include gaming, life annuities and insurance; and finally suretyship.

We have stated earlier that Islamic law, like early Roman law, failed to develop a general theory of contract and instead recognized specific forms of transactions into which contracts fit to be valid. While Book II of the code deals with particular contracts, its purpose and underlying principles are completely different from those of Islamic law. It will be useful to dwell briefly on this difference.

Contracts law in Islam was mostly a "by-product" of the Islamization process of existing pre-Islamic forms of transactions.[33] Islam did not come into a social and economic vacuum whether in Arabia or the countries of North Africa and the Middle East to which it eventually spread. What Islamic jurists did at first was to ensure that existing contracts did not conflict with the tenets of Islam prohibiting for example usury (*riba*) and risk taking or uncertainty (*gharar*) even when economic necessity demanded it. This resulted in a number of strict stipulations for the validity of particular contracts.

The Arab code instead adopted the modern theory of obligations which is based, as is also the case with both the civil and the common law, on the twin pillars of the freedom of contract and economic necessity. This theory was developed in Book I of the code. Book II provides the rules governing contracts with special purposes and characteristics without sacrificing in their formation the same underlying principles of freedom of contract and economic necessity. Consequently the code has introduced new types of contracts unknown to Islamic law, such as insurance and public concessions, and dealt with others, such as contracting and services, in a manner which reflects the modern, more complex, contractual relations in these fields.

The code has also done away with irrelevant contracts which had evolved in Islamic law simply to circumvent the restrictions Islam imposed on certain transactions because of its prohibition of usury and risk taking and have therefore lost their justification in a secular legal system. Such a contract is a sale of real property with the right of redemption, known as *bay' al-wafa'*. Whether intended as an arrangement similar to the mortgage of property common today, with the vendor guaranteed payment over time, while benefiting from the free use of his house in the meantime; or simply as a device to obtain a loan, in which case the vendor became a borrower and the temporary purchaser the lender who benefited from the use of the property until the vendor redeemed it, constituted a form of usury prohibited in Islam.

Sale: The contract of sale was regarded as the basic form of contract in Islamic law. Of the sixteen books of the Ottoman Majallat, the first codification of Islamic law in the 19th century, sales constituted the first and largest book, which contained many of the conditions for the validity of a contract generally. It was the conditions attaching to transactions such as sales which troubled Islamic jurists and produced voluminous opinions about those conditions which were valid, voidable, or null and void and the effect of each on the contract as a whole.

The Arab code represents a break with the stringent rules of the Islamic law of sales. If it in turn introduces conditions of its own, it is to facilitate the sale, give effect to the intent of the parties, and avoid controversy between them. One of the significant departures from Islamic law to reflect the new economic conditions and the conduct of business in the world today is the distinction the

Arab code makes in the sale of goods between the transfer of the corpus and the title to it. Islamic law insisted that the object of sale be existing, specified and capable of immediate delivery if it is to be valid. Indeed, things whose use is forbidden by Islam, such as wine, pork, carcasses of animals, and things which do not have material existence, such as electricity, credit, could not be the object of sale. As the Majallat put it, "the sale of a thing which is not generally recognized as property is void."

The only exception to future sales was the sale of parts coming successively into existence with those already existing in the case of fruits or vegetables which do not mature simultaneously. But the general rule prevailed and its justification is indicative of the pervasive effect the prohibition of usury and risk taking have had on the Islamic law of contracts. With modern law, whether civil or common, granting the intention or will of the parties to a contract a preeminent position, these rules against risk taking in Islamic law were bound to unravel when it came to formulating the new rules of obligations in the Arab code. Title itself is after all not corporeal; rather an invisible concept of intention which passed from owner to buyer when it was intended to pass. It was actually around this concept of title that the law of sales grew in the 19th century.[34]

Hire and Lease: The second most important nominate contract in Islamic law was that of hire and lease, which governed equally the benefit accruing to the hirer or lessee in the usufruct of property and the use of transport or animal, the work of a laborer and the skill of an artisan. The Arab code, reflecting the European civil law doctrines, shifts the essence of the contract of hire or lease from the mere passive use by the hirer or lessee, to the positive requirement of the owner or lessor to make sure, as far as the condition, utility and upkeep are concerned, the hirer or lessee will be able to enjoy the benefits he contracted for. In the words of the code: "Lease is a contract by which the lessor undertakes to enable the lessee to benefit from a specified thing for a specified period of time and in return for a known rent."

Some of the Arab codes which portray greater influence of Islamic law among their provisions have retained the concept that the contract of hire or lease grants the lessee in fact "ownership" of the usufruct. Thus the Jordanian code defines lease as "the lessor permitting the lessee to own the intended benefit of the leased thing for a specified period of time and in return for a known compensation."

This difference between Islamic and modern law over the nature of the contract of hire or lease is due to the greater emphasis the former placed on the object of the contract, which in this case is the benefit of hire or lease, compared to the greater importance the latter gives to the intention of the parties, what they committed themselves to do or refrain from doing. By adhering to the notion of ownership of benefit in a lease, Islamic law denied the right to lease except to the actual owner of the property, whereas the Arab code recognizes a lease by a third party, at least between the parties to the contract, and with the rightful owner if he consents to it, since no transfer of ownership is contemplated in the contract, only the commitment of the lessor to see to it that the lessee benefits from what he has leased.

Labor and Contracting: Reflecting the law's changing view of the position of labor and contracting in the market place since the industrial revolution, the Arab code allocates separate sections for labor contracts and contracting agreements. As was alluded to above, Islamic law saw these work relations in the nature of a lease contract, governed by the same requirements of specified object, duration and compensation. Contracting for the "manufacture" of something new suffered from the same doubts which militated legally against the rent of an undefined space or a sale in futuro. Labor was bound by the ties of servant to master, not far removed legally speaking from the indentured servants, the farm and household workers, in colonial America.[35]

The code defines the nature and the constituent elements of the labor contract and the contracting agreement in terms compatible with the will theory applicable in the code to contracts generally, taking into consideration the respective rights and obligations of either party to the contract. These provisions of the code are today supplemented in practically all Arab countries by specific labor codes and social security legislation.

Under this section, the Arab code provides also for the rules governing concessions for public utility services and the duties and responsibilities of the concessionaire, particularly the need to deal fairly and equitably with the consumer.

Loan and Deposit: The Arab code lays down the basic rules of lending and safekeeping generally, which in their specialized, financial sense, such as banking, are, as in the case of labor, the subject of specific comprehensive legislation. Already however in these basic rules the code digresses from the tenets of Islamic law in two important points essential for modern business practices: It does not consider loan and deposit agreements in the nature of proprietary contracts requiring actual, physical delivery of the property for their conclusion, and it does not question the legitimacy of lending with interest, which it goes on to legalize and set at what amounts to market rates or the agreement of the parties.

Islam considered any monetary return on capital not associated with labor, service or use as usurious. Islamic scholars even today rationalize this rule with arguments which were quite familiar in the Middle Ages to Christian scholastics.[36] This led to the widespread use in Muslim society of legal devices to get around the prohibition of usury. There was for example the contract of *mukhatara* by which a person contracted to sell another a thing for say $120 to be paid in a year's time and buys it back immediately for $100 paid on the spot. In this way he lent the other person the $100 to be returned to him in a year's time as $120 all in the name of purchase and sale. This type of contract was so widespread that it found its way to Europe at the time as the *contractus mohatra*.

During the 1980's a number of private and state sponsored Islamic banking institutions came into being in Arab and European financial centers raising the issue of accommodation on both the national and international plane between these institutions and the conventional system of banking.[37] Their purpose was to steer away from the Islamic prohibition of usury by taking deposits and issuing loans free of interest, utilizing in the process the depositors' funds in profit and loss sharing investments or equity participation transactions known in Islamic law as *mudaraba*.

It is often overlooked that the emergence of banking in the 17th century had to await the resolution in Europe of the issue of usury. It was a long and exacting journey from the teachings of Thomas Aquinas who condemned all interest as usury to Adam Smith's justification of a fair rate of interest as revenue for the use of money, just as rent is for the use of land, wages for labor and profits for stocks.

Having dismissed the Islamic prohibition of usury in lending, the Arab code went on to legitimize insurance in all its forms which Islamic law also prohibited together with all other aleatory contracts for the elements of chance and risk taking they involve.

ENDNOTES

1. Subhi Mahmasani, *Falsafat al-Tashri' fil-Islam* [The Philosophy of Legislation in Islam] Beirut (1975) p. 94-97
2. Ahmad al-Khamlishi, "Kayfa Nagra' Zahir al-Iltizamat wal 'Uqud" [How to Read the Code of Obligations and Contracts] in *Al-Majalla al-Maghribiya lil-Qanun wal-Siyasa wal-Iqtisad,* Casablanca, No.7 (1984) p. 7-29.
3. Kanzo Takayangi, "A Century of Innovation: The Development of Japanese Law 1868-1961," in Arthur Taylor von Mehren ed. *The Legal Order in a Changing Society*, Cambridge (1963) p. 27.
4. Abdel-Razzaq al-Sanhuri, *Al-Wasit fi sharh al-Qanun al-Madani al-Jadid* [Interpretation of the New Civil Code].Cairo (1952) vol. I, p. 2-10
5. Takayangi, *A Century of Innovation,* op.cit. p.30.
6. Alan Watson, "Legal Transplants and Law Reform", 92 *Law Q. Rev.* (1976) p. 79
7. Al-Sanhuri, Al-Wasit, op.cit. p. 56-57.
8. Ibid. p. 45-50.
9. See generally Harold J. Berman, *Law and Revolution: The Formation of the Western Legal Tradition*, Cambridge (1983).
10. Shafik Chehata, *Al-Ittijahat al-Tashri'iya fi Qawanin al-Bilad al- 'Arabiya* [Legislative Trends in the Laws of the Arab Countries] Cairo (1960) p. 60-61
11. John Henry Merryman, *The Civil Law Tradition: An Introduction to the Legal Systems of Western Europe and Latin America*, Stanford (1969/1985) p. 92.
12. Roscoe Pound, *The Spirit of the Common Law,* Boston (1921) p. 141-142.
13. Konrad Zweigert & Hein Kotz, *An Introduction to Comparative Law,* Oxford (2nd ed. 1992) p. 87f.

14. See generally Albert Hourani, *Arabic Thought in the Liberal Age 1798-1939*, Cambridge (1962/1983).
15. Farhat J. Ziadeh, *Lawyers, the Rule of Law & Liberalism in Modern Egypt*, Stanford (1968) p. 99f.
16. Berman, *Law & Revolution*, op.cit. p 197.

*This section is based in the main on the Egyptian Civil Code, articles cited are those of that code, unless otherwise stated.

17. Lawrence M. Friedman, *A History of American Law*, New York, (1973/1985) p. 299-302 and 467-487.
18. S. Chehata, "L'influence du Code Civil dans le Mond," in *Travaux de la Semaine Internationale de Droit*, Paris (1950-1954) 854 at p. 857
19. Morton J. Horwitz, *The Transformation of American Law 1780-1860*, Cambridge (1977) p. 180f.
20. Zweigert & Kotz, *Introduction to Comparative Law*, op.cit. p 451.
21. P.S. Atiyah, *An Introduction to the Law of Contracts*, Oxford (1961/1989) p. 124-125.
22. Zweigert & Kotz, *Introduction to Comparative Law*, op.cit. p 424-425.
23. Subhi Mahmasani, *Al-Nazariya al`Ammah lil-Muwjibat wal-'Uqud fil-Shari'a al-Islamiya* (The General Principle of Obligations and Contracts in Islamic Law] Beirut (1948), vol. II, p. 42-44
24. Abdel-Razzaq al-Sạnhuri, *Al-Wajiz fi Sharh al-Qanun al-Madani* [The Concise Interpretation of the Civil Code], Cairo (1966) vol. I, p. 70.
25. Zweigert & Kotz, *Introduction to Comparative Law*, op.cit. p. 662-663.
26. Friedman, *History of American law*, op.cit. p. 262-263
27. Mahmasani, *Al-Nazariya al-'Ammah*, op.cit. p. 80 and 106
28. Zweigert & Kotz, *Introduction to Comparative Law*, op.cit. p. 575-577.
29. Ibid, p. 519.
30. Abdel-Razzaq al-Sanhuri, *Masadir al-Haq fil-Shari'a al-Islamiya* [Sources of Right in islamic Law], Cairo (1957), Vol I, p. 17-29.
31. Zweigert & Kotz, *Introduction to Comparative Law*, op.cit. p. 471-487.

32. Abdel-Mun'im Faraj al-Sadda, *Muhadarat fil-Qanun al-Madani:Nazariyat al-'Aqd fi Qawanin al-Bilad al-'Arabiya* [The Civil Code: Theory of Contract in the Laws of the Arab Countries], Cairo (1960), vol. 3, p. 24-37.
33. M.E. Hamid, "Islamic Law of Contract or Contracts," *Journal of Islamic & Comparative Law,* vol. 2-6 (1968-76) p.2.
34. Friedman, *History of American law,* op.cit. p. 262-263.
35. Ibid. p. 82.
36. See John Thomas Noonan, *The Scholastic Analysis of Usury,* Cambridge (1957).
37. George N. Sfeir, "Accommodating Islamic Banking: A U.S. Perspective," *Arab Banker* (Journal of the Arab Bankers Assoc., London) vol. V, no. 6 (1982) p. 24.

CHAPTER FOUR

Crime and Punishment

More than any other branch of the law, the criminal law of the Arab states was bound to undergo a profound change in the overall process of legal modernization. Family law was left essentially unchanged from its Islamic origin, and the Islamic law of contracts and obligations, except for the theological admonitions against usury and risk taking, was mostly patterned after customary usage, which made the transition to the European-based civil codes less problematic. The principles and purposes of crime and punishment in Islam, on the other hand, are so ingrained in the faith that modernization which implied secularization was bound to radically alter some of their basic assumptions, assumptions that are at the root of Islamic legal culture. That is why today the re-imposition of the principal Islamic crimes and punishments found in the revealed law is one of the main demands of Muslim fundamentalists.

It will therefore be necessary to preface the discussion of the contemporary, Western-based criminal law of the Arab states with a comparative look at the nature of crime and punishment in Islamic law which was until the end of the 19th century the prevailing law in all Arab states. Not only has this law left its mark on the new law and on the retained customs of Arab society, it remains to this day the applicable law in some of the Gulf states, particularly Saudi Arabia.

Historically, the influence of religion on criminal law and on law generally is too well known to require further elaboration. But while modern legal systems have sufficiently evolved beyond that stage to be able to distinguish between sin as a breach of one's relation to God and crime as a violation of positive law, Islamic scholars today continue to subscribe to the definition of crime formulated by their medieval predecessors as, "those forbidden things which God has admonished against whether by determinate or indeterminate punishment."[1] A broad definition no doubt which captures every infraction of the revealed law, be it religious, social or economic in nature, of whatever degree of severity, and whether the result of forbidden acts or failures to act. It comprises the entire spectrum of human actions and interactions, from failure to fast during Ramadan and abstain from drinking alcohol at all times, to blasphemy and fornication. to embezzlement and theft, to usury and gambling, to homicide and rebellion.

In its classification of crimes, however, Islamic law is not guided, as is the case with modern law, by the severity and nature of the crime. There is no distinction between felonies and misdemeanors or social crimes and victimless crimes. What it does is to identify crimes as *hudud* or nominate crimes with predetermined punishments in the revealed law, as *qisas* crimes justifying retaliation for homicide or bodily harm, and finally *ta'zir*, a catch-all category of unspecified offenses with undetermined punishments not falling under either *hudud* or *qisas.*

The *hudud* are the mainstay of Islamic criminology and the limits of transgression. In the words of the Qoran, they represent "the bounds of God's magnanimity which no one shall approach" (ii.187). They include the crimes of adultery or fornication (*zina*), false accusations thereof (*qadhf*), apostasy *(radda*), alcohol drinking (*shurb*), theft (*sariqa*), armed gangstery (*hiraba*), disobeying and rebelling against the ruler (*baghiy*). Their predetermined punishments range from flogging, to stoning, to severing of the limbs, to crucifixion, to death by beheading. Having been prescribed by the revealed law, these punishments are in the nature of God's right against the transgressors. Under no circumstances can they be the subject of bargaining, mitigation or commutation; only penitence (*tawba*) will absolve the accused of his or her sin.

Notwithstanding the tremendous developments in the science of criminology since the Middle Ages when Islamic criminal law was formed, and the radical changes introduced by modern Arab legislation, the reinstatement of the crimes of *hudud* remains for Muslim fundamentalists the test of Islamic revival. So much so that some Arab states who had earlier adopted modern criminal codes, such as Libya and Sudan, subsequently reintroduced some of the *hudud* crimes with their harsh punishments.

It was simply not possible to retain some of the *hudud* crimes under modern conditions. Apostasy, for example, had to be dropped from the new legislation if the freedom of belief provisions in the state constitutions were to make any sense. Likewise the crime of adultery or fornication had to undergo major restructuring to take cognizance of changing social mores and the rights of consenting adults. And as will be brought out in a subsequent section of this part, the new criminal codes adopted a totally new approach to punishment, moving away from the medieval notion of ritual justice and what Michel Foucault has called "the art of unbearable bodily sensations."[2]

Qisas, on the other hand, is based on the ancient concept of retaliation, of subjecting the perpetrator to the same pain and penalty he inflicted upon the victim. Its a carry over of the Biblical an eye for an eye. Indeed the Qoran, alluding to the Biblical text, states: "And therein we ordained for them, life for a life, eye for eye, nose for nose, ear for ear, tooth for tooth, and for other injuries equal retaliation. And whoever waives the right thereto, it shall be an expiation for his sins. Those who judge not by what God has ordained, they are the wrongdoers" (v.45). In other verses the Qoran elaborates further in the case of homicide: "O ye who believe, *qisas* is ordained unto you that in homicide, the free for the free, the slave for the slave, and the woman for the woman...(ii.178).

Qisas therefore comprises the crimes of homicide, manslaughter and any bodily deformation, injury, or harm. But in every verse in which this crime is mentioned, the Qoran asks believers to show compassion and remission by compensating the victim's family with the customary *diya* or blood money. But unlike *hudud*, the punishment of *qisas* is a right of the victim and his family. It is up to them to exact justice or grant forgiveness. The judge would abide by their decision.

As a right of retaliation, *qisas* was done away with where modern criminal codes have been adopted. Homicide and bodily injury however have been retained as crimes only to be prosecuted by the state.

Finally, there are the crimes of *ta'zir*. Except for a number of offenses specifically mentioned in the revealed law, such as usury, bribery, vituperation, deception, the crimes covered by *ta'zir* represent all the moral and material transgressions and infractions under the revealed law which do not fall under either *hudud* or *qisas*. They are generally captured by the sweeping Prophetic admonition, "command that which is agreeable and interdict that which is reprehensible," (*al-amr bil ma'ruf wal nahi 'an al-munkar*). With no specific punishment given for these offenses, it is left to the judge to devise one. Depending on the circumstances of the case, punishments can range from a mere reprimand, to compensation, flogging, incarceration, or even death, so long as they do not exceed the specified punishments of *hudud.* Unlike the latter however, *ta'zir* punishments may be the subject of mitigation, suspension or commutation.

As we shall see later however, the discretionary power given the judge under *ta'zir* to determine what conduct deserves punishment and what punishment to apply defies the principle of legality in modern penal law.

The Comparative Characteristics of Islamic & Modern Penal Law.

To be meaningful, any comparative analysis of law must necessarily take into consideration the differences in the legal culture and philosophical outlook of the societies whose legal systems are considered in the analysis. Already within the Western or modern legal tradition, with which Islamic law is here compared, there are conceptual differences between the common law and the continental law systems, and within both among the positivists and the sociologists, to name but two major schools of jurisprudence. Where does Islamic criminal law, which is part and parcel of the religious precepts and structure of Muslim society, fit when compared with these Western legal systems.

On the one hand, Islamic criminal law appears to favor legal positivism with its emphasis on the revealed source and text, the Qoran. On the other hand, its emphasis on the morality and security of the Muslim Community recognizes the importance of the sociological context of crime and punishment, albeit the ethical, religious meaning of these terms. Of immediate concern to a comparative study of crime and punishment is the question whether one can identify a penal law theory and the principle of legality within that theory.

The revealed text of Islamic criminal law leaves, as we have already seen in the discussion of *ta'zir* crimes, a great deal of criminal conduct devoid of specific description or punishment. The principle of legality as developed in continental law is premised on the specificity of codification, and by extension to common law on the recognized precedent of case-law.[3] Islamic penal law has neither been formally codified so far despite the expressed intention of fundamentalist scholars in recent years to do so, nor does Islamic legal procedure recognize the doctrine of stare decisis.

1. A General Theory of Penal Law: The observation made in an earlier part of this book that the Islamic law of contracts lacked a general theory of obligations applies equally to penal law in Islam. That law draws on the individual admonitions, rules, reprimands, postulates, and precepts in the revealed law, supplemented by the reported practices of the Prophet and the early Caliphs and elaborated upon by the religious scholars (*ulema)* of the various schools of Islamic jurisprudence of the 7th and 8th centuries. Only in this century did Arab jurists trained in Western legal science deduce from these sources a structured and methodical body of criminal rules comparable to modern penal law. Far however from systematizing and rationalizing the precepts of the revealed law in the light of modern conditions, they limited themselves to categorizing crimes in accordance with the Qoranic distinction between crimes with predetermined punishments or *hudud,* crimes of retaliation or *qisas,* and offenses with undefined punishments or *ta'zir*. Their new contribution was to relate to these various categories of crimes the principles of responsibility and justifiability found elsewhere in the revealed law.[4]

In recent years the tendency has been for monographs on Islamic criminal law to apply a comparative approach to the subject, underscoring the superiority of the preventive qualities of the harsh punishments of *hudud* crimes compared to the leniency of modern law punishments, and generally the effectiveness of the revealed law in preserving the moral virtues of society in the face of changing circumstances and the capriciousness of legislators.

A cursory look at the subject matter is sufficient to show that to do otherwise would have been a formidable task without abandoning completely the religious basis of the law. As we have seen the entire concept of *hudud*, the pillar of Islamic criminology, rests on a few singular verses in the Qoran. The prescription against adultery simply states, "Nor come ye nigh of adultery; it is shameful and leads to evil" (xvii.32). Many verses later comes the punishment: "The woman and the man guilty of adultery or fornication, flog each of them with a hundred lashes...and let a party of believers witness their punishment" (xxiv.2). Another states: "If any of your women are guilty of lewdness, take the evidence of four witnesses from amongst you and if they testify against them, confine them to their homes until death claims them or God finds them another way." (iv.15). Taking into consideration subsequent sayings and practices of the Prophet, the commentaries of the religious scholars interpret the admonition against adultery to mean that death by stoning should be meted to a married person, or single woman, and flogging of 100 lashes for an unmarried man. These commentaries are rich with detailed and formalistic explanations of what physically constitutes licit and illicit sexual acts, but little attention is given to the circumstances of the act or the state of mind of the accused.

When it comes to alcohol drinking, the Qoranic admonition does not even specify a punishment: "O ye who believe, intoxication and gambling...are an abomination and Satan's handiwork, eschew them that ye may prosper" (v.90). The punishment of 80 lashes is not based on any text, but on what was reported to have been the practice of the Prophet and the early Caliphs in dealing with drunk people. Although the admonition was against coming to prayer while drunk, the interpretation put on the revealed text by the religious scholars was to prohibit even the mere intake of alcoholic beverages no matter that the amount taken was not enough to intoxicate. An attempt in recent years by a state statute in the United Arab Emirates to allow an element of personal freedom in drinking and view drunkenness as a crime only in the context of a public nuisance, ran against the Islamic law provision of the federal constitution.[5]

With regard to theft, the Qoranic verse simply states: "As to the thief, male or female, cut off their hands for what they had gained as a severe reprimand from God, for God is exalted and wise" (v.38). The lack of exactitude in the definition of theft led to divergent views among the religious scholars with regard to the circumstances in which to apply this harsh penalty. The generally accepted view is that for theft to deserve such a harsh sentence it must involve the taking of things held in secure place often referred to as "protective custody" (*hirz*). Theft which occurs with the knowledge of the person from whom it was taken or from an unprotected place, is punishable by the more lenient punishments of *ta'zir*. Scholars also disagreed whether repentance, which is mentioned in the Qoran as acceptable to God "who is forgiving" (v.39), should absolve the thief of his guilt and escape punishment in this world, or was it intended for the hereafter only.

The very serious crime of apostasy is dealt with in the revealed law in similar summary fashion: "...And those among you who disavow their faith and die in blashpehmy, their work shall bear no fruit on earth or the hereafter, for they are the companions of fire where they shall remain eternally" (ii.217). Whether the abandonment of the Muslim faith is for another faith or simply turn agnostic, Muslim religious scholars consider apostasy a "retreat" (*radda*) from the rightful path intended to undermine the moral fabric of Muslim society.

The problem with such an offense is its imprecision. It has been held to mean any deviation from the faith; anything said or done which can be interpreted an affront to Islam, comparable to high treason in modern states. But this view is no longer tenable. This may have been the case under common law before the United States Constitution put a limit on its content. That ended the tendency of some States to label treason any petty crime against state functionaries and property.[6] The definition in the Constitution is plain and clear: "Treason against the United States, shall consist only in levying War against them, or in adhering to their Enemies, giving them Aid and Comfort" (Article III, Section 3). It is interesting to note in this connection the analogy made in medieval Europe between the canon law's repression of heretics and the Roman law's severe rules for the crime of treason. Heresy as an offense 'against divine majesty' was assimilated to affront to the 'imperial majesty.'[7] In Islam the equivalence between the sin of apostasy (*radda*) and the crime of rebelling against the authorities, that is, *hiraba* becomes obvious when one considers how similar their punishments are.

But the repercussions of the crime of apostasy upon the civil status of the accused remain far reaching even after the death penalty had been done away with in modern legislation. In a 1995 case in Egypt, a Muslim professor of Arabic literature was accused of apostasy and ordered to divorce his Muslim wife by the court in a suit brought by a total stranger on the grounds that the professor's lectures and writings on the literary aspects of the Qoran amounted to apostasy. Islamic law of domestic relations applicable in Egypt prohibits a Muslim woman from remaining married to an apostate from Islam, while the law of inheritance denies him his lawful share in the estate.

Although some of the elements which authorities today consider essential for the development of a general theory of penal law--principles, doctrines, rules and all the matters falling under intention, justification, excuse and responsibility,[8] can be found in the revealed law; they appear here and there in contexts which are not necessarily related to the criminal acts they are now used to qualify. The personality of crime and punishment, for example, is attributed in contemporary Islamic criminal law monographs to a verse in the Qoran unrelated to the commission of any crime. This is how that verse reads: "And they who believe and their seed that follow them in the faith, We will unite them with their offspring and will deprive them not of their work. *Every man is liable for what he had earned*" (52.21). Religious scholars interpreted this last phrase to mean that no one shall be made responsible for the sin of another.

The subject of responsibility generated an endless controversy in Islam between those who believed that human acts, the just and the unjust, were predetermined (*jabr*) and those who believed they were freely willed (*qadr*). But contemporary Muslim scholars seeking to develop a doctrine of responsibility in Islamic criminal law limit themselves to citing the solitary verse in the Qoran which states: "God shall not burden a soul more than it can bear; it shall receive what it had earned and suffer what it deserved" (ii.286).

If Islamic law lacks a general theory of penal law, it certainly is not devoid of a rationale and a method of its own. Contemporary Muslim scholars underscore the role of strict morality in the making of a good society, a kind of morality they ascribe to the religious law. They have also identified those elements which constitute the focus of morality and therefore worthy of protection. They are faith, self, progeny, property, and honor.[9] Each of these elements has an active and a passive aspect to it; that which the revealed law requires the faithful to do and that which it implores them to refrain from doing. For example when it comes to faith, the Qoran calls on the faithful to be knowledgeable of the religion of Islam and remain devoted to it. On the other hand, it implores them to make war on those who seek to oppress the Muslims and cause dissension among them. With regard to matters of honor or virtue, the emphasis is on sexual purity, particularly in women. On the passive side, several verses in the Qoran demand of the women to dress and act modestly and avoid anything which would arouse the sexual instincts in men, while on the active side every mature, responsible Muslim (*mukallaf*) is urged to combat immorality wherever it is encountered. Individual Muslims believe this gives them the right to take the law into their own hands, so to speak, whenever the Government fails or is unwilling to act against those who defy the revealed law.

One of the first ideas Beccaria developed in his pioneering work,[10] on modern criminal law is that vice and virtue are vague and fluctuating terms not suited to be the scale of punishments and crimes. "They are so murky because they change with time, which makes names outlive the things for which they stand, and because they change with rivers and mountains, which often mark the boundaries not only of physical but of moral geography."[11]

But Beccaria's lasting influence on the modernization of penal law is in identifying a measure of crime in society and the purpose of punishment--the two essential features of the theory of penal law today. He considered the true measure of crime 'the harm done to society.' Without however overlooking their changing nature in different times and places, he classified crimes in this descending order: offenses against the state or high treason, offenses against the security and liberty of private persons, offenses against the public tranquillity and the peace of citizens.[12]

When it came to punishments and the method of inflicting them, he underscored the need for proportionality between the crime and its punishment: "to make the most effective and lasting impression on men's minds and inflict the least torment on the body of the criminals."[13]

2. The Principle of Legality: As must have become clear by now, Islamic criminal law consists of first, a limited number of crimes with prescribed penalties to be strictly adhered to, the *hudud* crimes, even where their definition was left imprecise; second, homicide and bodily injury which is subject to retaliation that is *qisas* and/or compensation by blood money (*diya*); and third, all other criminal conduct which has neither a precise definition nor a prescribed punishment, the *ta'zir* offenses, left to the discretion of the judge to specify.

A modern theoretician of penal law would consider this wide ranging power of the judge the antithesis of the principle of legality in penal law. Citing an opinion of the International Court of Justice, Jerome Hall says that "the essence of this principle of legality is limitation on penalization by the State's officials, effected by the prescription and application of specific rules."[14] In European legal parlance where it originated, the principle is rendered by the Latin phrase, *nulla poena sine lege*. It is the product of the 18th century Liberalism and the French Declaration of the Rights of Man which contained a provision to that effect, and the movement for codification which advanced the technical ideas underlying the phrase no penalty without a law.

Anxious to show that Islamic penal law had many of the characteristics of modern law long before they figured in the Western legal tradition, Islamic scholars today point to those tenets of the Qoran which in their own way uphold the principles of no retroactivity and no punishment without law, particularly with regard to the crimes of *hudud*.[15] What these scholars miss are the far-reaching changes in the medieval concepts and institutions of public law brought about by the intellectual revolution in Europe. In tracing the effect of this revolution on the development of the Civil Law tradition, Merryman points out three major accomplishments: (a) the complete break with religious doctrine, brief or authority in favor of secular natural law which brought forth the notion of individual fundamental rights; (b) the separation of governmental powers, particularly the independence of the judiciary from the legislative and the executive; and (c) the rational approach to the law and legal institutions which could now be rationally repealed and new ones put in their place without defying unimpeachable tenets.[16]

How does Islamic penal law compare with these modern characteristics of public law of which penal law is a part? To begin with, the revealed text of Islamic law is immutable for being divine. This has hindered the evolution of a rational theory of criminal law without defying its unimpeachable tenets. Not only is man-made change in the revealed text unthinkable, any attempt at reducing its precepts into a coherent and systematic code gets bogged down in the mass of conflicting commentaries and interpretations on the revealed text by religious scholars (*ulema*) of the 8th and 9th centuries. And where agreement among these scholars was achieved, it assumed the status of a consensus (*ijma'*), which subsequent generations erected as Gibb has described it into a "theory of infallibility."[17] Not unlike the councils of the Christian Church in their pronouncements on the doctrines of the faith, the probative quality of *ijma'* in Islam is for all practical purposes on a par with that of the revealed text.

With such insurmountable hurdles to codification, the technical ideas underlying the modern principle of legality were simply unattainable. The law's prescribed penalties (*hudud*) are left unavoidable and must be strictly applied; the role of the judge being limited to pronouncing the prescribed punishment no more and no less and without the right to suspend or commute the sentence, no matter what the circumstances are.[18] But the crimes of *hudud*, serious as they are, are but a few in number which leaves a considerable segment of Islamic penal law (*ta'zir*) subject to the discretion of the judge to find the rule of law which fits the crime and prescribe the right punishment. Unlike the case of *hudud*, he is at liberty to pass, suspend or commute the sentence, taking into consideration the circumstances of the case and the status of the accused.

It must be obvious that a law saddled with such conditions cannot be amenable to the development of a modern principle of legality. Consequently, anything considered contrary to the faith or detrimental to the interest of the Muslim Community at large can validly be judged criminal conduct. As Hall has pointed out with regard to certain epochs of European law, enjoining unrestricted legal analogy ended in "widening the net of punishability" and encouraging repressive government not only in the interpretation of the law but also in the finding of facts.[19] Pursuing this line of thought would lead to the wider subject of the limitation on the power of the State and the rights of the individual which although an essential aspect of the principle of legality is better left to the part dealing with constitutionalism.

The Transition to Modern Law

The extent of the change brought about by the adoption of modern penal codes in this century is quite apparent in the first articles of these codes establishing the principle of legality. The articles take various forms, but the intent is the same:

> "No punishment shall be prescribed.for a crime which when committed the law did not provide for it." (Lebanese code).
>
> "No one shall be punished except in accordance with the provisions of a previously promulgated law." (Tunisian code).
>
> "No conduct shall be considered criminal and no punishment shall be prescribed for it except in accordance with a provision in the law." (Kuwaiti code).
>
> "The provisions of this law shall apply to anyone who commits one of the crimes provided therein." (Egyptian code).

Such provisions were only possible in the context of the modern territorial state and its power to legislate free of the constraints of the religious law. This sea change from the medieval to the modern was pioneered by the Ottoman Turks and mirrored after European legislation, particularly the code Napoleon.[20] And as was the case in other fields of the law, the change affected the Arab provinces of the Empire.

The first Ottoman penal code of 1840 was a hybrid of Islamic and European provisions. It was reformulated in 1851 and reissued in 1858 in its most modern form. The code remained applicable in modern Turkey until 1926 and in the former Arab provinces until the 1940's.

Modeled after the French code of 1810, the 1858 Ottoman code was a marked transition to modern criminal law, the process being quite obvious in the first article of the code. Instead of the outright declaration of the principle of legality found in more recent Arab legislation, the Ottoman code began with a statement of justification if not vindication for deviating from the Islamic norm:

> "Just as it is the obligation of the Government to punish crimes which are committed directly against it, it is also its obligation to punish crimes directed against individual persons because of the disturbance of public tranquillity they cause. Therefore this law is intended to obligate and incorporate that which is legally [by Islamic law] (*shar'an*) the duty of the authorities that be (*uwliya al-amr*) in defining the different kinds of *ta'zir*

> crimes and their procedures. It being understood that nothing in this shall in any way detract from personal rights recognized *shar'an* [by Islamic law]."[21]

To justify the new rules the code invoked what was known in Islam as *siyasa shar'iya,* literally legal policy, a prerogative of the Caliph to decree, when necessary, laws which would supplement but not contradict the tenets of the revealed text. The specific reference made in the article to the *ta'zir* offenses as the category of crimes left by Islamic law to the authorities to identify and punish as they see fit was intended as a cover from the past to what was certainly new categories of crimes and punishments.

Nevertheless, the code did make a significant break with Islamic law. Instead of the *hudud/qisas/ta'zir* categories, the code divided crimes into felonies, misdemeanors, and contraventions. It discarded the bodily punishments of amputation, flogging and stoning, and replaced them with the death penalty, life imprisonment with hard labor, banishment, incarceration, fine, and loss of civil rights, with strict rules for imposing and executing these punishments. But these rules left intact the traditional public spectacle to which convicts were subjected. The code required those convicted of heinous crimes to be paraded in chains with a placard hung on their bodies describing in large letters the nature of their offense and punishment; a residue of the kind of ordeal practiced in Europe until the beginning of the 19th century which Michel Foucault desscribed in his book on prison reform, *Surveiller et Punir.*

The code's 265 articles, began with crimes against the internal and external security of the state, a novel category of crimes brought about by the nature of the sovereign territorial state. Here treason rather than apostasy was the great offense. Still, "defaming" the Prophets brought the accused one to three years in prison, while "defaming" the Sultan prison with hard labor. Bribery, corrupt practices, embezzlement of state funds and misuse of office by government employees were among the many new offenses of the modern state the code introduced.

It was however the manner by which the code dealt with the *hudud* and *qisas* crimes, whose punishments are prescribed in the revealed law, that the transitory nature of the code in trying to bridge the old and the new, came clearly through. Intentional homicide elicited the death penalty, according to article 171. But the language of this article and the one succeeding it left room for the Islamic punishments of retaliation *(qisas)* and blood money (*diya*) to be invoked by the victim's family. Similarly, the punishment for bodily injury was no longer retaliation, only a prison term with a sort of fine (blood money?) to compensate for the medical expenses and lost income of the injured party.

The crimes of adultery and fornication were reduced in stature and their punishment limited to a prison term where a minor was involved or duress used. However a husband who surprises his wife or any other female member of his extended family in bed with another man committing the "disgraceful act" and kills either or both of them his conduct was labeled justifiable homicide and forgiven. But homosexual acts with minors and with adults under duress, sexual harassment, and abortion were made punishable by prison terms.

The punishment for theft, which under Islamic law brought about amputation of the hand, became under the code a maximum of fifteen years to life with hard labor if it involved breaking in, conspiracy or other aggravated circumstances.

With all its technical and formal advantages over the old law, the Ottoman code could not improve much on the autocratic rule of the Ottoman sultans. The revolutionary cultural and political changes which laid the ground for the Code Napoleon in France were simply not there. Nor did the Ottoman authorities adopt the companion French law to the penal code, the Code of Criminal Procedure, until twenty one years later. And as far as the Arab provinces of the Empire were concerned, both the law and the proceedings of the court were in Turkish, a language unknown to the majority of the people there.

A Modern Penal Code

By the 1930's the deficiencies of the Ottoman Penal Code had become quite evident. Not only had the French code by then come under increased criticism in France itself, in the 1920's and 1930's a world-wide surge of legislation was breaking new ground in the criminal law field. It is said that the committee charged with drafting the current Lebanese penal code in 1941 had before it no less than 60 foreign codes of recent vintage to consult and compare. And although it was originally drafted in the French language, the influence of the French Penal Code cannot be said to be more than the influence of other European codes, such as the Italian and the Swiss. Indeed as some Lebanese authorities in the field have pointed out the variations between the French and the Lebanese codes are quite substantial.[22] While its rendition into Arabic left much to be desired from the point of view of legal drafting, its principles and provisions were highly praised, and became a prototype for other Arab codes including the Syrian (1949) and the Jordanian (1960) codes.

National legislation in Egypt (as distinct from the law of the Mixed Courts catering mostly to foreigners) goes back to 1855 when a penal code patterned after the first Ottoman code of 1851 was adopted. This law like its Ottoman model combined both Islamic and customary rules. Its improvement on the former was in specifying some of the punishments of *ta'zir* crimes which were not prescribed in the revealed text. However it left some of the harsh bodily punishments intact, except that persons with means were given monetary fines while the poor continued to be subjected to flogging and other bodily sanctions.[23]

The shift away from the Islamic rules of crime and punishment did not come until 1883 with the establishment of the national courts side by side with the Mixed Courts, and the adoption of comparable modern laws including a penal code modeled after the French code of 1810. But as was the case with the 1858 Ottoman code, the 1883 Egyptian code, lacked the social context and procedural safeguards which its French counterpart enjoyed. The result was socially unsettling resulting in an upsurge in crimes, until the authorities stepped in and tightened the procedural safeguards, giving the courts the investigatory powers the law had left in the hands of administrative commissions.[24]

The current 1937 Egyptian Penal Code came with the end to foreign concessions and the assumption of Egyptian courts competence over all criminal matters. It has since been amended and revised with inputs from Italian, Belgian and Lebanese sources.

Meanwhile European inspired legislation in the criminal law field came as early as the turn of the century in the North African Arab states which came under French influence. The current Tunisian penal code dates back to 1913. It has since been through numerous amendments to bring it up to date with changing social conditions. In Algeria and Morocco, new legislation coincided with the unification of the countries' judicial systems after the demise of the French presence. The current Moroccan Penal Code was adopted in 1962 and the Algerian code in 1966. The two codes and their procedural counterparts follow closely the continental European system and French practice in particular.

British administered Arab territories became the recipients at first of penal codes modeled after the Indian code of 1860. This was evident in Sudan with the promulgation of the first modern penal code in 1899 to replace what was essentially a regime of Islamic and customary rules, later to be followed by the 1925 code. In recent times however, Sudan was to experience a reversal in the modernization process. Since the 1970's succeeding regimes resorted, whether for reasons of ideology or simply to enhance their claim to legitimacy, to the Islamization of the country's penal code. This was evident in the reintroduction in the 1974, 1983 and 1991 codes of the Islamic crimes of *hudud* and in various versions and application their corporeal punishments.

British influence brought about also the first Iraqi Penal Code of 1918, which was promulgated soon after the British occupation of the country in World War I. It displaced the Ottoman code of 1858. But the defects of this first code and the need, in the words of the Explanatory Memorandum of the current code, "for the law to adjust to the changing spirit of the times and the conditions in society," soon became obvious. Planning for a new code began in 1929 and various drafts were prepared, but none saw the light until the current 1969 code was promulgated by the newly installed Baathist regime. It benefited from the latest Arab and European legislation in the field, including a 1966 Egyptian draft penal code which was never enacted.

As far as the other Arab states are concerned, the modernization of the criminal law has not been as thorough or complete. Saudi Arabia and Yemen continue to adhere to the Islamic law rules of crime and punishment unchanged except for statutory improvements in court organization and procedure. In the smaller Persian Gulf states of Kuwait, United Arab Emirates, Qatar, Bahrain and Oman, the law evolved gradually along British inspired reforms, until their independence in the 1960's when new codes combining Islamic and modern law began to be adopted. Typical of this amalgam is the United Arab Emirates penal code of 1988 whose first article reads:

> "Crimes of *hudud*, *qisas* and *diya* shall be governed by Islamic Sharia, while crimes and punishments of *ta'zir* shall be determined in accordance with the rules of this and other criminal laws."

The result is a dual categorization of crimes, the one following the modern three categories of felonies, misdemeanors and contraventions, and the other the crimes of *hudud*, of *qisas* and of *ta'zir*. The code then attempts to bridge the two by defining felonies as the crimes whose punishments are those of *hudud* or *qisas*, death and prison sentences, and the punishments for misdemeanors prison, fine, *diya*, and flogging, which correspond to the *ta'zir* punishments.

Libya, which adopted in the 1950's a modern criminal code based on Italian and Egyptian laws had second thoughts after the Qadhafi regime came to power. While that code remains essentially valid to this day, the Qadhafi regime enacted in 1972, 1973 and 1974 legislation which reintroduced some of the Islamic *hudud* crimes and their punishments, including those of theft and highway robbery, fornication, unfounded accusations of fornication, and alcoholic drinks. However it is not certain to what extent these crimes and their punishments are being applied by the country's regular, civil judiciary.

The Salient Features of the Arab Penal Codes

Directly or indirectly, the Arab penal codes are a product of the schools of criminology which flourished in Europe around the turn of the century and their scientific methods and modern policies in dealing with crime. Among the early new codes the 1943 Lebanese penal code is a prototype of the new Arab legislation in the field. Despite its hurried drafting and lack of formal legislative enactment, it comprehended all the modern principles in the field that practically none of its subsequent amendments were intended to introduce new ideas. What they did was only to adapt its prescribed punishments to new forms of crime, such as the use of drugs and illicit financial transactions.[25]

Here then are some of the essential features of the Arab penal codes

1. Legality and Non-Retroactivity: The principle of legality which has already been noted above, implies also the principle of non-retroactivity. Nevertheless, in some Arab states, such as Egypt, the principle shows up also as a constitutional provision, while in others it appears as a companion principle to that of legality in the penal code itself. There is however one important exception to the non-retroactivity rule, and that is the adoption, following the commission of the crime, of a new law more favorable to the accused. In that case the new law will generally apply. What the Arab codes differ over however is the stage in the proceedings at which the new law will take effect. The majority favor giving the accused the benefit of the new law even after judgment had been rendered if the new law no longer considers the crime for which the accused was convicted punishable. In the words of the Lebanese code:[26] "A crime shall not be punishable if abrogated by a new law; any criminal ruling made in the case shall have no effect."

2. Territorial Competence: The majority of Arab codes address the question of territorial application of the law, whether the extent of the territorial limits are defined in the code or not. The Lebanese code is quite comprehensive in this regard. After stating that the provisions of the code apply to all crimes committed on Lebanese soil, it goes on to describe both the relevant elements of the crime and the territorial limits which justify the application of the law. The former includes the actual or prospective consequences of the crime, any component of it, or any act of a series of acts constituting the crime if committed on Lebanese territory. The latter includes Lebanese soil, the territorial waters, the air space above, and Lebanese ships and aircraft. Crimes committed on foreign aircraft and ships are excluded, even if committed within Lebanese air space and territorial waters, unless the accused happens to be a Lebanese national. This is in conformity with the accepted international practice known as the law of the flag.

The territorial competence of the Arab codes extends also to nationals and foreigners alike who, outside the territory of the state, abet, participate in, or commit "crimes against the security of the state, forge or counterfeit the seal of the state, its currency or national and foreign legal or customary tender. These rules shall not however apply to a foreign national whose actions were not contrary to international law."

Although some Arab codes, such as Egypt's, exempt from the enforcement of this rule persons tried and convicted or declared innocent in a foreign court, others, including the Lebanese code, specifically state that, unless the foreign judgment was rendered at the request of the Lebanese Government, Lebanese law would still be enforced if the crime in question was committed on Lebanese soil.

3. Nationality Competence: The competence of the Arab States' codes extends to crimes committed abroad by their nationals. While some, such as those of Egypt and Kuwait, require that the crime be punishable in the country where it was committed, others such as the Syrian and the Jordanian do not. The latter states follow the Lebanese law which applies to all Lebanese nationals "who commit outside Lebanon a felony or misdemeanor punishable by Lebanese law, even if the accused relinquished the Lebanese nationality following the commission of the crime."

Specifically mentioned generally in Arab codes as subject to this rule are crimes committed abroad by Government officials and members of the diplomatic and consular services. By the same token, the Arab codes exempt from applying their law to crimes committed in their territories by members of the foreign diplomatic and consular services who enjoy internationally recognized immunity in accordance with the 1961 Vienna Treaty.

The nationality competence of some Arab codes takes on a wider, universal application, however, when it is made to extend to domiciliary foreign nationals who commit abroad crimes punishable under the codes. For example, Lebanese law will apply to "any foreign national domiciled in Lebanon who abetted or committed abroad a felony or misdemeanor and whose extradition had not been requested or approved."

4. Application of Foreign Law: The majority of the Arab codes give only indirect cognizance to foreign law in a criminal case to determine whether the criminal conduct perpetrated by a national is punishable under the law of the place where the crime was committed. In cases where the foreign law and the local law are at variance, the judge is required when passing judgment to take into account this variance in favor of the accused.

Others, such as the Jordanian code, which do not even allude to whether the crime is or is not punishable under the foreign law, have decided to completely disregard the possibility of the application of that law.[27]

Part of the problem which the Arab penal codes face in this regard are the restrictions which the civil codes impose on the application of foreign law if the rules of that law are contrary to public order and morality. While the civil codes do not specifically define public order and morality, it is generally accepted to include the moral and religious principles on which matters of personal status and domestic relations are based in the Arab countries.

Thus the Lebanese code and others influenced by it, require the courts to apply in the case of crimes committed locally or abroad the national (personal) law of the accused when any element of the crime involves some aspect of personal status or civil competence. This means that in those cases the foreign law is definitely blocked by the application of the personal law of the accused. It is a deprecation from the general rule previously alluded to and found in the Lebanese and other Arab codes that the courts will apply the law more favorable to the accused.

5. Enforcement of Foreign Judgments: Generally speaking, the Arab codes, as is the case with the laws of most other states, do not grant unqualified recognition to foreign judgments. This is an area of criminal law more often left to bilateral or regional treaties, such as the League of Arab States Extradition Treaty of 1953. Article 17 of this treaty requires a member state of the League to execute the judgment of the other member state rendered at its request and the state holding the convict agrees. This requirement is limited to judgments imposing a prison term with or without hard labor.

Nevertheless, the Arab codes are not totally oblivious to foreign judgments. The Lebanese code is the most accommodating in this respect. Other than cases involving the security of the state or counterfeit of its legal tender, no person whether a national or an alien tried abroad, and the sentence was executed or waived by pardon or statute of limitation, may be sued again in Lebanon. Foreign judgments in cases involving crimes against the security of the state or counterfeit of its legal tender, as well as crimes committed on Lebanese territory, will only be recognized if rendered in pursuance of official notification from the Lebanese authorities. This last condition gives the recognizing state the satisfaction that its sovereignty was not completely disregarded but had somehow participated in the prosecution of the accused.

Otherwise Arab codes give cognizance to foreign judgments to the extent that these judgments call for precautionary measures against the accused, his loss of civil rights, and reimbursement of damages, if they comply with local law. Contrary however to accepted international practice, the Lebanese and other Arab codes give the judge the right to go beyond the procedural to the substantive aspects of the case in determining whether the foreign judgment was properly rendered.

6. Extradition: The increase in international crimes and acts of terrorism world wide has not generated a similar growth in national legislation for extradition. This remains in the main the realm of bilateral and regional treaties. Reference has already been made to the 1953 Extradition Treaty of the League of Arab States to which most Arab states have adhered. These states have also a number of bilateral treaties with other Arab and foreign states. But the only bilateral treaty between the United States and an Arab state so far, is the 1995 extradition treaty between the United States and Jordan. Jordan is also one of the very few Arab states with an extradition law which dates back to 1927.

Requests for extradition are usually regulated in the Arab states by the Criminal Procedure Law or the Penal Code, which generally forbid extradition except under the terms of the extradition treaty where it exists or according to the provisions of the law. As the Lebanese code shows, the terms under which extradition may be granted are quite limited:

(1) The requesting state must be legally competent, that is, the crime is committed by one of its nationals, on its territory and its courts have jurisdiction. Furthermore, the crime must be against the security or financial well-being of the requesting state. Crimes falling within the territorial and personal jurisdiction of Lebanese courts are therefore excluded.

(2) The state from whom the extradition is requested does not have jurisdiction in the case. On this ground Lebanese courts will deny the extradition of an accused if he is a Lebanese national.

(3) The criminal conduct must be a felony or a misdemeanor in both the requesting and the requested states. This eliminates from extradition persons accused of contraventions under Lebanese law.

(4) Extradition will not be granted if final judgment had been returned in Lebanon or the public claim against the accused had lapsed by the force of law in either the requesting or the requested state, if the crime itself or the motive for the extradition is political in nature, and if the punishment for the crime in the law of the requesting state is contrary to the public policy of the requested state.

The Anatomy of Punishment in the Arab Penal Codes

Judging from the text, the Arab penal codes comply in the main with the basic principles which determine the imposition of punishments in modern criminal law. These are the legality of punishment, the individuality of punishment, the specificity of punishment, the equality of punishment, and finally the juridical nature of the punishment, that is, handed down by a court of law.[28]

Having established the principles guiding their application, the division of punishments in the Arab codes is synonymous with the types of crimes--felonies, misdemeanors, contraventions. A crime is a felony if the prescribed punishment is the death penalty, hard labor or long prison term; it is a misdemeanor if the punishment is a shorter prison term or fine; and it is a contravention if the prison term is days and the fine nominal.

All Arab penal codes prescribe the death penalty, especially by hanging, for such felonies as murder in the first degree or aggravated circumstances, arson or attacks against means of transport resulting in the death a person, and crimes against the security of the state. But to take effect, a death penalty requires a consensus judgment, a concurring opinion by the court of cassation, and approval of the head of state.

The Arab states have not been spared the world wide controversy over the death penalty. But it remains well entrenched, particularly that it is set by the revealed text of Islamic law for murder and other heinous crimes. The only relief in the majority of the codes is granted to pregnant woman whose death sentence is temporarily lifted until she had delivered and nursed her baby for two months, as most Arab codes hold, or her sentence is commuted to life in prison, as the Kuwaiti and Jordanian codes provide.

The next punishment in the scale of severity is prison with hard labor which is the penalty for murder without premeditation and the theft or destruction of state property. Like the death penalty, hard labor is also a common feature of Arab penal codes. The Lebanese code describes it as "Forcing the prisoner to undertake such strenuous work as is consistent with the sex and age of the prisoner." But most Arab codes permit a convict sentenced to a life term with hard labor to be paroled after the lapse of twenty years.

The punishments of prison and/or fine may be punishments for felonies, misdemeanors or contraventions, the difference between them being the prison term and the amount of the fine. The Lebanese code has the interesting provision which states that if the motive for the crime was illicit gain and fine was not the punishment for that crime, then the accused shall be subject to a fine as well as the punishment prescribed in the code.

In addition to these so-called original punishments, the Arab penal codes prescribe additional and complementary punishments as well as preventive measures. Additional or complementary punishments include deprivation of certain civil rights, denial of public service, confiscation of property involved in the commission of the crime, and police supervision, all provided by law and not at the discretion of the judge.

Precautionary or preventive measures are invoked by law when a suspect is a habitual criminal, deemed a clear and present danger to public order, or sufficient suspicion exists that a crime is about to be committed. These measures can be anything from posting a sort of bail for good conduct to a restraining order and non-prison confinement to suspending a newspaper and closing of a place of business. Questions have been raised about the legality of these precautionary measures which are not limited to the Arab penal codes but are also found in a number of European codes, for their intervention in *ante delectum* situations and the consequent contravention of the personal freedom of the suspect. But the conflict which these situations raise between the principle of legality and the security of society has been resolved in favor of the latter with the adoption by the penal codes of what are essentially administrative measures.[29]

Now that we have described the nature and types of punishments two questions need to be addressed. Are these punishments applicable to any kind of crime, and are juristic persons subject to them in the same way individuals are?

Certain Arab penal codes differentiate between a political crime and a regular crime as far as punishment is concerned. The Lebanese and Syrian codes, for example, exclude the death penalty and prison with hard labor from punishments prescribed for political crimes. Political crimes are described as those crimes which are committed with a political motive in mind or are directed against the political rights of individuals or society as a whole. Attempted coups or conspiracies to change the form of government are the classical examples of political crimes, and they should be distinguished from crimes against the security of the state and acts of terrorism which are treated as ordinary crimes in the penal codes.

On the culpability of juristic persons, such as corporations and associations, itself a highly controversial subject in comparative criminal law, the Arab penal codes assume differing stances. The reason is that these codes treat differently the causal relationship between the party abetting or instigating and the actual perpetrator of the crime if the latter is irresponsible by reason of ignorance or lack of competence. The officer or employee of the corporation is often after all the innocent executor of corporate decisions.

Whatever the differences in their provisions however, the Arab codes do in practice allow for the culpability of juristic persons, particularly where the law considers the act of abetting or instigating a distinguishable act of participation in the crime whose author is answerable for it. This is the case with the Lebanese code which takes the position that a juristic person is responsible for the conduct of its directors, officers, and representatives when the conduct is undertaken on its behalf, a position which renders the juristic person liable for penal prosecution, except that in the case of criminal bankruptcy of a commercial enterprise the officers of the corporation alone are held liable.[30]

Penalties for the crimes of juristic persons, whether they are construction violations, fraud, unfair competition, or other such criminal conduct by corporations or associations, are usually limited to fine, confiscation, and dissolution or cessation of operations.

Grounds for Non-Culpability and Justifiability

The internal and external manifestations of criminal conduct in the Arab penal codes are not much different from what one finds in their European counterparts. This reduces the need in this survey of Arab law to discuss in detail the moral and material elements of criminal conduct, the act whether it is commission or omission, the resulting harm or violation, and the causality between the two. Instead, we shall concentrate here on the grounds which would render an otherwise criminal conduct justifiable and non-culpable, an area of criminal law where remnants of Islamic law rules and traditional social mores have survived in the new codes.

Nevertheless the basic principles and overall approach of the Arab codes in this field are generally the same as those which inform European law, a situation which is not devoid of some irony. That the Islamic rules of crime and punishment which constitute a major premise of Islamic law, should be displaced by European rules whose evolution was greatly influenced by canon law. It was the medieval canonical theory of culpability which prepared the way for the development of modern rules for determining volition, premeditation, recidivism, mitigating circumstances, and others, whereas primitive criminal law was interested above all in the harm done and in compensation.[31]

Because of the fine line which separates the legal difference between non-culpability and justifiability, the one denying liability and the other dismissing criminality, some Arab codes treated the subject under various parts of the code while others pooled them together under one heading. They all agree however on three main causes of justifiability. These are crimes committed in the exercise of a right, in the exercise of a duty, and in legitimate self-defense. In addition to these some codes recognize also necessity, coercion, and consent of the victim as grounds for non-culpability or justifiability. Generally speaking the occurrence of any one of these grounds in the circumstances of the crime sap it of culpability and transform it into a justifiable act.

1. **In the Exercise of a Right**: While the language used in the codes vary, what constitutes an act in the exercise of a right is essentially the same--the legitimate exercise of a right for the purpose it was intended. The Egyptian code adds that the exercise of the right be carried out "with good intentions," while the Lebanese code qualifies the exercise "without excess [abuse]." The Moroccan and Tunisian codes, on the other hand, state simply that the act be "perpetrated in accordance with the provision of the law."

Examples of such acts which otherwise may be punishable are those which normally happen in sports, medical treatment, and parents' chastisement of their children, provided these acts are necessary, relevant, and legitimate. The latter which negates the abuse of rights, hence justifiability, is based on a cardinal principle of the civil code, the code which, for all practical purposes, is the general law of the Arab states which have adopted a civil code.

According to this principle the abuse of right occurs when the purpose of the act was sheer aggression, if the benefit sought from the act is illicit or disproportionate with the harm done, and goes beyond what is reasonable and customary. With such limitations on the use of rights the following acts cannot be justified: a husband's abuse of his wife to enforce her duty of obedience to him under a domestic relations law, the resort by an attorney to defamatory utterances in defense of his client, or a doctor aborting a woman unnecessarily.

2. **In the Performance of a Duty**: The Moroccan and Tunisian codes, following the French example, combine in the same provision acts undertaken in the performance of a duty and in the exercise of a right. The Lebanese and Syrian codes while segregating at first acts in the exercise of a right, which is taken to mean in accordance with the law, speak in a subsequent article of an act "in compliance with a provision of the law or a legitimate order of the authorities." The reason for this apparent confusion is the need to provide for two different but not unrelated situations, the one concerning acts by ordinary persons and the other acts by government officials.

Whether it is that of an ordinary person or a government official, to be justifiable the act must be in compliance with the law or in pursuance of a legal order issued by a competent authority. Although certain laws allow ordinary citizens to inform about or help in apprehending culprits without contravening the provisions of the criminal code against divulging secrets or constraining the freedom of others, and are therefore not culpable, most of the acts envisaged by the criminal codes as justifiable for being in the performance of a duty are the acts of government officials. This has led some codes, such as those of Egypt and Kuwait to provide specifically for acts by government officials acting in the performance of their duties or in compliance with orders they are legally bound to obey.

Government officials are however absolved of responsibility by these and other Arab codes, such as the Lebanese and Syrian codes, if they mistakenly believed that they were acting in the course of their duties in compliance with a legitimate order. But they are not so absolved if the act is contrary to the law such as the torture of a prisoner in order to extract a confession from him, in which case both the employee and his superior who issued the order become culpable.

3. **In Self Defense**: Because of its particular relevance in Arab society to the crimes of passion and of honor, self-defense is better understood in the context of Islamic and customary rules and social values which place a high premium on the integrity of the individual's relations to others as well as family honor especially as it relates to the chastity of women. As Lawrence Rosen has put it in describing Moroccan society, each individual stands at the center of a web of obligations and incorporates in his or her network of ties the features of social background (*asel*) and situated encounters (*hal*) by which they will be known to others.[32]

Self-defense is generally recognized as legitimate in fending off harm or danger to one's self or even to others. Arab codes identify it as a right. In the words of the Lebanese code, "any act necessary to ward off an illegal, unprovoked, imminent threat to self or property or the self or property of another, is considered an act in pursuit of a right." The condition that the act of self-defense be necessary, unprovoked and commensurate with the danger posed is brought out elsewhere in the code in the section dealing with necessity as ground for justification.

Although all the Arab codes require for self-defense that the danger be imminent, not all of them go along with the condition that the defendant did not provoke or incite the circumstances which necessitated his self-defense, which, according to one criminal law authority,[33] is bound to create unsavory situations difficult to justify. Such a situation would be a claim of self-defense by an adulterous wife and her lover in fending off the threat of her husband who surprised them together in bed. The tendency in more advanced codes, according to this authority, is to do away with this condition, leaving it for the courts to assess the particular circumstances of the case irrespective of what the perpetrator did before.

Because aggression constitutes a negation of the right of the victim and self-defense is a refutation of that negation, the law generally allows it for the protection of one's own self, property or honor, as well as the self, property or honor of another. Some codes, such as that of Jordan, however, set certain limits on acts of self-defense to protect property. In order to justify the claim of self defense, the theft or other attacks against the property must be accompanied by violence leading to considerable harm against the person or his proprietary rights. The Tunisian code gives instances of violent robbery such as forceful break-in or climbing over a fence at night as justifying murder and injury of the criminal; to which the Egyptian code adds arson, destruction of property and entering of another person's home.

Causing death or severe injury in self-defense is not uniformly recognized in the Arab codes. It is specifically mentioned in the codes of Algeria, Morocco and Tunisia as justified if it occurs in only three situations--in defense of life, in night break-in, and in violent robbery. Not specifically mentioned and left to the particular circumstances of the case to determine whether its was justifiable, are the codes of Jordan, Lebanon and Syria.

In a number of Arab criminal codes justifiable self-defense is specifically extended beyond the threat to life, to include bodily harm, defamation of one's honor or integrity, abduction, sacrilegious utterances against religious personalities and beliefs, encouraging pornographic acts, sexual enticement and abuse of the young, rape, and the mere violation of female premises.

This wide definition given to self-defense represents a clear concession to the particular human condition and mores of Arab society, where passions and emotions are easily aroused in defense of personal honor, the integrity of family relations and religious beliefs. This concession was well recognized in the first modern criminal code, the Ottoman code of 1858, where article 186 provided the general principle that murder and bodily harm are justified "in defense of self or honor." Such a wholesale ruling is quite at variance with American jurisprudence which generally speaking limits the use of deadly force likely to inflict death or serious bodily injury to those situations in which it is reasonably necessary to prevent immediate death or serious felony from being committed.

These variations in the law of different environments are bound to raise the philosophical question of the relationship between social values and the rules of law on the use of deadly force, as well as the practical question of the symmetry between the harm averted and the harm inflicted by the act of self-defense. It will not be hard today to find a consensus in Arab society on the proposition that the chastity of a woman is more valuable than the life of a man accused of adultery or rape, or the sanctity of religious belief over a person's right of dissent.

Partners in Crime

While all the Arab codes subscribe to the unity of the *actus reus* or criminal act even were there were more than one party to it, they differ in their assessment of the roles of the various partners in the crime. Following the French code, the Tunisian and Moroccan codes do not distinguish between principal and partner or accessory whether he is aiding, abetting or participating in the crime. In the words of the Moroccan code, "Whoever participates directly or indirectly in a criminal act shall be subjected to the punishment prescribed for that criminal act." As the Tunisian code makes clear, the criminality of the partner is dependent upon the criminality of the principal; or in the words of the code, "without a principal in the crime there can be no partner and if the former is let go the latter must also be set free." While American law subjects an accessory to the same punishment as the principal, it makes sure that he is punished irrespective of whether the principal is convicted or not.

Closer to this American position are the codes of the Arab states to the East which distinguish between principals and partners, whether aiding, abetting or participating, and deal with them separately.

The Lebanese and Syrian codes, for example, subject the abettor but not the actual participant, to the punishment prescribed for the intended crime no matter at what stage of the criminal act--initiated, arrested or consummated. In the Jordanian and Egyptian codes, on the other hand, for an abettor or participant to be held liable the criminal act should have actually taken place. But a partner in a crime may still be found culpable even if the principal was able to benefit from any of the causes of justifiability and is exonerated.

The Egyptian code also condemns participants in a crime even if the crime actually committed was not the intended crime but was a probable outcome of the abetment, agreement or assistance which actually took place. And in a provision which might come handy in the fight against international crime, the Egyptian code reaches out to punish a partner outside Egypt if the crime in which he acted as abettor or participant took place wholly or partially on Egyptian territory.

These differences in the Arab codes are due to the lack of clarity as well as uniformity in their conceptions of what constitutes aiding, abetting and participating in the *actus reus*. The Moroccan code includes under "participation" in crime, "abetting, providing guidance and means, aiding and supporting." The Egyptian and the Kuwaiti codes identify three types of participation: abetting, agreeing and aiding in the commission of the crime.

The Lebanese and Syrian codes, on the other hand, distinguish clearly between abetting and participating, calling the latter literally "interference" in the sense of complicity and aiding in the commission of the crime by providing the perpetrator with guidance, aid and support, and "strengthening in any manner his determination". The latter is distinguished from abetting by coming after the perpetrator had decided to commit the crime, while abetting precedes it, as an accessory before the fact.

Nevertheless the Lebanese and Syrian laws have been criticized for creating two types of abetting, the one independent of the criminal act and the other a participation in it, just as they provide for two types of aiding, the one direct and essential to the commission of the crime and the other indirect and incidental to it, when in fact any type of aiding is an essential ingredient in the commission of the crime.[34]

The Arab codes differ also over the punishment to be meted to the partners in crime. Those of Egypt, Iraq, Kuwait, Morocco and Tunisia follow the French example of prescribing the same punishment for principal and participant. Those of Jordan, Lebanon and Syria, following the Belgian example, provide for a lesser punishment for the participant in the second degree than what is prescribed for the principal, while giving in the process consideration for the usual mitigating or aggravating circumstances.

Liability of Minors

The liability of minors for criminal acts is uniformly provided for in the Arab penal and procedural codes and complemented in some jurisdictions with special laws dealing with juvenile delinquency.

As is the case at common law, a child under seven years of age is presumed to be incapable of committing a crime and is neither prosecuted nor punished under the Arab penal codes. In the words of the Egyptian code, "a child at this age is presumed to be incapable of comprehending the criminal act or its consequences." This age of innocence ends according to varying provisions of the Arab penal codes at the age of 12 (Egypt, Jordan, Morocco), 13 (Algeria, Tunisia),

14 (Kuwait, Libya), 15 (Iraq, Lebanon, Syria), when the minor is subjected to protective and reformatory measures or to reduced penalties if the presumption of incapacity can be rebutted. By the age of eighteen the child ceases to be a minor and becomes subject to the general provisions of the penal codes.

Special care has been taken in the Arab penal and procedural codes to ensure that minors are dealt with at all stages in the investigation and trial by officials specialized in the treatment of minors. These officials are required to look into the particular circumstances which led to the delinquency of the child, his physical condition and social background. Juvenile courts have been set up in most Arab jurisdictions to try minors as delinquents rather than as criminals before the criminal courts. In most cases, juvenile courts hold their proceedings in private, open only to the parents, guardian and counselor of the minor. Judgments which may include protective and reformatory measures may be reviewed at the behest of the minor, or his parents, guardian or counselor.

ENDNOTES

1. Abdel-Qadir 'Awdah, *Al-Tashri' al-Jina'I al-Islami Mugaran bil Qanun al-Wad'i*, [Islamic Criminal Legtislation Compared to Positive Law] Cairo (1985), citing with approval the 11th century Muslim scholar Al-Mawardi (d. 1057) in his *Al-Ahkam al-Sultaniya.*
2. Foucault, *Surveiller et Punir*, Paris (1975), Engl. transl. Discipline & Punishment (Vintage Books, 1979) p. 11
3. Jerome Hall, *Principles of Criminal Law*, 2nd. ed. Indianapolis and New York (1947) p. 52
4. See 'Awdah, op. cit. Cf. the contribution of medieval canonists to some modern legal theory. "In criminal law, the canonical theory of culpability prepared the way for modern criminal law, which attaches prime importance to determining culpability (voluntary or involuntary, premeditation, recidivism, mitigating circumstances, and so on), whereas primitive criminal law was interested above all in the harm done and in compensation," R.C. van Caenegem, *An Historical Introduction to Private Law,* Campridge (1992) p. 67
5. See George N. Sfeir, "Source of Law and the Issue of Legitimacy and Rights," 42 *Middle East Journal* (Summer 1988) 436
6. Muhammad Abu Zahra, *Al-Jarima wal-`Uquba fil-figh al-Islami* [Crime and Punishment in Islamic Jurisprudence] Cairo (1966) vol. 2, p. 192-204; Lawrence M. Friedman, A *History of American Law*, 2nd. ed. New York, (1985) p. 291-92
7. van Caenegem, op.cit. p. 66
8. Hall, op.cit. p. 14f
9. Ahmad 'Uthman, *'Uqubat al-Jinayat bayn al-Shari'a wal Qanun* [The Punishments of Crimes in Islamic and Positive Law], Al-Azhar Univ., Cairo

(1974) p. 19f

10. Secare Beccaria, *On Crime and Punishment* (1764), Engl. transl. by David Young, Indianapolis (1986)
11. Id. p. 15
12. Id. p. 17-23
13. Id. p. 23
14. Hall, op. cit. p. 28
15. See 'Awdah, op. cit.
16. John Henry Merryman, *The Civil Law Tradition*, Stanford (1969/1985), p. 14f
17. H.A.R. Gibb, *Mohammedanishm*, New York (1962) p. 95-98
18. 'Awdah, op. cit. p. 82
19. Hall, op. cit. p. 50-51
20. The Napoleonic code was made up of five different codes which appeared consecutively over a period of 12 years: Civil Code (1804), Code of Civil Procedure (1806), Commercial Code (1807), Penal Code (1810), Code of Criminal Procedure (1811)
21. The text of the Ottoman code used here is the Arabic version found in the Sader collection of laws applicable in the former Arab Provinces of the Ottoman Empire. Yusuf Sader, *Majmu'at al-Qawanin*, vol. I, Beirut (1937), p. 6-102
22. Farid Zughbi, *Al-Mawsu'a al-Jaza'iya al-Lubnaniya al-Haditha* [The New Lebanese Compendium of Criminal Law] Beirut (1979), vol. I p. 208-209
23. Shafiq Shihata, *Al-Ittijahat al-Tashri'iya fi Qawanin al-Bilad al-'Arabiya* [Legislative Trends in the Laws of the Arab Countries] Cairo (1960) p. 26
24. Id. p. 38-40
25. Zughbi, op. cit. p. 204-205
26. Unless otherwise identified, code citations are from the Lebanese penal code.
27. Kamil al-Sa'id, *Al-Ahkam al-'Amma lil Jarima fi Qanun al-'Uqubat al-Urduni* [General Principles of the Jordanian Criminal Code], Amman (1981) p. 96-97
28. See Muhammad Zaki Abu 'Amir, *Qanun al-'Uqubat al-Lubnani, al-Qism*

al'Am [The Penal Code of Lebanon: The General Provisions] Beirut (1981) p. 351f

29. Mahmud Mahmud Mustafa, *Usul Qanun al-'Uqubat fil Duwal al-'Arabiya* [Sources of the Penal Law in the Arab States] Cairo (1970), p. 140-42
30. Zughbi, op. cit. p. 314-15
31. van Caenegem, op. cit.
32. Lawrence Rosen, "Islamic 'Case Law' and the Logic of Consequence," in *History and Power in the Study of Law: New Directions of Legal Anthropology*, June Starr & Jane Collier eds., Ithaca & London (1989) 302 at p. 306
33. Al-Sa'id, op. cit. p. 105-110
34. Mustafa, op. cit. p. 84-86

CHAPTER FIVE

Constitutionalism

Just as the modernization of the law in the Arab states owed much to the 19th century Ottoman and European-inspired reforms, constitutionalism in the modern sense of the term, that is a fundamental law whose basic principles include limiting governmental powers, recognizing citizens' rights and imposing a rule of law, was first introduced into the region by the Ottoman Sultans in response to the growing European challenge to their antiquated system of government. But unlike the direct borrowing of European codes which typified the reform of the law, the constitutional changes evolved over time.

They began with the charter like *firmans* of basic rights granted by the Sultans to their subjects, something they had not known since the establishment of the Ottoman state in 1517. The first of these *firmans* was the Hatti Sharif of Gulhane of 1839 which launched the *tanzimat*, the state reorganization, and began the codifiction of the law along European lines. It was followed in 1856 by the Hatti-Humayun, which affirmed the civil equality of all Ottoman citizens, their regional representation at the Delegates' Assembly in Istanbul, and the traditional status of the recognized religious communities in regulating their own spiritual and domestic affairs. As far as the religious non-Muslim communities were concerned, the Charter's regulation of their affairs meant limiting those affairs to matters of family law only.

The culmination to this liberalizing trend would be the adoption in 1876 of the first, albeit short-lived, Ottoman constitution, which would not be revived until 1908 when the temporal might of the Sultanate and its spiritual concomitant, the Caliphate, were on the verge of extinction at the hands of the Young Turk movement.

Modeled after the Belgian constitution of 1831, the *kanun-i Esasi*, that is, the fundamental or basic law as it was dubbed, combined modern principles of parliamentary government and equality of citizens before the law, with the Islamic practice of exalting the sultan as defender of Islam and undisputed head of the Community. Such obvious conflicts in constitutional principles which, in the case of the Ottoman regime, may have been unavoidable by the uncharted transition from the old to the new, would find their way, more recently, into many of the post World War II constitutions of the Arab states.

The first modern Arab constitution was that of Tunisia of 1861. Although it preceded the Ottoman constitution by fifteen years, it was itself an outcome of the Ottoman reform *firmans* and drew on some of their provisions. Having gained a measure of autonomy from the High Porte with the help of the local Ottoman garrison, the Bey of Tunisia, prodded by the European powers, had no alternative but to enact a constitution. It provided for an appointed Council made up of 60 members to make laws and control expenditures by the government, established a hierarchy of courts and named the Bey the hereditary ruler, defender of the Islamic faith and supreme head of the state.

Although the French, through their consul in Tunis, had a hand in its preparation, the 1861 constitution would be short-lived, suspended by the French themselves who by 1881 had established their protectorate over Tunisia. Subsequent attempts at constitution making in 1907 and 1920 would also fail, partly because of competing generational interests within the country itself, and partly because of conflict with the French colonial interests in the region. It was not until the emergence of a strong nationalist party, the Neo-Destour Party under the determined leadership of Habib Bourguiba, and the achievement of independence in 1956 that the current 1959 Constitution would be adopted.[1]

The Tunisian experience is a microcosm of constitution making in the rest of the Arab World where emergent new states embarked between world wars I and II upon building a new legal order upon the ruins of the old. Arab political and religious reformers of the turn of the century whose "constitutional" ideas grew in tandem with the Ottoman reforms or out of opposition to them were, as was the case with Tunisia, stymied by internal discord, lack of a mediating political mechanism, and external force.

The proponents of the European liberal state and the adherents to traditional values in the form of a revived Islamic order went their separate ways; and, as the current wave of Muslim fundamentalism has shown, were never assimilated or reconciled. At that formative stage in the evolution of the Arab state system, the debate remained largely academic because of the absence of a fully developed political process. Except for the historically recognized rights and privileges of religious communities and the traditional clannish and tribal allegiances, neither of which was germane to the emerging territorial state, there were no mediating institutions to speak of which were capable of defining, asserting or reconciling the new political ideas and orientations propagated by the small intellectual leadership.

Nor were such mediating institutions able to develop and operate freely while the colonial presence remained and no sooner did the fledgling independent regimes bring an end to this presence than they themselves had to cope with the rising popular demand for greater individual freedoms and participation in government. Add to this the Zionist colonization in Palestine which mushroomed into an all out Arab-Israeli conflict, the newly installed parliamentary regimes in Amman, Baghdad, Cairo, and Damascus, in particular, suddenly found themselves besieged by a dual threat: the internal pressure for reform, and the external expropriation of Arab land. The immediate change on the political scene was the emergence of the military as the only institution with the requisite discipline and force to put the Arab house in order and at the same time meet the Zionist threat.

The fatal blow dealt by military rule to the fledgling parliamentary regimes happened unfortunately at a time when the purpose of the political process in the Arab states was undergoing a change from trying to preserve and assimilate the traditional system of the past, as the religious reformers hoped, to creating a system which was possible to maintain under modern conditions of society, as the proponents of the liberal state would have it.[2] Consequently, the constitutional process has remained inconclusive. Repeated political upheavals and military coups invariably ended up with their proponents facing the problem of justifying the change of regime or rewriting the constitution. This raises the question whether it was the constitutional contradictions which have hindered the process of mediation and modernization, or was it the unrealized demands of mediation and modernization which have created the constitutional crises that have so far remained unresolved.

In his study of constitutionalism, McIlwin subscribed to the notion, originally advanced by Thomas Paine, that a nation's government is only the creature of the constitution and not its creator; pointing out that the American Constitution, which became a model to be emulated, "consists mainly of a codification of institutions and principles long in actual force." That this constituent act of the people is in fact an expression of the phase they had reached in their political development, explains McIlwin's assertion that "legal limitation on government" has been the one essential quality of constitutionalism in all its successive phases.[3]

A review of current Arab constitutions will readily bring out the discrepancies that exist in varying degrees among the Arab states between constitutional provisions and practices. It is a situation common to most newly independent states where constitutions provide ample security for the rights of citizens and clear limitations on the institutions of government, when in fact these rights are still groping for recognition and the institutions for roots.

As far as Arab society is concerned, such disharmony between formal provisions and actual practices has frequently led to a breakdown in the constitutional process. It seems to revive an old tradition in Islamic history which goes back to the 10th century: the uncoupling of rule from law in times of crises. Following the demise of the Arab founding dynasties, military adventurers and aspirants for power were left to rule the Islamic dominions according to their own devices provided they steered clear of the *ulema*, the guardians of the revealed law, whose preoccupation was not so much with the legitimacy of rule as with the preservation of the law.

It is not simply a question of political immaturity of the social forces which usually sustain the constitutional process, the inherent contradictions in the constitutions themselves continue to work against ensuring their stability. These contradictions represent many of the issues which normally plague constitution making, from issues of national identity to that of civil society and the break with the past, to the practical means of upholding the separation of powers, establishing the rule of law and protecting individual rights.

A review of a select number of individual constitutions will easily show a commonality of certain issues particular to the Arab states.

SAUDI ARABIA: A Basic Law for an Islamic Society.

The newest Arab constitution is the 1992 Basic Law of Saudi Arabia. For a country which has not ceased since its inception in 1932 to declare that the Qoran and the Traditions of the Prophet are the law and constitution of the land, the enactment of a man-made basic law must be quite significant. And yet one cannot attach undue legal importance to this document which on the face of it represents a departure from a hallowed tradition of Islamic society going back to medieval times. While it commits to writing for the first time the ideological, social and economic objectives of the Saudi State and the rights and obligations of its citizens, it makes sure that these remain in the end subject to the tenets of the Qoran and the Traditions of the Prophet.

Already in its first article the Basic Law pronounces the country an Arab Islamic state "whose constitution is the Book of God and the Traditions of His Prophet." While this provision may be intended to give the Saudi regime an Islamic legitimacy, in practice it is bound to detract from the juridical value of the Basic Law itself. By deferring to a higher law, the status of the document as the law of last resort is open to question.

This is no idle speculation. The constitutional uncertainty of the legal status of the Basic Law is underscored by the provision in article 7 which reiterates the doctrinal and juridical supremacy of the revealed text. "The regime (*hukm*) draws its authority (*sultan*) from the Book [the Qoran] and the Sunna [the Traditions of the Prophet]." And as if to give credence to the proposition that restoring past values would inevitably mean restoring old relationships, article 44 designates the King as the "authority of last resort (marji')" when it comes to the various powers of government, "judicial," "executive," "organizational."

The notable absence of the "legislative" from the Basic Law is again a reflection of past relationships in the Islamic legal order where the already revealed law excluded the need for a legislature in the modern sense: the process of creating the law with the consent of the representatives of the people. It is a premise of the modern liberal state which was first advanced in the sixteenth century by Humanists to challenge the Christian medieval theories of divine right and natural law.

What the Saudi Basic Law creates instead is an administrative, or "organizational" as it is dubbed, organ of government entrusted with the drafting and preparation of decrees and regulations for enactment by the Council of Ministers presided over by the King. According to articles 55 and 70, the enactment of regulations and the ratification of international agreements are the prerogative of the King. Indeed he is entrusted with overall responsibility of "overseeing the application of the Sharia [the revealed law], the regulations [man-made laws complementing the Sharia], and public policy." The latter comprises in Islamic jurisprudence what Western legal systems distinguish as the realm of morals and morality.

More than any other Arab state, Saudi Arabia is in search of constitutional identity. Regimes of the former states which began earlier and have progressed further on the road to modernization evoke the past simply to win legitimacy when popular backing is lacking. In the case of Saudi Arabia the restoration of past constitutional structures serves to put a break on modernization which is threatening traditional values and structure of Saudi society.[4] Furthermore, the constitutions of most other Arab states are associated with revolutions, which seems to be a common phenomenon world wide, in Saudi Arabia the regime is more like the product of a medieval compact between a temporal ruler and an ecclesiastical authority.

In the mid-eighteenth century, Muhammad bin Abdel-Wahhab, a former adherent to the mystic calling of the Sufis, takes up the cause of the fundamentalist, puritanical Hanbali school of jurisprudence and its adherence to the strict application of the rules of the Qoran and the Traditions of the Prophet, unadulterated by subsequent interpretations and innovations. Intent upon seeing his reformation succeed, Abdel-Wahhab entered into an alliance with Muhammad ibn Saud, the ruler of a local market town in Najd, an alliance which, as it turned out, laid down the foundation of the future Kingdom of Saudi Arabia.

Being on the periphery of the Ottoman Empire whose effective rule did not extend beyond the Hijaz, the Western flank of Arabia, Najd was gradually brought under Ibn Saud's rule as Abdel-Wahhab moved in to enforce a strict application of the revealed law against the tribal custom of its Bedouin inhabitants.[5]

But it will not be until the 1920's, following the defeat of the Ottomans in world war I, that Abdel-Aziz Ibn Saud, the son of the founder of the dynasty, would proclaim himself king of Najd and proceeded to bring the Hijaz as well under his rule. In 1927 Abdel-Aziz proclaims himself "King of the Hijaz and of Najd and its dependencies," in a premature bid for the unification of the two provinces,[6] only one year after a constitution for "the Kingdom of the Hijaz" under the stewardship of King Abdel-Aziz was proclaimed.[7] Finally on September 18, 1932, responding to "our subjects in the Kingdom of the Hijaz, Nejd and its Dependencies [who] petitioned us," Abdel-Aziz decrees that the name of his dominion be changed to that of The Kingdom of Saudi Arabia and his title to that of King of the Kingdom of Saudi Arabia.[8] But the two provinces would retain temporarily their separate and divergent governmental structures, the Hijaz having benefited from the 19th century legal reforms in the Ottoman Empire while Najd did not.

In the end however it will be the Ikhwan, Ibn Saud's Najd fighters, the religiously zealous Wahhabi preachers and the clannish-tribal allocation of power which would prevail in the dual kingdom. The Constitution of the Hijaz, the highly elaborate document for its time and place, would be discarded in favor of the bare bones Council of Ministers appointed by the king in Najd. Not until 1953 would a unified government, headed by the king's eldest son, Crown Prince Saud, be set up, and its structure and prerogatives subsequently defined in the Organization of the Council of Ministers decree No. 38 of May 12, 1958. Repeated promises since then of a constitution and a consultative assembly to complement the Council of Ministers and provide a semblance of participation in government remained unfulfilled until 1992 when the Basic Law was enacted.

Given this background to the nascent Basic Law, it will be both futile and unfair for the Western reader to try and compare its provisions with their counterpart in their own national constitutions. One needs to view them in the context of Islamic legal culture and the nature of authority in Islam, particularly those provisions dealing with the transmission of power and succession, state control of value preferences and individual rights and obligations of Saudi citizens.

The 16th and 17th century European notions of social contract, whether those expounded by Hobbs, Pufendorf or Locke, have yet to find acceptance even in modern Islamic political thought. If there is a contractual obligation in Islamic juridical thought it is one sided. Muslim scholars often point to the Qoranic dictum, "Obey God and the Prophet and those of you in authority" (sura iv:59), (whose scriptural equivalent in Christianity is Romans 13: "Obey the powers that are ordained of God, for there is no power but of God") as the Islamic alternative to social contract since it implies obedience by the ruled in return for the ruler's compliance with the revealed law.

In the absence however of an elected body to give expression to the will of the people, which is the case in Saudi Arabia, by what legal devise is power constitutionally acquired and transmitted? Historically, the closest in Islam to such a devise has been the *bai'ah* by which the first Caliph following the death of the Prophet was confirmed in office. The term *bai'ah* is from the root word for sale agreement or deal, and is best rendered in English as acclamation or declaration of allegiance. Ibn Khaldun, the celebrated Arab historian, called it "a promise of obedience" on which the authority of the ruler rested. This is in fact what it amounted to in practice. The notables of the Community would come forward to hail the new ruler and declare their allegiance to him on the implied understanding that he would well guide the Community and uphold the revealed law. It is not unlike the medieval form of fealty which lasted in Europe way into the 17th century.[9]

True to this tradition, article 6 of the Saudi Basic Law calls on the people "to acclaim/declare allegiance to the King." What the Law left out unsaid however is who among the people and by what legal mechanism or institutional arrangement this may be done. Under modern conditions of economic free enterprise and egalitarian ideas (which are Islamic values as well), it will be difficult, in the absence of some form of popular elections, to determine who the representatives of the people are. The old alliance between religious leaders and tribal chieftains which the founder of the Saudi state had forged in the 1920's has been sapped of its traditional integrity by the creeping process of bureaucratization and division of labor brought about by industrialization and modernization.

Succession to the throne is regulated by article 5 which gives the reigning king the right to nominate a successor and appoint him by Royal Order. Because this provision occurs prior to that in article 6, it means that if *bai'ah* or acclamation is required to confirm the current holder of office, then *bai'ah* will also be required to confirm the successor even though he was appointed by the reigning king. For one thing, *bai'ah* in Islam does not admit of heredity, just as precedent does not bind the judge in a court case. For another, the Saudi king is also the Prime Minister and the Commander-in-Chef of the armed forces, according to the Basic Law, and *bai'ah* represents, under the circumstances, the only form of legitimation for his extensive executive and legislative powers.

Even more troublesome for the Western reader familiar with the constitution of the liberal state today, are the provisions of the Basic Law which define the nature and purpose of the Saudi State and the rights and obligations of its citizens. Here again the problem lies in some of the old concepts and institutions these provisions revive and over which Muslims have disagreed in the past and are bound to create more discord in the present with the greatly changed conditions of society.

It is the articles which define the attributes of Saudi society and underscore the ideological mission of the state which are susceptible in practice to conflict and dissension. According to article 8, the principles on which the regime is based are "justice, *Shura* (consultation), and equality, compatible with Islamic Sharia." Article 9 requires Saudi families to raise their children in accordance with "Islamic doctrine and its requirements of fidelity and obedience to God, His Prophet and those in authority." The Basic Law interjects in articles 11 and 17 the medieval Islamic concept of *takaful*, a socio-economic principle which prescribes cooperative and mutual support in society for the common good. While article 9 states categorically that society is "based on *Takaful*," article 17 provides that "ownership, capital, and labor are fundamental components (*maqumat*) and private rights which serve a social purpose compatible with Islamic Sharia." The purpose of education, according to article 13, is to "inculcate in the souls of the youth the Islamic doctrine," and vide article 23 the State shall "defend the ideology of Islam, order that which [the revealed law] considers acceptable while prohibiting that which [it] denies, and undertake to summon [the people] unto God."

At the height of its achievements, Islamic civilization embodied highly developed systems of theology, philosophy, science and law. But its grandeur lay in its diversity; and as more recent research has shown, what made it a global civilization was its ability to receive and absorb culture from one end of the world and pass it on to other parts of the world.[10] With this in mind, the reader is bound to ask, who is it who will decide which of the ideas of the past constitute the ideology of Islam or any of the concepts and institutions the Basic Law provisions invoke from the past? The question becomes particularly crucial when the Saudi government moves, as it is empowered to do by article 12, "to prevent anything which would cause discord, dissension and disunity," or generally acts in the spirit of the Basic Law to safeguard Islamic values.

No one would disagree that Saudi Arabs have their particular moral and social values, and, as is the case with most other people, they are a continuum of historical, environmental and religious factors and characteristics which have over the ages determined their outlook to life. The question however is at what stage in the evolution of these values (and they are definitely changing in Saudi Arabia as they are in the case of practically all other people) should the state intervene and "freeze," so to speak, the moral and social values of its citizens?

Associating the state constitution with a particular religious identity will certainly imply censoring those who dissent from or disagree with it. This is particularly relevant to the provisions of the Basic Law dealing with the rights and obligations of Saudi citizens. Not only are the precepts of Islam in this area not codified, the opinions of the classical jurists which interpreted the revealed law are often contradictory.

By article 26, the Saudi State undertakes to protect human rights "in accordance with Islamic Sharia (law)." By this qualification, Saudi Arabia perpetuates its long-standing objection to the 1948 United Nations Universal Declaration of Human Rights on the ground that its language is at variance with Islamic law and morality. What brings about this variance are essentially the notions of freedom of belief and of natural rights and equality historically associated in Western thought with the ideas of Humanism, ideas by no means alien to Islamic thought either.[11]

In their practical application however, human rights are of very recent origin in any legal system. It was not until the Enlightenment that the naked will of the sovereign or the charisma of transcendental law began to be questioned and the need for a new relationship between the individual and the state became imperative. They are therefore bound to conflict with some of the precepts of the Sharia formulated by Muslim jurists in the eighth and ninth centuries to suit the needs of Muslim society at that particular stage in its development. This becomes quite obvious when one examines the purport of those provisions of the Basic Law safeguarding privacy and freedom of expression.

Article 37 provides for the "sanctity of the homes," which shall not be entered or searched "except in accordance with the law." And according to article 40, postal, telephone and other forms of communications, shall not be interfered with "except in cases specified by law." But that law, the general precepts of the Sharia, prohibits all sorts of things of a private nature, from what you drink and eat to what you read, see, and believe, a fact well brought out in article 39 which deals with the media and all other methods of expression:

"It is incumbent upon all forms of information, publication and expression to adhere to the agreeable word [*al-kalimah al-tayibah*] and the State's regulations, and to take part in educating *[tathqif]* the nation and shoring up its unity. That which leads to dissension and strife or harms the security of the state and its public relations or degrades from man's dignity and rights, shall be prohibited in accordance with relevant regulations."

In the absence of any qualifying phraseology, such as 'with the intent to,' or 'in bad faith,' the provision discourages public discourse and debate. Despite the growing number of Saudi nationals engaged in various trades and professions, the only association or organization permitted to operate in the country is the Chamber of Commerce and Industry, whose Board of Directors and budget are partly controlled by the government.

The other objectionable premise of the Universal Declaration of Human Rights, gender equality, remains the most controversial in Islamic society, despite recent scholarship which downplays the role of Islam in gender arrangements and looks instead to the historical context of the time and place, where Islamic ideology intersects with predominant patriarchal systems.[12] The views of the classical Muslim jurists continue to uphold the stark differences between the sexes in inheritance, the right to marry and divorce, to travel, to the weight given to testimony before the courts, to mention but a few examples. Relative to their status prior to the coming of Islam, women became the beneficiaries of a social reformation when Islam granted them the right to own property, to engage in business and work. This reformation has taken on a deeper meaning and a wider scope under modern conditions, making the continued segregation of the sexes and the subordination of the women in the name of religion a contradiction in terms.

Another area of potential contradiction in the name of religion are the economic provisions of article 17 of the Basic Law. By declaring ownership, capital and labor "fundamental attributes of the social and economic structure of the Kingdom," it goes on to define these attributes as "private rights serving a social purpose in accordance with Islamic Sharia."

It is not the intention here to take up the economic theories attributed to Islam. But what these provisions may very well allude to is the principle of *takaful*, requiring the cooperative, mutual support of all Muslims of legal capacity in the promotion of public interest and the economic and social welfare of the Muslim Community as a whole. Classical interpretation of Revelation on this point is somewhat contradictory to the extent that the Qoranic precept that the owner of all things is the Creator who has dominion while man has only the temporary benefit of possession or use, is sometimes imbued with a collectivist sense. In the spirit of *takaful*, therefore we find that *zakat*, a form of tithe imposed on Muslims by the Qoran, made mandatory by article twenty one, while income tax and duties shall not, according to article twenty, be imposed "except when the need arises and then on equitable basis." The on again, off again, income tax in Saudi Arabia reflected the uncertainty in theological circles whether Muslims may be subjected to anything other than *zakat*.

LEBANON: A State of Religious Communities.

If the constitutional paradox of the Saudi Arabian State is to modernize and liberalize without abandoning its absolutist singular religious identity, in Lebanon it is the paradox of a unitary, non-sectarian, territorial state accommodating the multiple identities of some sixteen different religious communities.

Recent events indicate that in neither state has the paradox been resolved constitutionally. In Saudi Arabia, no sooner was the Basic Law enacted than a Committee for the Defense of Rights Under the Sharia was formed with a platform which says that the Saudi regime is not Islamic enough and needs to be more vigorous in its application of Islamic law. Since political parties are not permitted in Saudi Arabia, by setting out to mobilize public opinion for political action, the Committee was destined to be banned. In May 1993 the Council of Senior Theologians, a government appointed body, and at the behest of the government issued a religious opinion denouncing the Committee and its activities as contrary to the precepts of Islam.

In Lebanon on the eve of the fiftieth anniversary of the adoption of the constitution, the talk of politicians and journalists alike was how to make the constitution more responsive to the ideas of the National Pact, the unwritten 1943 understanding between the Muslim and Christian communities, to abandon the sectarian distribution of posts in the government and promote the concept of shared and equivalent responsibility of both communities for the preservation of the Lebanese State. As a leading journalist prophetically put it at the time, there is need for a true revolution to do all that and it is going to be either a legitimate revolution of constitutional reform or else the constitutional atrophy is going to lead to a revolution of violence.[13] Shortly thereafter, the Lebanese sectarian war broke out.

The Lebanese Constitution is the oldest surviving Arab constitution. It has survived a number of political crises and social upheavals, not so much because of the dedication of the country's leaders to the constitutional process; it was rather their realization that the survival of the Lebanese State, an island of relative freedoms in the region, depended on balancing the interests of all its religious communities.

Initiated by an order of the then French mandatory authorities in compliance with the terms of the 1922 League of Nations Mandate, the Constitution was prepared by a commission of the Lebanese Assembly and promulgated by the full Assembly on May 26, 1926. Contrary to popular belief, it was not the work of the French or a copy of the French Constitution. If anything, it reflects some of the provisions of the Belgian Constitution of 1831 (as was the case also with the first Tunisian Constitution). But as was the case with many of the early Arab constitutions, the Lebanese Constitution had to endorse the extensive authority of the French Government in Lebanon, including foreign representation, and name the French Republic in the final provision of the text the "custodian" of the Constitution. The Constitution however established some of the more enduring characteristics of the Lebanese State.

The first article of the 1926 Constitution declared "Greater Lebanon" a single and independent State "whose frontiers are those which have been officially recognized by the Government of the French Republic." It will be recalled that the territory of geographical Syria which under Ottoman rule comprised present day Syria, Lebanon, Jordan and Palestine/Israel was, contrary to the wishes of its inhabitants,[14] partitioned by Britain and France at the end of World War I in accordance with their secret Sykes-Picot agreement of 1916. France, who took over the northern territories, expanded the autonomous region of Mount Lebanon by adding to it the littoral area between Tripoli and Tyre which comprised a considerable number of Sunni and Shiite Muslims to create with the previously mostly Maronite and Druze communities the religious conglomerate of Greater Lebanon or the Republic of Lebanon as the country became known upon achieving its independence in 1943.

The other characteristic of the Lebanese constitutional make-up which distinguishes it from other Arab states is the politicization of religious affiliation and the non-identification of the State with any particular faith. According to Article 9 of the Constitution "there shall be complete freedom of conscience. And the state, while rendering the duty of reverence to the Most High, shall respect all creeds and religions and safeguard and protect the free exercise of the rites of worship..." But this salutary provision goes on to perpetuate the traditional sectarian divisions of the people of Lebanon, first established by the Arab/Muslim conquest in the 7th century and reinforced by the millet system of the Ottoman Empire, by guaranteeing that "the personal status and religious interests of the population, to whatever creed they belong, shall be respected."

If one were to point to the root cause of political sectarianism in the Lebanese state it is this traditional confessional structure of society which the Constitution simply perpetuates. Given the historical record of communal differentiation in the region on religious grounds since the ascendancy of Islam as state religion, the emergent multi-confessional Lebanese State found itself compelled to recognize, even valorize, communal differences in the interest of freedom and equality.

Article 95, appearing at the end of the constitutional text as a transitional provision, proved that only the provisional lasts:

> "As a temporary measure and in the interest of justice and harmony, the [religious] communities shall be equitably represented in all public positions and in the composition of the Cabinet, provided the [measure] shall not cause any damage to the interests of the State."

On the confessional distribution of the seats in Parliament, Article 24 was non-committal. It simply provided that the number of representatives and their mode of election shall be in accordance with applicable law. Upon independence, it was agreed that the ratio of Christian to Muslim deputies of various sects be 6:5. By this formula it became imperative that any change in the total number of deputies must always be divisible by 11. In 1990, a constitutional amendment, reflecting the Ta'if agreement which brought an end to the civil war, specified in the new article 24 that the seats in Parliament must be divided equally between Christians and Muslims and proportionately among the various sects in each of these two communities. Once again this change was described as temporary "until such time as the Parliament enacts a non-sectarian election law."

Similarly the 1990 amendment to article 95 which was again dubbed transitional, until Parliament takes the "appropriate measures to eliminate political sectarianism," requires that the Christian and Muslim communities be "equitably" represented in the Cabinet, and in the higher level posts of the government. This has presumably left intact the unwritten rule which requires that the President be from the Maronite Christian Community, the Prime Minister from the Sunni Muslim Community, the President of the Parliament from the Shiite Muslim Community and his deputy from the Greek Orthodox Christian Community, with the other communities well represented in other important executive posts. This sharing of power extends to the enactment of laws by Presidential decree cosigned by the Prime Minister signifying thereby the concurrence of the two major communities, the Maronite Christian and the Sunni Muslim.

All this is done in the name of "participation" in government, not in the democratic sense of participation by the people; rather in a sentinel sense, with the representatives of the religious communities in public office standing guard over the interests of their communities to ensure that they are not encroached upon by the others.

It is a phenomenon born of the 1943 unwritten National Pact which heralded the independence of Lebanon from France towards the end of world war II. The Pact was intended to shore up the national unity of the Lebanese and their bid for independence in the face of France's last colonial gasp to hold on to its position in Lebanon. To do that Lebanese political leaders had to concoct a compromise between the Muslim communities' desire to associate with their Muslim brethren in neighboring Syria and the Christian communities' wish to bring to an end their status as a protected minority in an Islamic dominion. The National Pact, was said to have been a compromise of historic proportions which promised, in the words of the popular adage at the time: "From now on, Lebanon shall be neither a conduit for colonialism, nor an abode for sectarianism." The former euphemism alluded to France's colonial ambitions in Syria via a sympathetic Christian Lebanon, and the latter to the end of political Islam and its communal differentiation between Muslims and non-Muslims.

What this compromise overlooked was that its success was predicated on the separation of government and religion. The constitutional neutrality of the Lebanese State in matters of religion, which surpasses anything one finds in the other Arab states, is complemented by the constitutional equality of all citizens before the law, and in their civil and political rights and obligations "without any distinction whatsoever between them," as article 7 asserts. But the State's recognition of freedom of belief, equality, and non-interference in the affairs of the religious communities, does not necessarily guarantee by itself the separation of politics and religion.

In Germany, for example, churches and religious sects are recognized as bearers of fundamental rights, including the right to regulate their own religious affairs. This recognition has been based on article 19(4) of the Basic Law of the Federal Republic of Germany which extends the application of basic rights to domestic juristic persons "to the extent that the nature of such rights permits." Similarly in the United States where the Constitution and the Bill of Rights are premised on respect for individual rights, there has been a tendency on the part of the courts to recognize institutional rights as well, whether in the case of church properties, business entities or academic institutions. But in neither case did this erode the constitutional principle of the separation of Church and State or blemish their constitutional identity in any way.

For all its perceived diplomatic astuteness, the National Pact failed to resolve Lebanon's enduring political problem, that of its constitutional identity. By declaring that "Lebanon is an independent state with an Arab face," the Pact sought to reconcile Muslim public opinion, but ended up adding a new dimension to the problem. How much less Christian or more Muslim should Lebanon be to become fully Arab? Unable or unwilling to conceive of the separation of politics and religion, Muslim public opinion has traditionally equated Arab with Islam.

This is because historically their emergence on the world scene overlapped and, until modern times, politically coincided, a fact which highly complicated the evolution of constitutionalism in the Arab states.

To Lebanese Christians, and no less to secular-minded Muslims, there is history before Islam which constitutes part of their cummulative consciousness just as Arab history does. Nor where they less forthcoming towards the latter. The idea of Arab nationalism was in great measure the brain child of Christian Lebanese literateurs of the turn of the century, and many Maronite Lebanese families, among them the author of this book, trace their origin to the Christian Arab tribes which moved North from the Arabian Peninsula and even fought side by side with the Muslim armies which advanced against the Byzantine forces in Syria.

All of which goes to show that Lebanon's national complexion has not been of particular relevance to the emergence of a Lebanese constitutional identity. What is relevant are the means by which communal religious differentiation is minimized and certainly de-politicized, without compromising any of the features of modern constitutionalism--the separation and limitation of the powers of government, the rule of law, and fundamental rights.

As has already been pointed out, it is not sufficient for the Lebanese State to be neutral vis-a-vis the religious communities to achieve a separation of politics and religion. Nor is it, for obvious reasons, disposed, as is the case with other Arab states, to sacrifice freedom of belief and deny the right of dissent in order to do that. Lebanon has therefore no alternative but to purge the constitution of its religious components and secularize its purport and attendant regulations (from appointments to government positions, to election of the National Assembly to the regime of personal status and domestic relations) if it is to minimize the religious differences and shift the focus from these areas of discord and division to areas of accord and common identity. One way to realize this is by a self-imposed "gag rule" when it comes to matters of religion. By agreeing to privatize religious problems which cannot be resolved rationally and politically, religious attachments would gradually become dissociated from political differences and political divisions would no longer reduplicate religious cleavages.[15]

For Lebanon, the idea of secularization is neither new nor simple, given the country's highly literate leadership and particular social composition among Arab societies. Lebanese Muslims who, in the Lebanese state, lost the traditional preponderant position they enjoy elsewhere in the Arab World, tend generally to favor the abolition of confessionalism but only as far as the apportionment of seats in Parliament or the appointments to public office, generally the sharing of power, are concerned. Lebanese Christians, on the other hand, having attained in the Lebanese state political equivalence with Muslims unlike anything found in other Arab states, are wary of the abolition of confessionalism and the loss of their guarantees until such time as the Muslims relinquish the theocratic notions of Islam which, among other things, have traditionally differentiated between Muslims and non-Muslims in matters ranging from personal status to marital relations and national identification.[16]

Paradoxically, what this spells, for Christians and Muslims alike, is the perennial fear of majority rule, the basis of democratic government, so long as constitutionalism, in its modern secular sense, is prevented, by the persistence of communal religious loyalties, from taking root in Lebanese society.

In bringing to an end the fifteen-year civil war, the national reconciliation of 1990, not unlike the national pact of 1943 before it, was an agreement between the Christian and Muslim communities over the sharing of power and participation in government. As the amendment to the Constitution[17] enacted in 1990 by the reconstituted parliament clearly shows, little attempt has been made to bring about a resolution of the constitutional contradictions which brought about the communal strife in the first place.

In fact, the prologue which the amendment now adds to the Constitution, where none existed before, reiterates many of the ideas and euphemisms of the National Pact--Lebanon's Arab identity, its separate and independent status, and equal sharing of power between Muslims and Christians. What is different this time is that the long hoped for elimination of "confessional sectarianism," is designated in the prologue a "national objective" to be achieved in accordance with a "gradual plan." Besides that, the amendment is steeped in the same concerns about the religious differentiation between the two major communities and the balancing of their interests.

One of the obvious aims of the amendment was to reduce the powers of the President of the Republic, who is traditionally a Maronite Christian, and increase those of the Council of Ministers and its Sunni Muslim Prime Minister. Among these powers previously exercised by the President and now require the consent of the Council of Ministers include the right to introduce legislation in Parliament (article 18), return a law for review (article 57), recall parliament for special session or disband parliament (articles 33 and 65).

As far as sharing of power is concerned, the old wording of article 95 which simply called for an "equitable" distribution in the appointments to public posts and the formation of the Council of Ministers, now speaks of the "elimination of the confessional system" in the appointment to public posts, except for the senior posts in the government which must be "equally divided" between Christians and Muslims. In filling other posts, the government must now be guided not only by the requirements of "specialization and qualification," but also by the "requisites of national reconciliation," which implies once again the equitable distribution of posts between the two major communities. On the formation of the Council of Ministers the article maintains the old text which spoke of "equitable" representation of the communities..

A major segment of the new amendment to the Constitution is devoted to a reformulated Part IV with separate sections defining the responsibilities of the three components of the Executive Power of the state: the President, the Prime Minister and the Council of Ministers, which in the old Part IV were dominated by the position of the President. The purpose of this new reformulation is clearly intended to redress the balance between the Christian presidency and the Muslim premiership and its cabinet, some of which may have already become apparent from the revised articles referred to above. What then are the main tasks and responsibilities of the three component elements of the reformulated Executive:

The Presidency: According to article 49, the President of the Republic is the head of the state and the symbol of its unity. He defends the constitution and the country's independence and the unity of its territory. He presides over the Higher Defense Council and is the Commander-in-Chief of the Armed Forces which are however subject to the authority of the Council of Ministers. He is elected by Parliament for a term of six years and may not be re-elected except after an interval of six years. He nominates the Prime Minister designate following consultation with the speaker of Parliament and in agreement with the Premier names the Council of Ministers. He may preside, without the right to vote, at Cabinet meetings, and may propose items for discussion outside the formal agenda. The negotiation and conclusion of international treaties which previously were the sole responsibility of the President of the Republic, must now be undertaken in conjunction with the Prime Minister and the approval of the Cabinet. Treaties however with financial implications, of a commercial nature, and all others which are not renewable annually require ratification by the National Assembly.

The Premiership: The Prime Minister is the head of the government and responsible for its public policy. He presides over the Council of Ministers and deputizes at the Higher Defense Council. Conducts consultations for the formation of the government which must obtain the National Assembly's vote of confidence within thirty days of its formation in order to be confirmed in office. He cosigns with the President of the Republic all decrees, including those for the review or enactment of laws. He convenes the meetings of the Council of Ministers and prepares its agenda after informing the President of the Republic of the items to be discussed. He presents the government program to the National Assembly and follows up on its execution with the various ministries and agencies.

The Cabinet: The Council of Ministers is the body in which the Executive

Power of the State is vested, a power previously held by it only if and when the post of President was vacant. It is also the body to which the Armed Forces are beholden. Another function in which the Council has now superseded the President is the hiring and firing of public officials of the State. The Cabinet lays down the public policy of the State and makes sure that the laws are effectively applied. While the President may attend and preside at Cabinet meetings, he does so without the right to vote. Decisions will be taken by consensus, except for matters considered "basic" which require a two-thirds majority decision. They include amendments to the Constitution, declarations of state of emergency, of war and peace, national mobilization, international agreements and treaties, the State budget, long range development plans, appointment of public officials in the top government positions, altering the administrative system, dissolution of parliament, election, nationality and personal status laws, and the resignation of the government. The Cabinet will be considered to have resigned in the following situations:

- Death or resignation of the Prime Minister.
- Loss of more than one third of its constituent number of ministers.
- When a newly elected President of the Republic takes office.
- When a newly elected National Assembly convenes.
- A vote of no confidence by the National Assembly.

What is certainly new in the revised Constitution is the prologue which for the first time since the country's independence presents in written form what has always been the understanding among its various communities of the basic premise on which the Lebanese state is founded:

The unity and independence of Lebanon, its Arab identity and membership in the United Nations, its covenants and the Universal Declaration on Human Rights. A democratic parliamentary republic, based on respect for freedom of thought and belief and equality between all its inhabitants without distinction. The people are the source of authority and sovereignty, and the political order is based on the principle of the separation of powers. The economic order is based on free enterprise and private property is guaranteed. The elimination of political confessionalism is a national objective to be achieved gradually. Lebanon belongs to all Lebanese who have the right to reside anywhere in the country. No legitimacy for any authority which contravenes the principle of *al-'aysh al-mushtarak*, that is to say, shared living.

Some commentators have gone as far as to say that, by incorporating these principles, the prologue has once and for all settled the debate which has raged since 1943 about the constitutional status of the unwritten National Charter and the "contradiction" or "duality" between it and the Constitution. In particular, the adoption of the principle of "shared living" in the constitutional text, these commentators say, introduces a new concept in constitutionalism, that of the covenant of the people, and its role in understanding and interpreting the written text.[18]

MOROCCO: Democracy and the Divine Right of Kings.

We have seen how Saudi Arabia and Lebanon have tried, without much success so far, to adapt the traditional religious foundation of medieval constitutionalism to the modern territorial state. In the case of the former the state identified itself totally with Islam, making strict conformity with its tenets the basis of the just political order. In the case of the latter, the state perceived justice and equality in granting all religious communities juristic cognizance in the new political order, while dissociating itself from any particular faith.

Morocco, which had neither the historical compulsion of Saudi Arabia nor the pragmatic need of Lebanon's multiple religious affiliations to formally identify itself with, or dissociate itself from, political Islam, resorted instead to another aspect of medieval constitutionalism, that of the divine right of kings, to ensure the legitimacy and continuity of the legal order.

The two dynasties which have ruled Morocco since the 16th century have based their right to rule on their status as *sharifs*, that is descendants of the Prophet Muhammad. This allowed the religious dimension of constitutionalism to become subsumed into this other component of medieval constitutionalism, the divine right of kings. As a matter of fact, the only instance of an Islamic ruler to be deposed by the *ulema*, the religious scholars and the elders of the Community, for contravening his *bai'ah* or acclamation and declaration of allegiance, happened in Morocco in 1908 when Sultan 'Abdel-'Aziz was accused of failing in his religious duties when he was unable to resist the French incursions which eventually led to the 1912 occupation of the country. From then on, the preponderant role of the Sultan and how to circumscribe his powers became central to the political process.

When it came to formulating a modern constitution after independence in 1955, the country lacked a duly elected popular assembly to draft and adopt a constitution. Neither the consultative assembly set up by Sultan Muhammad V upon his return from exile by the French in 1956, nor the constitutional assembly he formed in 1960 were elected or fully representative bodies capable of producing a constitution.[19] It was only after the death of Muhammad V and the ascension to the throne of his son Hassan II in 1961 that the first constitution was formulated and adopted by a general referendum in 1962.

Although it begins by describing Morocco as a "constitutional monarchy," the Constitution does not circumscribe the office of the king to any extent which would rightly earn it that description. The political and religious attributes of the office are extensive. To begin with, the king is "the Commander of the Faithful, symbol of the unity of the nation, guarantor of the perpetuity and continuity of the state, defender of the sanctity of the faith, protector of the constitution and of the rights and freedoms of its citizens, social groups and communities, and he is the guarantor of the independence of the country and the territorial integrity of the Kingdom within its rightful borders."[20] These attributes of the royal office have remained practically unchanged in the constitutions that followed in 1970, 1972 and 1992.

That these provisions of the constitution are not merely rhetorical in nature became quite clear in 1977 when the king invoked them to delay parliamentary elections and assume legislative powers for six years in the wake of Morocco's military intervention in the Western Sahara to suppress the independence movement there upon Spain's withdrawal from the territory. The specific powers of the King are spelled out in detail in articles 22 to 35 of the Constitution.

After stating that the person of the King shall be sacred and inviolable, the Constitution goes on to grant the monarch the right to name the Prime Minister, appoint and preside over the Cabinet and dismiss the government. To promulgate laws passed by the legislature and issue decrees in the exercise of his statutory powers. He may dissolve Parliament and, until such time as a new one is elected within three months, assumes legislative powers. In addressing Parliament, his speech shall not be subject to debate. The King is the Commander-in-Chief of the armed forces and makes the appointments to both military and civilian posts in the state, including the Chairman and half the members of the Constitutional Council, the President of the High Court of Justice, and, upon the recommendation of the Supreme Judicial Council over which the King presides, other members of the Judiciary. He grants pardons, accredits ambassadors to foreign countries, and concludes and ratifies treaties, except those with financial commitments which must first be approved by Parliament. He has even the right to initiate a revision of the Constitution by submitting his proposal for a referendum.

But the most troubling power of the King in a Parliamentary form of government, and one unfortunately common to other Arab states, such as Egypt and Jordan, is the right of the head of state to decree a state of emergency in the country and assume both executive and legislative powers. The circumstances under which the King may declare a state of emergency are described in article 35 of the Constitution:

> Should the integrity of the national territory be threatened or should anything occur which might interfere with the normal conduct of the constitutional institutions, then the King shall, upon consulting with the President of the House of Representatives and the Chairman of the Constitutional Council and addressing the Nation, declare by Royal Decree a state of emergency. Consequent [to such a declaration] and

> notwithstanding any provisions to the contrary, the King shall have the prerogative of taking all necessary measures that are needed in the defense of the national territory or are required for the restoration of normal operations to constitutional institutions and the proper functioning of the affairs of state.
>
> The 1992 Constitution brought about an improvement over its predecessors, in this regard, by providing that the declaration of the state of emergency shall not bring about a dissolution of the House of Representatives.

In addition to the powers vested in the person of the king, the royal office was made hereditary even before the adoption of the first Constitution when Muhammad V broke with the Islamic tradition of selecting the new ruler by acclamation or the *bai'ah* of the *ulema* and elders of the Community, and designated his son Hassan to succeed him. Every Constitution since then has prescribed that succession to the throne and its "constitutional rights" shall pass "by heredity" to the eldest son of the reigning monarch, unless the king should designate from among his sons other than the eldest. In the event there is no direct male descendant, then succession will go to the nearest male relative of the king, according to article 20 of the 1992 Constitution.

This latest constitution lowered the age of maturity of the Crown Prince from eighteen to sixteen at which he could assume the royal office, and changed also the composition of the Regency Council which will act for the Crown Prince until he is able to assume the office of king. Whereas the Chairman of the Council was in the 1962 Constitution the closest collateral male relative of the crown prince, it is now the President of the Supreme Court, and membership of the President of the House of Representatives, the Chairman of the Ulama (religious scholars) Council, and ten dignitaries, all appointed by the King. The replacement of the Islamic legal order, with its divinely ordained rule, by that of the modern territorial state, with its concept of popular sovereignty, was bound to lead to tension over the limitation and separation of powers.

The Moroccan constitution is by no means short on expressions extolling the modern concepts of popular sovereignty. Already in the first 1962

Constitution and carried over to the 1992 one, sovereignty is said to reside in the Nation who shall exercise it directly by referendum and indirectly through the constitutionally established institutions. This is followed by the declaration that the law represents the highest expression of the will of the Nation, before which all Moroccans are equal. Nevertheless, while recognizing the right of everyone to the free exercise of his or her religious rites, the Constitution provides that Islam is the official State religion and neither the monarchical regime nor the provisions relating to Islam are subject to change even by a constitutional amendment.

Because of Morocco's recent transition from an Islamic to a modern legal order, such provisions in the Constitution bring to mind how Christian thought in Europe struggled with the problem of sovereignty in the later Middle Ages, until Jean Bodin's discourses about sovereignty and legislative power led to the philosophical detachment of law from its religious foundations and consequently to the secular notion of sovereignty.[21] While associating sovereign power with legislative power, he made sure to distinguish statutory or human law from morals or natural law, an important distinction for the modern concept of law and the modern doctrine of state.

The legislative powers of the House of Representative are said to be mandated by the Moroccan People, but as we shall momentarily see these powers are less than supreme. Elected for a six-year term, the representatives are immune from prosecution and arrest for the opinions they express while in office, except those opinions which may be derogatory to the King or contradictory to the monarchical system and the teachings of the Muslim faith. But it is the limitations which the Constitution places on the legislative powers of the House of Representatives which create one of the glaring contradictions of the Constitution. While article 46 gives the Executive residual statutory powers in matters outside the purview of the legislature, article 45 restricts the competence of the House of Representatives of enacting laws to the following matters:

(a) The rights of individuals and groups enumerated in part one of the Constitution.

(b) The nature of crimes and punishments, penal and civil procedure, and the establishment of new types of courts.

(c) The fundamental law of the judiciary.

(d) The fundamental law for public offices.

(e) The fundamental guarantees granted to civil and military personnel.

(f) The electoral system of local councils.

(g) The regulation of civil and commercial obligations.

(h) The establishment of public institutions.

(i) The nationalization of enterprises or their transfer from the public to the private sector.

Furthermore, what the House of Representatives legislates can by no means be considered final. The Constitution grants the Executive the right to declare unacceptable any proposed law or an amendment to a law, and with the consent of the Constitutional Council, to modify by decree laws already enacted by the House. Other restrictions imposed by the Constitution on the work of the Legislature include its internal organization and financing, its approval of the budget and appropriations, and the enactment of organic or organizational laws.

The King, who has thirty days to promulgate a law passed by the House of Representatives, can forestall its passage while in draft form by requesting a second reading, which request cannot be refused by the House. If still unsatisfied, the King may by Royal Decree submit his own version of the bill or proposed law to a public referendum, unless the House, by two-thirds majority, had already adopted or rejected the bill or proposed law. Indeed, the King who has the prerogative under article 70 to dissolve the Legislature and hold elections for a new House of Representatives no later than three months, is required by article 71 to assume in the interval the legislative powers in addition to the other powers conferred upon him by the Constitution. With the Government made answerable by the Constitution to the King as well as the House of Representatives, the King is constitutionally competent enough to run the country on his own. This has in fact happened on several occasions in the 1960's and 1970's when parliament was suspended for extended periods of time.

Compared to other Arab states, Morocco's constitutional development since independence has been more steady and less prone to revolutionary break downs. Despite two attempted coups d'etat and repeated civilian opposition and agitation, the monarchy has held its ground and managed to steer the country back on a constitutional course. While constitutional conflicts may have abated, they have not been completely resolved.

In no other Arab country is the legitimacy and continuity of the regime more directly associated with the person of the ruler than in Morocco. The present dynasty of Sultan/King goes back to the year 900 AD when Idris bin Abdalla, a great grandson of Ali, came from Arabia to establish the independent sultanate of Morocco, justifying his claim to rule on his descent from the Prophet. In his *bai'ah*, or acclamation compact with the elders of the community, we get a sense of the fealty on the part of the subjects and their veneration of the ruler: "O you People, we have assumed this task in which the beneficent among you shall be doubly rewarded and the baneful reprimanded. As for us, thank God, we are of good intentions. Do not extend your necks to anyone else, for you shall find with us all you seek with regard to the establishment of justice."[22]

Today, in the relations between citizen and King, the acclamation compact has certainly been replaced by the constitution. Considering however the role of the King as giver and guardian of the Constitution, arbiter among the various institutions of the State, and the manner in which the will of the representatives of the People is mediated and constrained, it is not as certain where constituent power lies.[23]

In 1958, shortly after his return from exile, King Muhammad V issued what amounted to a royal charter in which he promised the establishment of constitutional institutions, including a legislative council, but left no doubt where supreme authority lies: "The sovereignty of the Nation is embodied in the King who is its custodian. The legislative authority shall be shared by the King and the constitutional institutions, while the Prime Minister and his Cabinet shall be responsible to the King..."[24]

The view of the Monarchy of itself did not change much after the adoption of the first Constitution in 1962. Upon approval of the Constitution which he submitted to a public referendum, King Hassan II gave a press conference in which he appraised the results of the referendum in the following terms: "The Moroccan Constitution did not come as a result of demands or intrigues. It was rather the product of an idea which has grown in the soul of the People and the King. An imposed constitution commits everyone to it as soon as it is signed or officially announced without consulting the People. The Morrocan Constitution is not of this type; it gave the King the opportunity to ask everyone whether they agree to it or not.

The referendum is considered the easiest and simplest expression of democracy, (since) I do not accept any mediation between me and the People. As to those who have remarked that the Constitution gave extensive powers to the King and did not grant similar authority to the (People's) Representatives, [I say] that the Constitution does not grant Representatives authorities, it imposes on them commitments and responsibilities. [That is why] the Constitution has made the King an arbiter, giving him only (those powers) which are necessary for him to intervene whenever a disequilibrium develops in the course of events.".[25]

The constitutional conflict in Morocco has since the 1950's centered on who can legitimately claim constituent power. Such phrases as constitutional monarchy, democratic ideals, constitutional institutions, national unity, public freedoms, legitimacy and the rule of law, commonly used by political parties, both loyalists and dissidents, during governmental crises are often mere euphemisms for saying who has the supreme authority in the State, where does constituent power lie, with God, King or Country. It is an issue not confined to Morocco. As we shall see later in this part of the book, it is a perennial problem for constitutionalism in practically all the Arab states.

SYRIA: The Search for National Identity.

While the ideological confusion of being Arab and being Muslim in a political sense remains a major obstacle to the development of the modern territorial national state in the Arab countries generally, nowhere is the problem of national identity more acute than in Syria which ironically alone among the Arab countries the state has no constitutional identification with Islam.

This has contributed to the fact that since its dissociation from the Ottoman Empire in 1918, Syria has been a virtual laboratory for constitution making. It experimented with practically every kind of regime one can think of: monarchical, presidential, parliamentary, military, democratic, socialist, just as it tried to accommodate every political ideology without great success.

But it was the Arab dimension of its national character that has engaged it most in its search for a constitutional make up. Having been historically the setting for the first Arab-Muslim regime, the Omayad Caliphate, and more recently, at the turn of the century, the standard bearer for the political ideas of Arab nationalism, Syria came out of the dismemberment of the Ottoman Empire with a dual consciousness of itself: independent and united in its natural boundaries (including present day Syria, Lebanon, Palestine and Jordan) and at the same time heir to the Arab Empire of the past. It went through a similar experience as an important Province of the Roman Empire, at once ruled and provider of emperors. As if it were Syria's destiny from time immemorial to be herself and something else as well. The acknowledged center of Arab self-determination was however too weak to be dominant in an Arab grouping.[26]

No sooner did the Syrian National Congress, which also acted as a constitutional convention, proclaim in 1919 the first Syrian Arab state with King Faisal, son of King Hussein of Hijaz, at its head, and adopt in 1920 its first constitution, than the British and the French moved to nip the new state in the bud. Acting on their secret war time Sykes-Picot agreement and the 1922 mandate of the League of Nations, the two colonial powers proceeded to partition the country between them by force, with Britain taking Jordan and Palestine, and France Syria and Lebanon.

They not only disregarded the Syrian people's declared desire for independence in a united Syria and their readiness to take charge of their own destiny without the need for a trustee to guide them,[27] the two mandatory powers went on to exceed their mandate by their heavy handed rule and their dismemberment of the territory placed in their trust. While the British promised the World Zionist Organization a national home for the Jews in Palestine, and established the state of Jordan, the French gave Turkey the Syrian districts of Antioch, historic seat of the Syrian Orthodox Church, and of Alexandretta, the vital northern port on the Mediterranean, established the Greater Lebanon state and attempted to partition what was left of truncated Syria into several petty states.

The trauma of this first search for constitutional identity has left an indelible mark on the political psyche of the Syrian people. They had staked the future of their country on the Arab Revolt against the Ottomans which Lawrence of Arabia had mediated in the name of Faisal's father, in return for British promises of independence for the Arab territories of the Ottoman Empire. By the time it had come to Syria, however, the Arab Revolt was actually Syria's revolt, her officers and men in the Ottoman army and the members of the secret societies which had already worked for secession from Turkey, and some of whom were condemned to death in 1916 by a Turkish military tribunal sitting at Aley, Lebanon. When the Lawrence-Faisal Arab forces which formed the eastern flank to the British Allenby army advancing north from the Sinai entered Syria in 1918, they had practically no Hijazi elements with them. They were made up for the most part of inhabitants of Syria, Palestine and Iraq, men who had a direct stake and a home in the country they were about to enter. And when the time came, at the end of hostilities, for the Syrians to taking a stand against the British and French imperialist designs, Faisal faltered. It is said that so convinced was he of the justice of the Arab cause and the promises of the British to his father, that he readily and naively accepted the European offers of compromise which in the end came to naught.[28] Forced out of Syria by French forces, Faisal was installed by the British as King of Iraq, just as they installed his brother Abdalla King of Jordan.

What followed was a protracted constitutional struggle between the French mandatory power and the leadership of the truncated Syrian state. No less than 15 French inspired organic decrees and two full fledged constitutions affecting the composition and administration of the country were issued between 1922 and 1943. Forced by the terms of the League of Nations mandate to formulate a constitution within three years of assuming the mandate, the French in 1928 permitted elections for a constituent assembly to take place and draft a constitution. But when the assembly moved to adopt the constitution, the French High Commissioner intervened and objected to a number of provisions which the French considered contrary to their international obligations under the mandate. The Syrians however insisted on retaining them. The provisions to which the French objected declared Syria sovereign and indivisible within its natural boundaries when it seceded from the Ottoman Empire, gave the President the powers to grant pardons, conclude treaties, appoint ambassadors, reorganize the army and declare a state of emergency. When the impasse persisted the French dissolved the constituent assembly and shelved the 1928 constitution.

Two years later, the French High Commissioner proclaimed a new constitution. It was basically the 1928 text amended in a manner which would maintain French control over the country. This 1930 constitution dealt with the controversial question of Syria's boundaries by simply ignoring them. "Syria forms an indivisible political unit," declared article 2. Other provisions permitted the official use of the French language in addition to Arabic, removed the right to legislate an election law from the assembly and gave it to the Council of Ministers under the supervision of the mandatory authorities, gave the latter the right to intervene in the deliberations of the House of Representatives, and subjected most internal decisions and external acts of the Syrian government to the consent of the French High Commissioner. This constitution fared the way its predecessor did. Three years after its adoption the French High Commissioner suspended it sine die and disbanded the constituent assembly which had endorsed it.

An attempt to end the mandate and conclude a Franco-Syrian treaty failed in 1936 when the French Parliament rejected the French High Commissioner's proposed treaty which the Syrian House of Representatives had accepted. Once again the stumbling block was the boundaries of Syria. The French Parliamentary majority which rejected the treaty insisted that the treaty provide in no uncertain terms that it did not apply to certain parts of historical Syria, such as Lebanon and others within the French administered truncated Syria, such as Latakia and Jabal Druze. Other provisions which the French Parliament could not support had to do with the abolition of the regime of capitulations which Europeans had enjoyed in the former Ottoman territories, and the conditions attending the retention of French military bases in Syria.

From 1939 the year World War II broke out to 1945 when the French finally left Syria, the country oscillated between periods when the 1930 constitution was reinstated and a semblance of normality prevailed to periods when it was yet again suspended and national agitation resumed. The formal recognition of Syrian independence in 1946 saw the election of a new House of Representatives and the establishment of a parliamentary form of government, following the appropriate changes to the 1930 Constitution, to permit the re-election of the incumbent president in the interest of continuity and the expansion of the membership of the Council of Ministers for wider political representation.

But the coming of independence, sharpened rather than relaxed Syria's search for constitutional identity. As was the case in the pre-independence era, the post-independence period witnessed between 1948 and 1971 when the incumbent President Hafiz al-Assad came to power and the current 1973 Constitution was adopted, no less than ten military coups and fifteen organic decrees and changes of constitutions. Interestingly enough in none of these did the religious dimension figure much as was the case with the other Arab states. As a matter of fact, Syria is the only Arab country (besides Lebanon) whose constitution does not declare Islam the state religion. Given the active Christian element in the Syrian leadership and, despite a Muslim majority, the highly diverse religious and social composition of Syrian society, the subject did not figure at all in the drafting of any of the constitutions except that of 1953.

Two factors at that time helped to engender a public debate of the subject. The Muslim Brotherhood, through its leader Shaikh Mustafa al-Siba'i and an active protagonist of political Islam, pressed for the establishment of Islam as the state religion. This was opposed by the Syrian Social Nationalist Party, whose organ the daily al-Bina' took issue with al-Siba'i's views and argued instead for the complete separation of "church" and state. Luckily, the views of both sides have been made available in the English language in this country.[29]

Although the subject is at the heart of any discussion of modernization, no such open public debate took place anywhere else in the Arab World. Only recently and in response to increasing acts of violence attributed to Muslim fundamentalists, that Arab voices have been heard acclaiming the peaceful and liberal nature of Islam, but not the advantages of secularism, a subject to which we shall presently return.

The first major attempt at constitution making since independence however came in 1950 in the wake of two military coups and the rise of political parties whose ideologies challenged the established leadership of traditional urban families. The first was the Arab Socialist Party, whose radical ideas of social reform were to impact greatly the 1950 Constitution. The second was the Arab Baath or Resurrection Party, whose notion of a single Arab nation, was to bring about in 1958 the short lived union of Syria and Egypt in the United Arab Republic. Although well organized the power of these two parties would gradually fragment and their appeal eventually dissipate; but the socialist and Arabist ideas they propagated would dominate the public debates over Syria's constitutional identity throughout the sixties and seventies.

Judging from the preamble to the 1950 Constitution, the debate was yet to move beyond the grandiloquent extolling of public freedoms and social welfare and begin to identify more precisely the national identity and the nature of the Syrian state. Even if one allows for the benefits of abstractness in the formulation of constitutions, the rhetorical power of the Arabic language is such that it often subverts the actual intent and purpose of what is being said. Here are some extracts of this grandiloquent preamble:[30]

> We, the representatives of the Syrian Arab people, meeting in a constituent assembly by the will of God and the wish of this free people, declare that we have adopted this constitution in order to achieve the following sacred aims:
>
> To establish justice on such solid ground that every person is guaranteed his/her right without fear or bias, and that by giving the judiciary all the support it needs to strengthen its independence under a free democratic republican regime.
>
> To guarantee the fundamental public freedoms for every citizen and to ensure that they actually enjoy them in accordance with the law and order; for public freedoms represent the noblest symbols of the meaning of the human being and human dignity.
>
> To spread the spirit of brotherhood and raise the social consciousness among the citizens, so that each person will feel that he/she is part of the fatherland and the fatherland is in need of them...
>
> To free every citizen from the afflictions of poverty, sickness, ignorance and fear by establishing the rightful economic and social order which would achieve social justice and protect the laborer and the farmer, assure the weak and the scared, and lead every one to the bounty of the fatherland...
>
> To strengthen the individual personality and educate it so that every citizen will feel responsible for the security of the fatherland, its present and future, and that the fatherland is the eternal and lasting truth, and that it is in the trust of all the Syrians until they hand it down to their children with pride and dignity, and that by providing the people with the right national training, by facilitating and extending education to everyone, and by promoting the sense of sacrifice for the common good...
>
> We declare also that our peoplė are intent upon strengthening the bonds of cooperation between them and the peoples of the Arab and Muslim worlds, and upon building our modern state on the basis of the upright morals revealed by Islam and the other heavenly religions, and upon combating heresy and the corruption of good morals...
>
> And we declare that our people who are historically, now and in future, part of the Arab Nation, look forward to the day when the Arab Nation

will be united in a single state, a sacred wish for which our people will strive under conditions of freedom and independence...

We, the representatives of the Syrian Arab people, appeal to the Almighty to protect our nation and people and safeguard them from all ills, to guide us in the fulfillment of our high ideals, to the renewal of the time-honored glory which our great ancestors had accomplished, and to pave the way to a glorious and mighty future for our children.

In formulating the constitution, the constitutional assembly consulted the texts of no less than fifteen Asian, European and American constitutions, in addition to the constitutions of the Arab states. This partly explains the remarkable part in the 1950 Constitution devoted to Basic Principles. The provisions of articles 7 to 31 represent one of the most comprehensive statements of fundamental freedoms to be found in an Arab constitution. Everything from freedom of the person, of thought and expression, of sanctity of the home and of communications, to freedom of the press, of association and the right to demonstrate, from the right of the accused to a lawyer, a hearing within twenty four hours, innocent until proven guilty and equality before the law, to prohibition of deportation of Syrians and to granting of political asylum, from guaranteeing private property, prohibiting expropriation without judicial decision, to distribution of public lands while limiting individual ownership of land, and improving the lot of farmers, from guaranteeing work and improving the conditions of labor, to the right of every citizen for state ensured health, unemployment, social welfare, and old age benefits, from free and compulsory public education and vocational training, to state support for the arts, learning, and scientific research.

The Constitution was adopted on September 5, 1950 and in a little over one year, on December 2, 1951, it was suspended by a military junta which dissolved parliament and took over power in yet another coup. The new military authority formulated a new constitution for the country, the 1953 Constitution, only to be set aside in less than a year also by a military coup and the reinstatement of the 1950 Constitution with the return to a civilian government.

From then on the country's political parties became increasingly radicalized as the younger, educated generations flogged to new ideologies to challenge the dominant traditional leadership. The Communist party which preached the classical Marxist program succeeded in tightening its grip on student and professional unions and associations, so much so that by the late fifties or early sixties was poised for a take over of power not only in Syria, but in neighboring Iraq and Jordan as well. The Syrian Social Nationalist Party also active at the time, had sufficiently revived, following the 1949 execution of its leader by the Lebanese authorities, to return its representatives to the Syrian parliament. Taking after 19th century European notions of secular nationalism, the SSNP's program promoted a uniquely Syrian national identity rooted in the historical and social conditions of the country within its natural boundaries. To a movement which won adherents from across religious lines, the Arab dimension in the Syrian national character was only one of many cultural layers the country had been exposed to since recorded time.

But the movement which would have the more lasting influence on Syrian politics was the Arab Baath or Resurrection Party. Although founded by a Syrian of the Christian faith, the Baath adhered to the notion of a single Arab nation with secular overtones. The fact that the Arab nation as we know it today came about only with the rise of Islam, its political platform asserted, should in no way detract from its essentially Arab character (as distinct from other Muslim nations) or give Arab Muslims a higher claim to it than non-Muslim Arabs. As the Party leadership gained influence within extant regimes and began to developed its philosophy beyond the question of national identity and into the realm of social and economic reform, its program became increasingly socialist, a development which was given added impetus with the rise to power of Gamal Abdel Nasser in Egypt. Nasser is said to have viewed Arab nationalism as a cause in search of a hero which Egypt, fully content until then with its own Egyptian identity, was destined to provide that hero.

That gave the Baath Party the only opportunity ever, as it turned out, to create an Arab union. In 1958 it engineered Syria's merger with Egypt, into the United Arab Republic, under a single presidential system of government and a constitution tailored after the 1956 Egyptian Constitution. The Syrian people gave overwhelming approval by referendum to the newly formed state with Abdel Nasser as its first President.

The union lasted until 1961 when it was brought to an end by a Syrian military coup, which went on to abrogate all the socialist measures of nationalization and land expropriation of the union authorities. It also restored the Syrian Constitution of 1950 only to have it suspended, amended, or replaced by subsequent coups in 1962, 1963, 1964, and 1966. The latter coup saw the consolidation by an Air Force lieutenant by the name of Hafiz al-Assad of his power in the regional (Syrian) command of the Baath Party and eventually his overthrow of the Party's leadership, some of whom fled the country and joined their colleagues in Iraq. This brought about the enduring bitter schism within the Party between its Syrian and Iraqi wings from which it has never recovered. By 1970, Assad was in a position to seize power in a bloodless coup and in 1971 to be nominated President of Syria by the regional command of the Baath Party.

Assad's coming to power coincided with yet another Arab union, this time the loose confederation between Syria, Libya and Egypt, labeled the United Arab Republics. The new union tried to avoid the hazards of a real unity which the Syrian-Egyptian merger experienced. The organic law of the confederation permitted each member state to retain its national sovereignty and foreign representation while sending delegates to the confederation legislative assembly, and the three Presidents of the member states would constitute the Presidential Council of the Confederation. More importantly, each member state would have its own constitution, although compliance with certain basic common principles was required. The Confederation, unlike its predecessor, the United Arab Republic, which took a military coup to dissolve it, simply wilted away. But it left behind, as far as Syria is concerned, a constitution for a socialist Arab state which together with the Assad regime has had the longest survival record for Syria since its independence.

Judging from the basic criteria which are said to inform its principles, the 1973 Constitution expressed with greater vigor Syria's erstwhile inclination to be herself and something else as well, something larger than itself. These criteria are:[31]

(1) The comprehensive Arab revolt is a continual necessity to achieve the aims of the Arab Nation for unity, freedom and socialism. The revolt in the Syrian Arab region is part of this comprehensive Arab revolt, and all its policies stem from the overall strategy of the Arab revolt.

(2) Any accomplishments achieved by any single Arab region under existing conditions of fragmentation will fail to attain the desired goal unless supported and protected by Arab unity.

(3) The march towards establishing the socialist order is not only a response to the needs of Arab society, but is also necessary to mobilize the capabilities of the Arab masses in the struggle against Zionism and Imperialism.

(4) Freedom is a sacred right and popular democracy is the ideal form which guarantees to the citizen the exercise of his/her freedom...Only free citizens can protect the freedom of the fatherland, and the freedom of the citizen will not be complete without his/her economic and social liberation.

(5) The Arab revolt is an integral part of the world liberation movement...for progress, freedom and independence. This Constitution shall be a guidebook to the masses of our people in carrying on the battle for liberation and reconstruction, guided by its principles and provisions...

The operative parts of the Constitution endorse a one party, republican presidential system of government. The President is to be nominated by the House of Representatives upon the proposal of the regional command of the Baath Party and elected by public plebiscite. The Baath Party is the lead party of a coalition of leftist forces. In addition to this political formation, the Constitution provides for workers and peoples organizations, cooperatives and associations to marshal and consolidate the Syrian people's capabilities in the service of the Arab Nation and its goals.

This explains the Constitution's division of property ownership into three categories: People's Ownership which comprises all natural resources and public and nationalized property; Collective Ownership which covers the properties of peoples' organizations, cooperatives and associations; and Individual Property which refers to privately owned property whose use may not contradict the public interest. Although the Constitution adheres to a planned socialist economy to complement and integrate with the economy of the Arab fatherland as a whole, in recent years the government of President Assad has begun to relax its economic strictures and permit greater leeway for private initiative and even foreign investment. As the country's economy stalled, and many of its stalwarts, the merchant class, stayed away, it became increasingly apparent that the planned socialist system did not suit the Syrian's traditional individualist temper and enterprising spirit, let alone the imperative of complementing Arab economy as a whole.

Not only did the socialist economic program of the Baath Party falter, its political vision of a single Arab Nation has also proved illusory. Neither concept has in any way helped in defining Syria's constitutional, nor for that matter national, identity. When one recalls that the origin of these Baath Party ideas lay, as Albert Hourani has noted,[32] in the intellectual debates about the national identity of the Syrians and their relations with the rest of the Arab World, one can begin to fathom the depths of the problem of Syria's constitutional identity.

As has been mentioned earlier in this section, these debates were forced upon the Syrians already in the immediate post world war I years when they found themselves caught between an uncertain self and a fading other: the dismemberment of the country at the hands of the British and the French left the

Syrians shorn of their historic setting, and the failure of the Arab Revolt which fed on their own ideas of Arab nationalism left them without their political alter ego. It has been Syria's historic problem all along--how to exist in the universes which continually rose and fell apart around her.

EGYPT: The Problem of Presidential Power.

Egypt's long, uninterrupted, socio-political setting since the time of the Pharoes, helped it realize its first modern constitution in 1923 without the hang ups of a religious or a national identity which troubled other Arab states. Until, that is, the coming of Gamal Abdel Nasser in 1952 and his vision of an Arab role in search of a hero.

More problematic however has been the extensive power which Egyptian constitutions have invariably bestowed on the head of state. Although Nasser's personal charisma helped ingrain this power in the contemporary Egyptian political fabric, he certainly did not originate it. It began in modern times with another strongman, Muhammad Ali, and the Khedieveal line of rulers he founded in the 19th century. In fact it was Muhammad Ali's descendant, Khedieve Ismail, who created in 1866 the first embryonic constitutional body, the 75-member *Majlis Shura an-Nuwwab*, or Consultative Chamber of Deputies, and issued the first fundamental law regulating its work. But the purpose of the Chamber was only consultative with complete control of the Government retained by the Khedieve, until a popular uprising led by an army officer by the name of Ahmad 'Urabi, and directed against the authoritarian rule of the Khedieve and the increasing burden of taxation to pay for his indebtedness to foreign financial interests, forced Ismail to limit his absolute powers. He established a Council of Ministers and entrusted it with many of his executive responsibilities. At the same time the Chamber of Deputies, in a move to assert its independence, prepared and adopted in 1882 Egypt's first written constitution. But Britain's military intervention and occupation of the country that year under the pretext of putting down the 'Urabi uprising, aborted Egypt's first attempt at a modern constitution.

It was not until the country gained a semblance of independence from British occupation in 1922 (except for certain concessions which Britain retained), that another attempt at a modern constitution would materialize. That year Khedieve/Sultan/King Fouad appointed a 30-member committee of leading politicians and government officials to draft a constitution which he promulgated by royal decree, after having tried but failed to amend certain provisions which detracted from his traditional powers. The 1923 Constitution is therefore Egypt's first experience with contemporary constitution making, and before examining its salient provisions, it is important to shed some light on what is often quite vague in the case of Arab constitutions: the constituent power which sustains them.

Because of the circumstances under which it was adopted, Egyptian jurists have over the years questioned whether the 1923 Constitution was in the nature of a royal charter granted by the King, a compact between King and People, or of a special type unlike anything known in constitution making.[33]

The preponderant view is that the King voluntarily relinquished many of his traditional prerogatives when he granted the People a constitution. Furthermore, at the time it was being prepared the power to issue organic laws, such as those establishing the Council of Ministers and the Chamber of Deputies, unlike ordinary laws, was the sole prerogative of the Khedieve (now King). Indeed, those of this view point to the preamble to the Constitution which states:

> We, King of Egypt, whereas we continue since our ascension to the throne of our forefathers to safeguard the trust which the Lord has placed in us and which requires that we provide our nation all the welfare within our power, and guide her along the right path to happiness, progress and the enjoyment of those things which free and civilized nations enjoy. And since that is not possible to accomplish properly without her having the most advanced constitutional system that the world has known, and since its achievement has always been one of our wishes and the greatest thing toward which we have directed our efforts, we have therefore ordered as follows..."

The minority view which considers the Constitution in the nature of a social compact between the King and the People, point to the provision in the

Constitution which recognizes the Nation as the source of all authority, and to the mutual oath taken by both King and members of Parliament to uphold its provisions.

What brought about this difference in views was the fact that the 1923 Constitution was neither the work of a constituent assembly nor was it put to a referendum before it was adopted. It is a question which has often arisen in the Arab states as constitutions are repeatedly adopted and abrogated. In the case of the 1923 Constitution, it is as hard to conceive of a truly social compact between King and People brought about by the voluntary joining of two free wills, as it is difficult to believe that the King would have agreed to grant the People a constitution without considerable public pressure. He had after all to agree to some limitation on his traditional powers which nevertheless remained considerable.

As was the case with the first Tunisian constitution, the 1923 Constitution was based on the Belgian and Ottoman constitutions. It began by declaring Egypt a sovereign and independent state with a representative form of a monarchical government. Although it clearly provided for separate executive, legislative and judicial functions for the state, it left the monarchy with much of its traditional powers despite the limitations introduced by the constitution. It gave the King concurrent legislative powers with both houses of Parliament; no law can be enacted without the approval of the King, who has also the right to introduce legislation; the King appoints and dismisses the Prime Minister, the Council of Ministers and government officials.

But the troublesome provision of the 1923 Constitution which has found its way to successive Egyptian constitutions, gave the King, who could dissolve Parliament at any time or declare a state of emergency and suspend the constitution, the right to legislate by decree if urgently required when Parliament is not in session. This type of power given to a head of state who, unlike the Council of Ministers, is not answerable to the Legislature is the most controversial provision of the Egyptian constitutions of recent time.

Until the Nasser revolution of 1952 ended the monarchy in Egypt, the constitutional upheavals saw the suspension by royal decree of the 1923 constitution, and its replacement in 1930 by another which restricted the powers of Parliament to withdraw confidence from the Government and correspondingly increased the powers of the Executive. Egypt's movement in 1936 towards greater independence and the replacement of the old relations with Britain by a treaty of alliance, resulted in the reinstatement of the 1923 constitution which Egyptian political parties demanded as a condition for their participation in negotiations with Britain.

The first act of the Revolutionary Council of Free Officers which brought about the change of regime in 1952 was the abrogation of the 1923 Constitution on the grounds that it had become a tool in the hands of the King and made a mockery of parliamentary government. "I therefore declare in the name of the People," said Nasser at the time, "the fall of the 1923 constitution, and announce at the same time that the government is proceeding to form a committee to prepare a new constitution to be approved by the People, a constitution which, unlike the old defective constitution, will realize the wish of the Nation for a clean and healthy Parliamentary government. And until the constitution has been prepared, a government responsive to the interests of all the People will exercise authority, without bias or discrimination, during the interim period."[34]

Two months later, the Revolutionary Council issues a second decree outlining the basic rules for the governance of the country in the interim. It began by declaring that the Nation is the source of all authority, that freedom of thought and belief are guaranteed, that the judiciary is independent and all Egyptians are equal before the law. In the section entitled System of Government, the decree provides that the leader of the Revolutionary Council shall assume the overall functions of sovereignty and in particular the measures he finds necessary (to take) for the protection of the revolution, its legal order and the realization of its aims. Legislative powers are entrusted to the Council of Ministers who are appointed and dismissed by the leader of the Revolutionary Council. Still, the decree expressed the leader's "unswerving belief in the establishment of a democratic, constitutional regime" at the end of this interim period.

Almost a year would pass since the military putsch before the Revolutionary Council decides to abolish the monarchy, send the King into exile and declare a republic. The July 18, 1953 decree attributed the move to perceived machinations by leaders of the dissolved political parties and other reactionary forces to re-ingratiate themselves with the King whom the decree denounced as a descendant of a line of foreign traitors to the land.

Although a committee is named in 1953 by the Revolutionary Council to prepare a constitution, no text seemed to reflect adequately the aims of the revolution to be acceptable, until 1956. But by the time the 1956 Constitution was adopted, the Revolutionary Council were contemplating the union of Egypt and Syria which materialized in early 1958 into the United Arab Republic, and a provisional Constitution that year superseded the 1956 Constitution. It was a constitution intended to be the basis for an ever widening union of Arab states. Soon however the United Arab Republic around which it was tailored would disband, but its basic principles of Arab nationalism, state socialism, and Islam, would radically change Egypt's constitutional identity.

The 1958 constitution was consequently replaced, first by a National Charter in 1962 and then by a provisional constitution in 1964, which provided for the appointment of a committee to undertake the drafting of a permanent constitution. But circumstances, both internal and external, including Egypt's defeat in the 1967 Israeli-Arab war, the death of Nasser in 1970, and the failed Egypt-Syria-Libya union of April, 1971, the country would remain without a permanent constitution until September 1971.

Except for a few but not insignificant amendments introduced into the text in 1980, to which we shall presently return, the 1971 constitution remains to this day the constitution of Egypt, with all the tenets and terminologies introduced by the Nasser era into the political life of Egypt. In fact it was based on the principles enunciated in 1968 by the national conference of Arab Socialist Union, the political organization of the Nasserite regime, for a permanent constitution. They included the following:[36]

= To ensure Egypt's belongingness to the Arab Nation in an organic union, above (the wishes of) any individual and at any stage;

= To safeguard the socialist gains (of the revolution) and strengthen them...

= To point out the close relationship between social freedom and political freedom including personal liberties...

= To ensure the establishment of the modern state...in which it must be made clear that the President of the Republic exercises his responsibilities through the Ministers and the specialized bodies and their highly capable and experienced staff...

= To clearly identify the responsibilities of the different state institutions, including those of the Presidency, the Legislative and the Executive...

= To underscore the importance of work as the sole criteria for human dignity;

= To guarantee public, cooperative and private property and the limitation and social role of each.

The constitutional text begins by stating that the Arab Republic of Egypt is a state whose system of government is socialist and democratic based on the alliance of the People's working forces, and the Egyptian People are a part of the Arab Nation, and intent upon realizing that Nation's complete unity. Makes Islam the state religion, and the principles of Islamic Sharia a source of legislation, which became in 1980 the principal source for legislation and create thereby continual questioning of the constitutionality of legislation.

Socialism is identified in the Constitution as the economic system of the state, and the Arab Socialist Union is the only recognized political organization which is said to include under its umbrella all the working forces, including farmers, laborers, soldiers, intellectuals, and those described as national capitalists. It is here that the 1980 amendment made a subtle, but far reaching, economic and political change in direction. While the 1971 text described the Egyptian economy to be based on the socialist, democratic system, for the purpose of eliminating the class differences in society, the 1980 amendment changed the purpose to *reducing differences in income, protect legitimate gain, and guarantee the just distribution of public responsibilities and costs*. The 1980 amendment also did away completely with the Arab Socialist Union and permitted since 1952 the formation of political parties. Article 5 now reads as follows:

> The political system of the Egyptian Arab Republic is based on the multiplicity of (political) parties, (acting) within the basic criteria and principles of the Egyptian society as stipulated in the Constitution. The law would regulate political parties.

These amendments to the 1971 Constitution which were introduced in 1980 by Nasser's revolutionary colleague and successor, Anwar al-Sadat, left intact the provisions dealing with the powers of the President which remain considerable. The provisions in article 3 that the People are the sole repository of sovereignty and the source of all authority notwithstanding, the Constitution is a hybrid of parliamentary and presidential form of government, in which the President is endowed with powers which he exercises independently or in conjunction with the Council of Ministers. Of the former kind, he is the chief of the armed forces, concludes treaties, commutes sentences, dismisses and recalls the National Assembly for regular and extraordinary sessions, returns legislation to the Assembly, declares state of emergency, or take emergency unspecified measures which he sees fit in the event of a threat to national unity, the security of the fatherland or detrimental to the proper functioning of state institutions. Above all it is the President's prerogative to issue executory regulations and even decrees having the force of law, whether delegated by the Assembly or on his own initiative when the Assembly is not in session, has caused certain jurists to call for a review of the 1971 Constitution if not for its abrogation and the adoption of a new one.[37]

Some of these extraordinary Presidential powers are taken from the 1958

French Constitution, without however the stringent restrictions it places on their use. Unlike its French counterpart, the Egyptian constitution does not require the President to consult the Prime Minister, the President of the National Assembly or the Constitutional Council before resorting to emergency measures under vague circumstances such as the threat to national unity or the proper functioning of state institutions. Similarly the President's prerogative to declare a state of emergency without any constitutional requirements except the requirement of notifying the Assembly within fifteen days to decide what it sees fit, has so often been resorted to in the past decades that a state of emergency has almost become the normal state.

Two other current constitutional practices which since the Nasser era have assumed the force of tradition, are the manner in which the President is elected and his right to seek a referendum on important issues. One third of the National Assembly nominates a candidate for President who, approved by two-thirds majority of the Assembly, is presented as the sole candidate for confirmation by plebiscite. This indirect form of election and the absence of a choice of candidates contradicts the pronounced leadership role and the extensive executive powers which the President enjoys under the constitution.[38]

Referendum is the other practice which the President may utilize to bypass the Legislature. Here again the constitution simply provides that the President may submit for public referendum important matters relating to the higher interests of the country. The counter provision in the French constitution restricts the referendum to those matters which the constitution has identified and Parliament had itself initiated or consented to.

CONFLICTS AND CONTRADICTIONS

In their rush to modernize, the Arab states superimposed European inspired constitutional principles on prevalent traditional social values and modes of authority. By thus acquiring the one without first evolving or repudiating the other, they created the conflicts and contradictions which have led to the recurring constitutional crises we have encountered in the preceding survey of constitutional development in individual states.

Viewed as a historical sociological phenomenon, the modern, liberal state has had two distinguishing characteristics: the differentiation of the political from the religious and the distinction between the private/social realm and the public/political realm, both of which required the disintegration of Community with its shared views of what is right and what is wrong.[39] Indeed the rise of the only modern secular state in the Middle East, that of Turkey, earlier this century has been attributed to the "disintegration of the Ottoman millet system, and the decline of the idea of *ummet* (community) and of the Islamic *dinu-u-devlet* (religion and state)."[40]

There is no evidence of such development in the Arab states' constitutions. Nowhere do we encounter an invocation of statehood with "We the People." Instead the constitutions are made by and in the name of God and His Prophet, of King, of a leader of a Revolution or of a Corrective Movement to a Revolution. And yet most of them declare: "The People are Sovereign!" What does this mean to a society whose politics are tailored to suit its patriarchal social condition and whose traditional legal culture has no conception of popular sovereignty? It is highly important to dwell on this concept because of the repeated confusion in Arab political discourse between it and the Islamic notion of *shura* or consultation.

The notion of *shura*, together with that of *ijam'* or consensus, has been touted by Muslim fundamentalists as the intrinsic democratic alternative in Islam to the principle of representative government in the modern state. The term *shura* appears in the Qoran among the ethical exhortations urging Muslims to avoid conflict and resort to consultation and reconciliation in the conduct of their affairs: "And those who answer the call of the Lord...and whose affairs are a matter of counsel...(xlii.38). As to the ruler seeking counsel from the Community, the closest is a verse that is ostensibly intended as a guide to the Prophet himself: "It was by the mercy of Allah that thou wast lenient with them (O Muhammad), for if thou hadst been stern and fierce of heart they would have dispersed from thee. So pardon them and ask forgiveness for them and consult with them upon the conduct of affairs...(iii.159).

It was Rashid Rida, turn of the century Muslim reformer, who attempted to read into these Qoranic verses the premise of a modern day Islamic legislature made up of the theologians and other wielders of power in society [*ahl al-hall wal rabt*] to interpret the law and advise the ruler/caliph. By the application of *shura* and *ijma'*, that is, Muslim society would duplicate what representative government does in the modern state without abandoning Islam's hallowed doctrines. What Rida however completely overlooked is the entire question of the legitimation of power whose elements - legality, justifiability of rules, and the expressed consent of the citizenry - depend in the modern state as much on the relationship of these underlying elements as on the institutions that embody or give effect to them.[41] Muslim fundamentalists continue to this day to dismiss the question of legitimation of power as totally irrelevant to an Islamic society governed by the revealed law. Which brings us to the subject of sovereignty, the source of, and the end to which, legitimate power is directed.

Elaborated by Jean Bodin in the 16th century, the concept of sovereignty was the product of the new thinking about political community and authority which began with the philosophical detachment of law from its religious foundations.[42] Particularly in its association with the will of the people as the source of law, sovereignty had no place in the theocratic doctrines of either Christianity or Islam where man's duty was to abide by the will of God whose revealed law was universal and eternal. As Hinsley has observed, whether the Pope ruled as vicar of St. Paul and the emperor by delegation from the Pope, and whether the Caliph ruled as successor to the Prophet for and under God, the notion of sovereignty was irrelevant to both. In giving due credit however to the rediscovery of Aristotle's humanist ideas of the polis in the evolution of the notion of sovereignty, Hinsley notes that this was made possible by the works of the Muslim philosophers Averroes and Avicena, which were far more influential in

Europe than in the world of Islam because of the material developments which created there the political circumstances in which the new ideas could take root.[43]

Since the establishment of the Arab territorial states in this century, Muslim jurists have had a hard time trying to conceive from their modern vantage point of what would amount to an Islamic notion of sovereignty. They admit that in a political sense, sovereignty is unknown to Islamic jurisprudence; only in an exalted sense it is said to reside with God who is the source of both law and dominion.[44] To say on the other hand that sovereignty emanates from the combined functions of the revealed law, the Sharia, and from the consensus of the Community, *ijma'*, is to simply say that the Islamic legal order is a government "of laws and of men;" an acceptable notion. But to say that either was sovereignty is to force an uncertain concept of law which never existed in Islam.[45]

The Religious Dimension & the Territorial State:

These conflicting philosophical and theological ideas permeate the Arab states' constitutions. Aware of the transformation taking place, but not fully cognizant of its far reaching implications, the framers of these constitutions welcomed the modern territorial state system without completely abandoning the medieval, religious trappings of the Islamic legal order.

Already in their first articles, the Arab constitutions fail to give formal recognition to the territory of the state with which they identify. Instead, they associate the people and the territory of the state with a larger, legally undefined and politically non-existent, entity, making the achievement of that entity's unity the first purpose of the constitution. "The Tunisian Republic is part of the Greater Maghrib and will strive to achieve its unity," declares article 2 of the Tunisian constitution. The Kingdom of Morocco's constitution also subscribes in the Preamble to the notion of a Maghribian union. These North African states, together with Algeria, Mauritania and off and on Libya, which constitute the Western flank of the Arab World, have directed their external efforts at realizing an economic and a political union between them.

The constitutions of the Arab states to the East commit their peoples and their states to yet another entity. "The Syrian Arab region is an integral part of the Arab fatherland (*watan*), and the people in the Syrian Arab region are a part of the Arab nation (*umma*), and they will strive and work to achieve its complete unity," declares article 1 of the Syrian constitution. Similar provisions are found in the Egyptian, Jordanian, Kuwaiti, and Iraqi constitutions. The latter goes even further by making the achievement of the unitary Arab state "the purpose" of the Iraqi Republic. Those longing for Arab unity could only see in Iraq's invasion of Kuwait in 1990 a valid undertaking in fulfillment of the two countries' constitutional obligations.

The newest Arab constitution, that of Saudi Arabia, as well as those of the smaller Gulf emirates, identify with an Arab Islamic configuration whose bounds extend to the Muslim World at large. A great deal of official effort is spent in realizing the political and economic objectives of the Organization of Islamic States which include the projected Islamic International Court of Justice as an alternative to the Hague Court for the settlement of disputes among Islamic states on the basis of Islamic law. Meanwhile, Saudi Arabia, Bahrain, Kuwait, Oman, Qatar and the United Arab Emirates, joined in 1981 to form the Gulf Cooperation Council to coordinate their policies, harmonize their economies and unify their laws.

The Explanatory Memorandum to the Kuwaiti Constitution is candid in its admission of the conflicting ideas which "inspired and guided" the formulation of the constitutions of some of these states:

> To Follow in the path of our Islamic heritage with regard to the structure of society and the foundations of government, the conscious desire to comply with the precepts of progress, the achievements of the human mind and the constitutional experiences of other states.

These groupings for larger unions seem to satisfy the need for political identity following the break up of the Ottoman Empire, the last embodiment of the Islamic legal order. More recently, as the wave of Islamic fundamentalism began to spread, the constitutional association of the territorial states with a larger union of historic standing provided the regimes of these states with a convenient political crutch to prop up their legitimacy in the face of their more fundamentalist detractors.

But the clearest expression of the religious dimension in Arab constitutions is in provisions which continue to reflect the sense of Community and declare Islam the state religion and Islamic law the source of legislation; and where Islam is not made the religion of the state, as is the case with Syria, then it is required to be the religion of the President. More pervasive, however, socially speaking is the constitutional recognition of the institution of personal status, or the millet system as it was known in the Ottoman Empire, which perpetuates the legal differences between religious communities and grants them exclusive right to legislate and adjudicate in a wide segment of private law, that of domestic relations.

What does it mean for a Constitution to provide that Islamic Sharia shall be the source of legislation, when the same constitution recognizes at the same time the autonomy of the state's legislative body, the representative of the will of the People? Besides matters of faith and rites, the Sharia is not an agreed codified text. It is a vast array of various interpretations and rulings placed on the meager texts in the Qoran dealing with social relations and economic transactions. The meaning of these texts and their incorporation into positive law will, under today's changed circumstances, depend more on the attitude of those who will legislate than on the thousand year old text itself. Left to those who believe Islam must regulate every facet of human life as it was at the time of the Prophet and the early Caliphs, would undoubtedly lead to the establishment of the erstwhile religious state.

In a move to appease Muslim fundamentalists, Egypt's President Anwar Sadat, pressured Parliament in 1980 to amend article 2 of the constitution and make Islamic Sharia the principal source of legislation, instead of simply a principal source. In so doing he gave fundamentalists the right to demand that all man-made law be subject to scrutiny against, and compliance with, the tenets of the revealed law. The measure naturally caused a great quandary in Egyptian legal circles.

Various interpretations were advanced by legal scholars in Egypt to assess the practical effect of the amendment on the country's rich legal heritage of civil law which goes back to over a century. Some took the position that the amendment established the supremacy of Islamic Sharia over the will of the Legislature, requiring it to abide by its tenets, and where these are nonexistent considering today's changed conditions, then by drawing on Islamic procedures for the deduction of rules from divine sources. Others subscribed to the view that the amendment bestowed on Islamic Sharia an intermediate position in the legislative hierarchy between the constitution, as the fundamental law of the land, and the ordinary laws enacted by the Legislature. However in complying with the rules of Islamic Sharia, this view contended that the Legislature must still do so without contravening the other provisions of the constitution. Still others surmised that the amendment by itself did not bestow on Islamic Sharia any legal effect; it rendered its rules effective only to the extent that these rules were formally enacted into law by the Legislature.

This last view appears to be the position taken by the Egyptian Constitutional Court on a petition by supporters of a return to Islamic law to declare existing Egyptian legislation unconstitutional for reason of non-compliance with Islamic Sharia. In its decision denying the petition, the court stated that the purpose of the amendment to article 2 of the constitution is to identify for the Legislature the source on which it should draw when enacting laws in future. The amendment has therefore no retroactive effect on existing legislation, the court opined. In its decision the court stayed clear of any discussion of the substantive issue whether Egyptian laws do or do not contravene the rules of the Sharia.[46] Nevertheless, at the urging of fundamentalist members, the Egyptian Parliament has had under advisement since 1985 the question whether existing legislation contradicts the Sharia.

It is by no means uncommon today, for an Arab ruler who, lacking the spiritual mantle and majesty of the Caliph, to bolster his power by declaring allegiance to Islam. Saudi Arabia is by no means the only one where the traditional authority of religion is used to bolster political legitimacy. As Beetham has observed, this was achieved by forging an organic connection between the definition of a religious purpose and the acknowledged source of authority in the state from which the rules of the political system are derived.[47]

What is at stake here is more than the compliance of a man-made rule of law with one based on the revealed text where the substance of the two may not be that different after all. The concepts of Community and communal loyalty are incompatible with the idea of citizenship and civil loyalty in a territorial state and constitute therefore an obstacle to the integration and consolidation of the emergent territorial state.[48]

By admitting a religious dimension to their state constitutions before having first achieved the total separation of religion and politics, Arab governments have served the interests of neither religion nor politics. Secularization has ironically been a precondition for religious revival, as religious groups found themselves compelled to adapt to changing circumstances in order to remain relevant in today's society.[49]

Nowhere is this more true than in the United States where the constitutional separation of church and state has enhanced rather than diminished religious activity. So much so that the First Amendment provision, "Congress shall make no law respecting an establishment of religion, or prohibiting the free exercise thereof...," and the religious pluralism it has engendered, has resulted in the last four decades in a shift in the jurisprudence of the Supreme Court towards greater engagement of religion in the political process.[50]

Fundamental Rights & Traditional Values:

Based as they are on the 18th century ideas of constitutionalism, the constitutions of the Arab states recognize for the most part what has since become the universally accepted principles of individual freedoms, equality before the law, and the limitations and separation of powers. They were first introduced into the region by the short-lived Ottoman Constitution of 1876 which, like the 20th century Arab constitutions we have been considering, had as its prototype the continental European constitutions. Its claim to fame however lies in the fact that it was the first time an Islamic regime conferred full citizenship on "all subjects of whatever religion or sect they may be," and guaranteed their "personal liberty" and "equality before the law." But what these European inspired constitutional concepts connote in the context of the modern liberal state is not exactly what their counterparts in the traditional legal culture of Arab/Muslim society convey.

The provisions which uphold such fundamental rights as freedom of belief, freedom of association and equality before the law, have been at the heart of enduring constitutional contradictions in practically all the Arab states. Typical of these provisions are the following:

Article 34 of the Syrian constitution: "Freedom of belief is guaranteed and the state respects all religious faiths, and guarantees the free exercise of all religious rites so long as they do not contravene public order;" article 40 of the Egyptian constitution: "All citizens are equal before the law and have the same public rights and obligations without discrimination between them on the grounds of race, origin, language, religion or belief;" article 16 of the Jordanian constitution: "Jordanians have the right to form political parties and associations whose purpose is legal, their method peaceful and their organization does not contravene the provisions of the constitution." The Moroccan constitution goes as far as to prohibit in article 3 a one-party system of government. And in an unusual gender gesture, both the Syrian and Algerian constitutions single out women as deserving political, economic and social rights of their own and full participation in society. As the Syrian constitution puts it in article 45, "The state shall guarantee for women all opportunities which shall enable them full and effective participation in the political, social, educational and economic life, and shall undertake to remove all restrictions which obstruct their development and sharing in building the Arab socialist society."

These and many more fundamental freedoms, such as freedom of the press, of travel and of expression, the inviolability of the person, the home and all forms of communications, the right to a fair trial and guarantee of personal property against expropriation, are not absolute freedoms; their exercise is often compromised or denied by conflicting provisions of the constitution, by limiting legislation or restrictive interpretation by the courts, on the grounds of public order and morality.

It will be beyond the scope of this monograph to examine all the restrictive legislation in the Arab states which hinder the full enjoyment of these liberties and freedoms and interfere with the citizen's right to participate fully in the political life of the country. A recent survey by a trustee of the Egyptian Human Rights Organization,[51] lists 56 laws and numerous ministerial decrees and orders which in one form or another impede or nullify many of the constitutional liberties and freedoms or those contained in international declarations and covenants to which Egypt had adhered. Common to other Arab states are the restrictions placed on the freedom of the press, the overpowering role of the Executive in the formation of political parties and in organizing and monitoring national and local elections, the pervasive inequality in rights and in law for women, and the recurrent declarations of states of emergency which invariably turn out to be a misnomer for martial law enabling the head of state to rule with extraordinary powers.

At the heart of these conflicting attitudes is a conceptual difference over human rights between Western and Islamic legal cultures; and if the World Conference on Human Rights held in Vienna in 1993 is any reliable indicator, the difference is part of the greater North/South economic divide. While the West stresses the universality of a standard of human rights acceptable to all civilized societies, developing countries insist that human rights, like most other social values, must be viewed in the context of differing historical, cultural and religious backgrounds.

Reference has already been made to Saudi Arabia's refusal in 1948 to adhere to the United Nations Universal Declaration of Human Rights and its subsequent adoption in 1992 of a Basic Law which guarantees human rights "in accordance with Islamic Sharia." Similarly, Egypt's ratification in 1981 of the 1966 International Covenant on Civil and Political Rights, was made conditional by the enabling Presidential decree No.536 that none of its provisions contravene the rules of Islamic Sharia.

Although historically speaking the Qoranic precepts of rights and justice, including the principle of human dignity and equality and the conferment of legal entitlements upon women are in many respects in advance of anything found in the other scriptural religions, they are like all religious precepts premised on man's duty towards God and the Community, rather than on his natural right as the autnomous human being.[52]

What do the constitutional provisions on freedom of belief mean in a state formally identified with a particular religion as Islam is in the case of most Arab states and Islamic Sharia the source of their legislation? The tenets of the Qoran and the pronouncements of the Prophet denying coercion in matters of faith notwithstanding, Islamic jurist scholars have interpreted this to mean only the freedom to belong to a particular religion, but not to change or opt out of one. Apostasy is a crime in Islam punishable by death where Islamic criminal justice applies, such as Saudi Arabia and the Persian Gulf states; and although it is not a crime where modern penal codes have been adopted, which is the case in most other Arab states, it is cause for social censor and condemnation. Its social repercussions however on marital relations is decisive. As we have seen in an earlier part of the book, the laws of domestic relations consider change of religion among spouses in an Islamic marriage a ground for divorce.

Islamic jurist scholars maintain that a person could still elect the religion of his choosing until he or she attains the age of maturity. But since most of us are actually born into the religion of our parents, the freedom to elect another religion at that early age though legally permissible, is highly improbable and morally reprehensible. The constitutional right to the free exercise of religious belief as enunciated by the United States Supreme Court is no where to be found in the Arab states:

> The free exercise of religion means, first and foremost, the right to believe and profess whatever religious doctrine one desires. Thus, the First Amendment obviously excludes all government regulation of religious beliefs as such. The government may not compel affirmation of religious belief...punish the expression of religious doctrines it believes to be false, impose special disabilities on the basis of religious views or religious status, or lend its power to one or the other side in controversies over religious authority or dogma.[53]

Freedom of religion is a matter of special concern to religious minorities, and in Muslim society religious minorities are granted by Islamic law a status different from, and historically inferior to, the Muslim majority, which is inconsistent with the concept of equality in the modern territorial state. What makes this attitude towards religious communities all the more incongruous in today's individualistic, mobile society is that Islamic law and therefore the personal status laws of the Arab states limit their formal recognition of religious communities to the three scriptural faiths: Islam, Christianity and Judaism. As has been more fully brought out in Chapter Two, this recognition entails extensive legal privileges including the right of the communities' ecclesiastical hierarchies to apply their own canon laws and conduct trials in their own tribunals in matters of personal status, marriage, divorce, paternity, and all other aspects of domestic relations of their members.

That that was the limit of the freedom of religion provision in the constitution as far as the state is concerned, was confirmed in a 1975 Egyptian Constitutional Court decision. At issue was whether the Bahai Sect was free to practice its religious rites. In its decision the court said that the lower court did not contradict the freedom of belief provision of the Constitution when it denied the Bahai Sect the right to practice its rites since this right was limited to the three recognized communities.

Welcome as the present situation may be to recognized religious minorities in the absence of a secular family law equally applicable to all citizens irrespective of their religious affiliation, it has had the unsalutary effect of perpetuating the traditional differences and inequalities between religious communities. Furthermore, Islam being the religion of the dominant majority, its precepts have been adopted by the courts as criteria for measuring ordre public and morality, not only in cases involving Muslim nationals but non-Muslim nationals and foreigners as well.

Linked inextricably to modern constitutionalism is the guarantee to all individuals the same fundamental rights, since the general tendency has been to associate equality with identity and inequality or inferiority with racial, gender and religious differences.[54]

In the Western legal tradition, tolerance and the free expression of opinion have been the underlying assumptions for the constitutional guarantees of freedom of belief and of equality before the law, assumptions far removed from the orthodoxy of the medieval, religious legal order. The rise of Liberalism in post medieval Europe owed a great deal to the religious dissenter, and its popularization was not possible without secularization. As Chadwick has put it: "Enlightenment was of the few. Secularization is of the many."[55]

Personal Power & Corporate Institutions:

In his comparative analysis of Islamic and Western institutions, Hodgson perceived a difference between the Muslim pattern of legitimation and authority which he called "unitary contractualism," and the Occidental pattern which he described as "hierarchical corporativism." While in both the impersonal, formal and contractual norms played a role, Islamic society was unable to emulate its Occidental counterpart where already by the late Middle Ages the "ultimate social legitimation and authority were conferred not on personal relationships nor on a given power structure but on autonomous corporate offices and their holders as such."[56]

In arriving at its corporate institutions, European society progressed from the tribal to the feudal to the liberal state, with feudalism constituting the essential bridge from the one to the other. Unlike the European experience, Islamic society moved from tribal to Community, missing thereby the basic legal contributions of feudalism to the modern state. What is popularly known in the Arab experience as feudalism (*iqta'*), a phenomenon which survived intact until the rise of the socialist doctrines and land distribution regimes in 1960's and 1970's, was simply the extension of the power and control of the urban leadership of the Community to the rural, agricultural countryside without however the benefits of the rules of primogeniture and the vassal-lord relationship which Europe had known.[57] The latter was based on reciprocity of rights and obligations, participatory adjudication, and objectivity which gave the West its first secular experience of mutuality of legal obligations between persons of superior and inferior rank.[58]

The personal patriarchal authority and the traditional tribal solidarity which the 16th century Arab historian, Ibn Khaldun, considered the essential, but transitory, motor for the development of the state,[59] survived unscathed the coming of Islam and its universalist ideology. They were only glossed over by the religious charismatic authority of the leader of the Community. What Islam added by way of legitimization to the authority of the ruler was the concept of righteousness, a metaphysical criterion. Absent any popular or legal means for the transference of power or the deposition of the unrighteous ruler, Sassanid and Byzantine concepts of absolute monarchy found ready accommodation. The only "constitutional" basis on which the authority of the ruler rested, was the personal, quasi-contractual *bay'ah,* the act of acclamation and the declaration of fealty by the chiefs of the tribes and leaders of the Community. It was a medieval practice common to Christianity and Islam in which the people promised obedience to the ruler in return for his promise of protection and of upholding the law, a practice followed to this day in Morocco, Saudi Arabia and the Gulf emirates.

When the emir Faisal of Hijaz assumed in 1918 the throne of the short-lived monarchy in Syria, he addressed the Syrian people to thank them for their expressions of sympathy and support and for their speedy acclamation (*bay'ah*) "in the name of our patron/lord, the sultan and Prince of the Faithful, Hussein;

may God grant him victory." He went on to "inform" them that he shall be to each one of them a "compassionate father" as well as the one who will "severely punish" whoever contravenes the orders of his government and violates its laws.[60]

Half a century and more later, the Moroccan King portrays a similar paternalistic attitude towards his subjects, an attitude which is clearly in the tradition of the authoritarian Caliphs and their all encompassing personal authority: "As far as I am concerned, there is no such thing as the separation of powers. I am the father of everyone, I am the legislator, and I am the executive."[61] Elaborating on this attitude in an interview with a French newspaper, the King gave what amounted to an honest opinion of the irrelevance of democratic institutions in the lives of many of the newly independent countries at this stage in their political development. He considered the personality of authority a "symptom of this age, both normal and necessary," inasmuch as democracy is really in the hands of the "ruler in whom the people have confidence and with whom they interact." He went on to say that the same situation pertains to Morocco where the personality of authority will remain essential until such time as representative institutions have fully evolved[62]

The *dhahir* is a form of royal edict or decree unique to the legal system of Morocco. Its origin has been traced to the 10th century Omayyad Caliphate in Spain and has been employed by the sultans/kings of Morocco to this day to introduce basic and organic laws with only the personal authority of the sultan/king behind them.[63] Today the King's power to issue *dhahirs* is conferred upon him by article 29 of the Moroccan Constitution in a wide range of activities, executive, judicial and legislative. Indeed most organic and organizational laws in Morocco, including the first three constitutions of 1962, 1970 and 1972 were the subject of the King's *dhahirs* or edicts.

Legal scholars have puzzled at its continued use and validity in the context of the modern system of constitutionalism. One plausible explanation is its relevance to the personality of power and the other aspects of the Islamic legal tradition which continue to overlap in Morocco the modern principles of constitutionalism, so much so that, as one legal scholar has put it, "the Moroccan constitutional system seems closer to the ideas of Mawardi than it is to those of Montesquieu."[64]

Beyond the extensive powers legally granted to the heads of state in all Arab constitutions, one has still to consider the pervasive traditional attitudes of a patriarchal society towards the concept of leadership, whether familial, tribal, religious or political. Constitutionally speaking, the use of power may very well be legal, but in order to be legitimate it must also be justified. This is one of the great hidden dilemmas of Arab constitutions. Invariably, these constitutions institute parliaments, grant universal suffrage and declare the People sovereign. But the power and the authority of the state is for all practical purposes identified with the person of the ruler and his party, clan, dynasty, fellow revolutionaries, or comrades in arms.

The following provisions of the Algerian Constitution provide a typical example of how constitutional contradictions thwart the underlying democratic principles the constitution seeks to espouse:

> Article 5: National sovereignty belongs to the People who shall exercise it by means of the referendum or through their representatives.
>
> Article 7: The National Assembly is the basic institution of the state, and the context within which the popular will shall be expressed and democracy realized.
>
> Article 94: The Algerian constitutive order is based on the single party principle.
>
> Article 95: The National Liberation Front is the country's sole party. It is the vanguard made up of those citizens who are of higher consciousness and motivated by the high ideals of nationalism and socialism, and who by their own free will are united within it [the Party] in accordance with the conditions laid down in the basic laws of the Party...
>
> Article 128: The members of the National Assembly shall be elected by direct secret ballot on the basis of nominations made by the leadership of the Party.

Similar provisions can be found in the constitutions of Egypt, of Syria, of

Iraq, where the will of the people is said to be supreme, but the free expression of that will is thwarted by restrictions on who may be nominated for election to the National Assembly. Prior to the 1980 amendments, the Egyptian constitution made it a condition that only active members of the Socialist Union qualify to be nominated for election to the National Assembly, and that termination of their membership in the Union would make them loose their seat in the Assembly. This in turn was a complete contradiction with the provisions of the constitution guaranteeing for every citizen the right of nomination and election, and declaring participation in the country's political process a "national duty."

In Iraq as in Syria, the Baath Socialist Party is the vanguard party to lead the Nation, according to article 8 of the Syrian Constitution. It, or whatever happens to be its current configuration, dominates not only government positions, but the electoral process and the Peoples Assembly as well, even though the next articles of the constitution uphold in no uncertain terms equality of opportunity for all the people and their right to free and democratic elections of their representative bodies.

Under such conditions, the constitutional division of powers into executive, legislative, and Judicial, takes on a mere symbolic expression of modern statehood, as do national flags, national airlines, national anthems and national broadcasting stations in most developing countries. Not only is such a concentration of executive power in a select person or body contrary to the basic principles of modern constitutionalism, it deflects from, if not completely deny, the emergence of a genuine expression of the popular will or a reflection of the actual political and social conditions in the country.

What we encounter here is a symptom of the unconsummated transformation, itself an aspect of the lag in modernization, from the medieval patrimonial centralization of power (both temporal and spiritual) in the person of the caliph/ruler to the modern impersonal, autonomous, institutional organization of state powers differentiated from society. Unlike the medieval, theocratic system of government where legitimacy required compliance with the revealed text, modern constitutionalism is much more a function of legal culture than a matter of text. In varying degrees, political authority in the Arab states has all the external symbols of modernity, from separation of powers to bureaucratization of governmental functions. In reality however it is very much the product of personal and social relationships which most often transcend the institutional structure of government.

If one were to apply McIlwin's criteria, that the essential quality of constitutionalism has been the legal limitation on government, the excessive authority of the Executive and the personality of power with which it is commonly identified represents, together with judicial review discussed in another part of this book, the two main problems of constitutionalism in the Arab states.

ENDNOTES

1. For highlights of the Tunisian Constitution in English, see "The Tunisian Constitution", translation and commentary by George N. Sfeir, *The Middle East Journal* (Autumn 1959) p.443
2. For the various strains of Arab political thought around the turn of the century, see Albert Hourani, *Arabic Thought in Liberal Age* 1798-1939, Cambridge (1983).
3. Charles Howard McIlwin, *Constitutionalism: Ancient & Modern*, Ithaca & New York (1947) p. 20-21.
4. Andras Sajo develops this attractiveness of past-oriented constitutional thinking in relation to constitutional making in post-Communist Eastern Europe: "A partial return to past constitutional thinking makes the modernization of political and social structures of these countries less compelling; it offers legitimate protection from menacing modernization. Andras Sajo, "Preferred Generations: A Paradox of Restoration Constitutions," in Michel Rosenfeld ed. *Constitutionalism, Identity, Difference & Legitimacy,* Durham & London (1994) 335 at p.342.
5. Marshall G.S. Hodgson, *The Venture of Islam*, vol.3, Chicago (1974) p. 160.
6. Royal Decree of Abdel Aziz by which he assumed the title of "King of the Hejaz and of Nejd and its dependencies," in response to the petition of those of "our subjects with the power to loosen and to bind," published in the Saudi official Gazette, *Umm al-Qura,* of April 8, 1927.
7. Constitution of Hijaz, August 29, 1926, in Helen Miller Davis, *Constitutions, Electoral Laws, Treaties of the States of the Near and Middle East*, Durham (1947) p.248.
8. Royal Decree No. 2716 of September 18, 1932.

9. In accepting the office, Abu Bakr the first Muslim Caliph, pledged his accountability to the Umma (Community), and that obedience to him be conditional upon his compliance with the revealed law. In a similar fashion, the Christian rulers of Europe in the early Middle Ages pledge their respect for customary law and release of their subjects from obedience to them if they abandoned their side of the bargain. See J.M. Kelly, *A Short History of Western Legal Theory*, Oxford (1992) p. 97-99.
10. See Richard M. Eaton, "Islamic History as a Global History," in Michael Adas ed., *Islamic and European Expansion: The Forging of a Global Order*, Philadelphia (1993) 1 at p.16.
11. Hichem Djait recalls how Islam harbored the cultural legacy of Hellenism until the 16th century when Renaissance Europe rediscovered it and integrated into its world view a new concept of man. "The self-affirming individual is a purely Western creation... Islam not only did not come up with the same results, it ignored them." Djait, *Europe and Islam: Cultures and Modernity*, Berkeley (1985) at p. 59.
12. Judith Tucker, "Gender and Islamic History," in Adas, *Islamic and European Expansion*, op.cit. p. 37.
13. Ghassan Tueini, *An-Nahar* newpaper, Beirut December 31, 1974.
14. These expressions of unity were made at the Syrian National Congress which met in Damascus in 1920 and in the findings of the King-Crane Commission which the American President Wilson sent to Syria in 1919 to investigate the wishes of its people.
15. See Stephen Holms, "Gag Rules or the Politics of Omission," in Jon Elster and Rune Slagstad eds. *Constitutionalism and Democracy*, Cambridge (1988) 19 at p. 45.
16. In an article published in a journal of the Maronite clergy, the writer using the initials M.D. sums up the Christian view in the following terms:

> "Islam in the 20th century continues to maintain the qualities of its first decades, in that it is theocratic, and any relinquishing of theocracy will be considered a depreciation in the essence of revelation. In this lies the knot

of knots which appears at its worst entanglement in Lebanon...so long as the Muslims refuse to distinguish between that which is Caesar's and that which is God's...This obstacle faces all citizens whether they are Christians or liberal Muslims, and who, even if they do distinguish between that which is Caesar's and that which is God's, and who would therefore agree to live in a secular state, are forced by the struggle for self preservation to assume the same attitude as the Muslims and refuse to give up theocracy...Either the Muslims will accept a secular state, in which case Lebanon would find stability, and then perhaps there would be no real reason for its existence [i.e. as a state separate from the rest of Syria], or they would refuse, in which case Lebanon would not be stabilized and its existence, though shaky, would remain essential for the preservation of basic freedoms." *Al-Sanabil*, Beirut, vol. viii, No. x, (October 1953) 577f.

17. Constitutional Law No. 18 of September 21, 1990, published in a special supplement to the *Lebanese Official Gazette* No.39 dated September 27, 1990.
18. Antoine Masarrah, "Al-Bahth al-Dusturi fi Lubnan: Hal Yatajadad Ba'd Ta'dilat 1990?" in *Al-Hayat al-Niyabiyah*, Beirut, vol. 10 (March 1994) 7.
19. Ahmad Jadirah et al eds. *Al-Tajribah al Dimuqratiyah fi al-Mamlaka al-Maghribiyah* [Arabic: The Democratic Experience in the Moroccan Kingdom] Proceedings of a symposium by Moroccan scholars and professionals, Published by Dar al-Mustaqbal al-'Arabi (Cairo 1987) pp.9-25.
20. Article 19, the Constitution of Morocco, 1962, in Yusuf Quzma Khouri, *Al-Dasatir fil 'Alam al-'Arabi* [The Constitutions in the Arab World] Beirut (1989) p. 69. The same provision is repeated in the Constitutions of 1972 and 1992.
21. See Carl Joachim Friedrich, *The Philosophy of Law in Historical Perspective*, Chicago (1963) p. 57-66.
22. Quoted in Jadirah, *Al-Tajribah al-Dimuqratiyah*, op.cit. p.58.
23. The recognition of a theory of popular sovereignty was slow to materialize even in European political thought. As late as the 18th century "a Monarchy which was constitutionally limited was not a Monarchy at all." See Otto Gierke, *Natural Law & the Theory of Society 1500 to 1800*. Engl. transl. by Ernest Barker (Boston 1957), p.141ff.
24. Jadirah, *Al-Tajribah al-Dimuqratiyah*, op.cit. p. 101.

25. Id. p. 109.
26. See George N. Sfeir, "Syria: the Raw Material," *Middle East Forum*, vol. xxxviii No. 3, Beirut (March 1962) 23.
27. See Ernest William Hocking, *The Spirit of World Politics*, (New York, 1932).
28. George Antonius, *The Arab Awakening*, (New York, 1938) p.235
29. See R. Baily Winder, "The Establishment of Islam as the State Religion of Syria," *The Muslim World* vol.xliv, No.3 (July October 1954) and George N. Sfeir, "Islam as the State Religion," Id. vol. xlv No.3 (July 1955).
30. Khouri, *Constitutions in the Arab World*, op.cit. p.259-260.
31. Id. p.315.
32. Albert Hourani, *A History of the Arab Peoples*, Cambridge (1991) p.404.
33. The discussion of this point is based on the information found in Ramzi Taha al-Sha'ir, *Al-Nazariyah al-'Amah lil Qanun al-Dusturi* [Arabic: The General Theory of Constitutional Law] Cairo, 3rd. ed. (1983) pp.152-177.
34. Khouri, *Constitutions*, op.cit. p.557.
35. Id. p.558.
36. Quoted in Sha'ir, *The General Theory*, op.cit. p.174.
37. Muhammad Rif'at 'Abdel-Wahhab, *Ta'dilat Daruriyah li-Dustur 1971*, [Arabic: Essential Amendments to the Constitution of 1971], *Majallat al-Huquq lil Buhuth al-Qanuniya wal Iqtisadiya*, Journal of law, University of Alexandria (1991) Nos.1 & 2, p.1.
38. Id. p.5.
39. See Bertrand Badie & Pierre Birnbaum, *The Sociology of the State*, Chicago (1983), and Gianfranco Poggi, *The Development of the Modern State: A Sociological Introduction*, Stanford(1978).
40. Niyazi Berkes, *The Development of Secularism in Turkey*, Montreal (1964) p. 318.
41. David Beetham, *The Legitimation of Power*, Atlantic High-lands NJ (1991) p. 158.
42. Friedrich, *The Philosophy of Law*, op.cit. p. 57.

43. F.H. Hinsley, *Sovereignty,* Cambridge 2nd.ed. (1986) 72-73.
44. Abdel Hamid Mutwalli, *Mabadi' Nizam al-Hukm fil Islam*, [Arabic: The Principles of Government in Islam] Alexandria (1966) p. 551ff.
45. Ezzeldine Foda, *The Projected Arab Court of Justice*, Martinus Nijhoff (1957) p. 99-100.
46. 'Adel 'Umar Sharif, *Al-Qada' al-Dusturi fi Misr* [Arabic: Constitutional Adjudication in Egypt] Cairo (1988) p. 208-236.
47. Beetham, *The Legitimation of Power*, op.cit. p. 202.
48. Clifford Geertz, "The Integrative Revolution Sentiments and civil politics in the New States," *The Interpretation of Culture*, New York (1973), cited in Holmes, *Gag Rules*, op.cit. p.28.
49. See N.J. Demerath III, "Religious Capital and Capital Religion: Cross Cultural and non-Legal Factors in the Separation of Church and State," *Daedalus* vol.120, No.3 (Summer 1991) 21, at 32-33.
50. Ruti Teitel, "A Critique of Religion as Politics in the Public Sphere," 78 *Cornell L. Rev.* 5 (July 1993) 747 at 765.
51. Abdallah Khalil, *Al-Qawanin al-Muqayidah lil Huquq al-Madaniyah wal Siyasiyah fil Tashri' al-Misri* [Arabic: Laws Restricting Civil and Political Rights in Egyptian Legislation], Cairo (1993).
52. For a clear and concise presentation of the subject, see Amyn B. Sajo, " Islam and Human Rights: Congruence or Dichotomy," 4 *Temple International Comp. Law Journal* (1990) 23.
53. Employment Div. Vs. Smith 494 US 872 at 877 (1990), cited in Teitel, A Critique, op.cit. p. 777.
54. Michael Rosenfeld, "Modern Constitutionalism as Interplay Between Identity and Diversity," in Michael Rosenfeld ed. *Constitutionalism, Identity, Difference and Legitimacy,* Durham (1994) p. 8-9.
55. Owen Chadwick, *The Secularization of the European Mind in the 19th Century,* Cambridge (1975) p.9.
56. Hodgson, *The Venture of Islam* op.cit. vol.II, p.342-343

57. See Fuad I. Khuri, *Imams and Emirs: State, Religion and Sects in Islam*, London (1990), and Maxime Rodinson, Islam and Capitalism, Paris (1966), Penguin Engl. ed. (1974).
58. Harold J. Berman, *Law & Revolution: The Formation of the Western Legal Tradition*, Cambridge (1983), p. 303-315.
59. Yves Lacoste, *Ibn Khaldun: The Birth of History and the Past of the Third World*, Paris (1966), Engl. ed. London (1984).
60. Faisal's address quoted in Munir al-'Ajlani, *Al-Huquq al-Dusturiyah*, [Constitutional Rights] Damascus, (1955) p. 71-72.
61. Muhammad Shuqair, *Al-Qarar al-Siyasi fil Maghrib* [The Political Decision in Morocco] Casablanca (1992) p.21
62. *Le Mond* (Paris) May 22, 1962, cited in Id. p.22. King Fahd of Saudi Arabia expressed more recently a similar view about the unsuitability of Western democracy for Saudi Society.
63. See Muhammad Ashraki, *Al-Dhahir al-Sharif wal Qanun al-'Am al-Maghribi* [The Royal Decree and Moroccan Public Law] Casablanca (1983).
64. Id. p. 174. Mawardi was a leading medieval authority on the structure and functioning of the Islamic state.

CHAPTER SIX

Judicial Review

Practically all the Arab states have written constitutions guaranteeing an independent judiciary and individual rights; but who is to guarantee a fair interpretation of the constitution and with it the proper functioning of the democratic process?[1]

The answer to this question depended on whether the constitution was viewed as a political manifesto, separate and distinct from the positive legal order, as the case was until recently in Europe,[2] or as part and parcel of the law of the land as it turned out to be in the United States where judicial review achieved from the beginning the unique position it enjoys today in the administration of justice.

It will be recalled that because of his belief that the function of the judiciary was to interpret the law in order to apply it, Justice Marshall developed in the 1803 case of Marbury v. Madison the principle of judicial review against great political odds and the lack of a clear mandate in the constitution. This attitude to the judiciary was also responsible for the decentralized form of judicial review which gives all courts the competence to determine the constitutionality of legislation.

In Europe, on the other hand, where civil law countries adhere more rigidly to the doctrine of the separation of powers and the supremacy of the legislature, the development of a system of judicial review was more difficult to achieve. Traditionally, the courts had neither the structure nor the attitude for effective constitutional review. At the top of the judicial ladder was the cassation procedure to ensure the legality of civil and criminal adjudication through ordinary appeal, while the council of state procedure guarded against administrative abuse on the part of the Executive. And when these countries began to evolve a system of judicial review in the post world war II era, it was a centralized system with special constitutional courts alone with the power to review and invalidate legislation on grounds that it does not conform to the constitution.[3]

Among the Arab States which generally adhere to the European civil law system, only Egypt has had since 1979 a full fledged constitutional court with a mandate for judicial review.[4] The 1971 constitution was the first since Egypt has had a modern constitution in 1923, to provide for a specialized judicial body responsible for exercising "judicial control over the constitutionality of legislation and regulations and for the interpretation of legislative texts."

Until then Egypt relied, as in the case of continental Europe, on the cassation procedure to ensure the rule of law, and the Council of State to guard against administrative abuse by the Executive. Although the latter was an administrative tribunal in the French tradition, it nevertheless established as early as 1948 the principle that there is nothing in Egyptian law which prevented the courts from reviewing the constitutionality of legislation. This encouraged ordinary courts to follow suit, until 1969 when the Egyptian legislature established the Supreme Court to do just that. It was replaced ten years later by the Constitutional Court which will be more fully discussed below.

In other Arab states only a highly restricted form of judicial review exists. Iraq has a Supreme Constitutional Court charged with: (a) the interpretation of the constitution, (b) review of the constitutionality of legislation, and (c) review of the legality of decrees and regulations. But access to the court is limited to the President of the Republic, the Prime Minister, the Minister of Justice, and the Court of Cassation. In Syria the Constitutional Court has the competence to review the constitutionality of a law at the pre-enactment stage at the request of the President of the Republic or one-quarter of the members of the National

Assembly. The Court may also review the constitutionality of a legislative or Presidential decree prior to its issuance if one-quarter of the National Assembly requests it. A negative finding by the Court would hold up the promulgation of the legislation or the legislative decree.

In Lebanon, the settlement of the civil war in 1990 brought about an amendment to the Constitution which among other things provided for the establishment of a Constitutional Council to review the constitutionality of legislation prior to its enactment. The mandate of the Council follows essentially that of the Syrian court, as well as the practice of the Conseil Constitutionnel of France, which gives Parliamentary minorities the right to challenge the constitutionality of legislation prior to its promulgation.

The Lebanese however have added to that the novel idea that the heads of the recognized religious communities of Lebanon may also seek judicial review before the Council in matters of concern to their communities. Article 19 of the constitution reads as follows:

> A Constitutional Council shall be established for the review of the constitutionality of the laws and the resolution of contests and challenges pertaining to presidential and parliamentary elections. The right of appeal to this Council for review of the constitutionality of laws shall be limited to the President of the Republic, the Speaker of the Parliament, the Prime Minister, and ten members of Parliament, and, to the extent that matters of Personal Status [i.e. domestic relations], freedom of belief, exercise of religious rites, and the freedom of religious education are involved, to the heads of the recognized religious communities."

The Constitutional Council became a reality in 1993 amidst doubts about its efficacy as an instrument of judicial review, from no less a source than Auguste Bachus, the Chairman of the Parliamentary Committee for Administration and Justice. In comments published in the Parliamentary journal,[5] Mr. Bachus questions the need for the President, the Prime Minister, or the Speaker of Parliament to refer legislation to the Council for judicial review. He does not see why the President would have to resort to this means when he already has the constitutional right to return to Parliament for reconsideration a bill he believes to be unconstitutional before he signs it into law. Likewise the Speaker of Parliament who has wide powers for steering legislation through Parliament has sufficient opportunity to withhold voting on a law he does not think it is constitutional. Nor does Mr. Bachus consider it realistic for a Prime Minister who serves at the pleasure of Parliament to risk a vote of no confidence by questioning legislation passed by the majority in that Parliament. This leaves the possibility for a minority of ten members of Parliament who disapprove of legislation passed by the majority to seek the judicial review of that legislation. While this Parliamentary minority represents the only realistic candidate for the Lebanese Constitutional Council, the step is no less fraught with difficulties. Even if one dismisses the possibility of ulterior political motives for their action, the most that such a Parliamentary minority can hope for even if it had a legitimate concern about the constitutionality of a law is to return that law to Parliament where the majority will probably pass it again.

Mr. Bachus refrained from commenting on the right of the heads of religious communities to appeal to the Constitutional Council for review of legislation pertaining to matters of concern to their communities. But the reader who has become familiar with the Institution of Personal Status described in Chapter Two of the book, will readily realize that this privilege given to the heads of the religious communities has very little to do with the core purpose of judicial review--the protection of constitutional guarantees of individual rights and freedoms. Instead it is intended to safeguard the communal standings of the religious communities in the Lebanese body politic as defined in the constitution and the relevant laws of personal status and domestic relations.

Another instance of judicial review system is represented by the Supreme Court of Jordan. It was established in 1992 as the "High Court of Justice," with competence more resembling that of the French *Conseil d'Etat* than the U.S. Supreme Court. In addition to the resolution of disputes pertaining to election results, administrative orders and civil service claims and compensations, the court is also designated the sole tribunal to hear petitions from individuals to suspend the application of, or stay the execution of an order or measure in accordance with, a law or regulation which is contrary to the constitution.

The law establishing the court makes it clear that only those with a personal interest or claim may petition the court and the petition is based on one of the following causes: lack of competence (on the part of respondent); contravention of the constitution, law, regulation or order, or mistaken application and interpretation thereof; misuse of authority. In finding that a law is not in conformity with the constitution, the court could do no more than refrain from applying it to the case at hand. This was borne by an early decision of the court, which stated that the court had no jurisdiction to question the competence of the Bureau for the Interpretation of Laws and Regulations or the form or subject matter of its decisions, since these are legislative matters removed from judicial supervision.

Judicial review in Morocco follows the pre-1974 French example. The Moroccan Constitution limits the functions of the Constitutional Council to pre-enactment review of legislation at the request of the King, the Prime Minister, the Speaker of the Assembly or one-fourth of its members. Its future evolution is very much tied to developments in the relationship between the three branches of Government and the competitive positions of Islamic and positive law in the legal system. It was therefore only natural for Moroccan jurists to raise the question: Is it conceivable to have judicial review of the constitutionality of legislation in an Islamic state?[6]

Here is a Muslim nation whose people profess and practice Islam and its king the defender of the faith and the source of power in the Calipheal tradition, but whose laws are either of French origin or modeled after those of France. One of the leaders of the independence movement, Allal al-Fasi, relates how as a member of a committee formed upon independence by Sultan Muhammad V to codify the Sharia and declare it the law of the land, only to have their work stymied by French specialists at the State Secretariat charged with the supervision of new legislation.[7]

The learned jurist that he was, al-Fasi was not oblivious of the need for the Sharia to be reduced to positive law if its rules were to assume the authority of law in the modern state. It is a point well developed by another Moroccan jurist trained in modern legal science, Muhammad al-Khamlishi, that the revival of Islamic law can only come in the normal course of the legislative process of the state.[8] But for al-Fasi "the religious consciousness" of the Nation is sufficient to impel it to follow the rules of the Sharia as laid down by the religious scholars and judges who are after all the "direct source of its authority."[9] In such a political environment the state is subject to the Sharia and the Nation guards against the failure of the State to abide by its rules.

If proof were needed that judicial review is necessary to ensure that constitutional rights and freedoms were protected, it was quite apparent in the case of Tunisia. Since its independence in the mid-1950's, Tunisia has followed a more assertive approach to the modernization of its legal system than elsewhere in the Arab World. The Constitution however failed to provide for means by which to test the constitutionality of legislation or ensure respect for the individual rights and freedoms it guaranteed, until almost thirty years later when in 1987 the authorities constituted the Constitutional Council.

In the meantime, the only judicial instrumentality outside the ordinary courts of justice were the Conseil d'Etat, an administrative tribunal to hear petitions by individuals against state acts, and the Court of State Security, a military tribunal for the trial of persons charged with political crimes against the state. In the 1980's a number of developments brought matters to a head: The excesses of the Court of State Security in what became known as the 'trials of the fundamentalists,' the change of regime from the authoritative, single party rule of President Bourguiba to the more pluralistic regime of President Ben Ali, and the decision of the Kairawan Court of First Instance which declared unconstitutional a provision of the Law of Associations requiring the permit of the Minister of the Interior for the formation of a political group on the ground that it contravened the freedoms of thought, expression and organization, guaranteed by the Constitution.

The question whether ordinary courts can pass judgment on the constitutionality of legislation, in the manner that it is done in United States courts, has always been controversial in the civil law system, where traditionally the judge is expected to apply the law not question its legitimacy. Six years before the Kairawan Court made its decision, the Tunisian Court of Appeal had upheld the constitutionality of the same provision of the Law of Associations. What the Kairawan court did was take the position that the judge in applying the law is under obligation to view the law in its entirety, that is, "all the legal rules which constituted The Law of the land." This the court said is particularly important when the defense in the case raises before it the question of the constitutionality of the legislation in question.[10] There has always been a preponderance of opinion among Tunisian lawyers and jurists in support of this view, even though the Court of Cassation and the State Security Court did not subscribe to it, so long as the country lacked an appropriate body for the judicial review of the constitutionality of legislation.[11]

The establishment of the Tunisian Constitutional Council came in response to these developments even though the idea was long before in the making but somehow missed the 1976 amendment to the Constitution. Nor was the manner in which the Council was constituted totally satisfactory to a good segment of the Tunisian law fraternity who would rather have a full fledged Constitutional Court.[12]

Instead, the Council, whose eleven members are chosen by the President of the Republic, was instituted on December 16, 1987 by Presidential Decree, a method by no means comparable to a constitutional amendment. As such its autonomy and constitutional status are, in the view of those in favor of a Constitutional Court, open to question. Nor is it fully competent to pass judgment on the constitutionality of legislation in the ordinary course of justice. Its primary duty is to review the constitutionality of legislation only at the pre-enactment stage and at the request of the Executive, including all matters pertaining to the functions of the public institutions of the Government.

In the Gulf states, except for Kuwait and the United Arab Emirates where a constitutional court exists, judicial review is complicated by the lack of a modern constitutional framework and the dichotomy in the legal system between civil and Sharia law and courts. This is particularly the case in Saudi Arabia. Given the preponderance of claims against the Government from foreign contractors engaged on development projects, and in an effort to consolidate the diverse administrative committees adjudicating disputes arising under the various civil regulations, the Saudi Grievance Board was reorganized in 1982 to cope with all administrative, commercial and civil service disputes in which the Government is a party.[13]

For a time it looked as if the Grievance Board would be on its way to becoming a council of state in the French tradition, particularly that the concept had long been widely copied in the Arab states, including Egypt, Lebanon and Tunisia. Being also the only high level civil juridical body in the country it had the wherewithal to develop the competence for judicial review. But that was not to be.

The Board was by the reorganization denied the right "to entertain petitions pertaining to acts of state or appeals by individuals against decisions or rulings of other courts or judicial bodies acting within their jurisdictions." This was intended to avoid any entanglement between civil and Sharia tribunals, and preserve the integrity of the latter which, despite the widening jurisdiction of the civil tribunals, remain the courts of general jurisdiction in the country.

The closest that Saudi Arabia has at present to judicial review rests with the Higher Judicial Council. The Council which has administrative, consultative and restricted review functions, is the highest juridical body in the Sharia court system. As such its mandate is restricted to expressing, at the request of the Minister of Justice, an opinion on matters requiring interpretation and determination of Islamic law principles, review of judgments imposing the death sentence, amputation and stoning, as well as administrative matters pertaining to the Sharia courts.

The future of judicial review in Saudi Arabia is complicated by the inherent dichotomy in the legal system and the consequent division of powers between the Grievance Board and the Higher Judicial Council. With the pre-eminent position given to Islamic law in the Saudi legal system, legislation is restricted to Executive decrees whose purpose is to supplement and complement the immutable rules of Sharia. Under the circumstances judicial review, if one can call it that, is limited to the possible conflict of these Executive decrees with the rules of the Sharia, a function of the Higher Judicial Council at the preenactment stage and at the request of the Executive. On the other hand, any dispute with the Executive arising under these Executive decrees is, because of the dichotomy in the legal system, a matter to be resolved by the Grievance Board, a civil tribunal with historical and administrative affinity to the Executive.

Islamic Law and the Problem of Judicial Appeal and Review

The case of Saudi Arabia typifies the problem which traditional Islamic law poses for the evolution of a modern system of judicial review. It is a problem faced to varying degrees by most of the Arab states where Islamic law is still very much a part of their legal tradition. It is a source of legislation according to their constitutions, and in some fields, such as domestic relations and crime, the applicable positive law. As such it remains an important element in the Arab legal culture leaving it ingrained with juridical ideas which do not fully conform with those of the modern state.

Judicial review subsumes a constitutional form of government where the right of appeal and the protection of individual rights are guaranteed by the constitution. It takes the form of a court action brought by the aggrieved individual against the state, the author of the public act or legislation. In other words, judicial review is an institution of the democratic state and the ideas of the Enlightenment. Even then, it wasn't until recently that the European states would overcome their traditional belief in the supremacy of Parliament and fully subscribe to the judicial review of the constitutionality of legislation. It took a lot of doing to begin to accommodate the potential conflict between legislator and judge, between law and adjudication which judicial review invokes, and resolve the "mighty problem" of its legitimacy in a system of government with clear separation of powers.[14]

Many of these concepts and conflicts are simply alien to Islamic law and its notion of statehood. Legislation as the expression of the will of the People, has no place in the Islamic legal order. Revelation took care of that. The law is the written word of the Qoran and the tradition attributed to the Prophet. Religious scholars of the first three centuries of the Islamic era sought to amplify, comment upon and interpret both text and tradition. Grouped into a number of major schools of jurisprudence, this historical material remains to this day the last word on the subject. If there is a sense of "constitution" in the Islamic legal order it is this plethora of text, tradition, and commentary. But it is too diffused and differently interpreted to constitute the kind of precise criteria conducive to judicial review. Drafts of "Islamic constitutions" circulated by Muslim fundamentalists as the alternative to modern secular constitutions, fail to circumvent this twin problem of diffusion and differentiation by repeatedly invoking the Sharia in its generic all-encompassing sense.[15]

Another impediment to judicial review in Islamic law is the absence of the notion of appellate jurisdiction as we know it in modern law. Some Western writers have recently argued what modern Arab/Islamist jurists have been wont to believe, that Islamic law recognized judicial review to the extent that under certain circumstances (an obvious contradiction with the revealed text, the Prophet's traditions, or *ijma*, the consensus of the scholars) it allowed for the reconsideration of a judicial decision by the same or an alternate judge.[16] The fact remains that Islamic law did not recognize any formal system of appeal, separate and distinct from the original jurisdiction.[17]

The single judge (*qadi*) remained throughout the Islamic era the sole, single forum for the administration of justice, with only the rudimentary form of procedure at his disposal. If recourse were contemplated from his decision, it was to the Caliph who appointed him, and only as a pleading for the Caliph's intercession against the iniquity (*mazalim*) of the judge and not as redress of a right. This *mazalim* procedure (revived in modern times by Saudi Arabia in a more judicial form as the Grievance Board) represented merely the natural effusion of the authority and prestige of the ruler and his compunction to rectify the failings of his functionaries, among whom was the *qadi*.

This brings us to the third difficulty of Islamic law with a system of judicial review--the absence of a clear cut separation of powers. With the law already revealed, the only notion of legislation left was the power of the ruler, in what became known as *siyasa shar'iya* or the political application of Sharia, to supplement the revealed law when practical needs demanded it with administrative decrees which would still adhere to the basic tenets of the Sharia. Although the Caliph was as much as anyone else in the Islamic legal order subject to the revealed law and expected to abide by its rules at pain of being deposed, he nevertheless combined in his office much of what we distinguish in the modern state as the executive, legislative and judicial powers. He was after all the guardian of the faith and of the law, the head of the administrative apparatus of the state, and the source of authority and the authority of last resort in the administration of justice.

Today those who support the revival of Islamic law have no quarrel with the notion of judicial review to test the constitutionality of legislation. What they object to is the supremacy of the Constitution. They view the Sharia, as the revealed word of God, hence far superior to, and more lasting than, any constitution. Man-made laws, no matter what their rank in the legislative hierarchy, are mere tools in the hands of often oppressive rulers, devoid of the moral imperatives of the faith.

In an attempt to present their views on the subject in a more modern garb, they speak of the similitude of Sharia in the Arab legal system with Natural Law in Western legal thought, a curious comparison since the concept of natural law is usually dismissed as irrelevant to Sharia which already comprehends all that which natural law connotes. Nevertheless, since most Arab constitutions declare the Sharia a source of legislation, shouldn't this be taken as a mandate to merge positive legitimacy (according to the Constitution) with Islamic legitimacy (according to the Sharia) to arrive at one single constitutional-Islamic principle of legitimacy.[18]

This type of reasoning was given a boost by the amendment in 1980 of article 2 of the Egyptian Constitution which changed the status of Sharia from being a source of legislation to being the source of legislation thereby making the revealed text the criterion for constitutionality over and above the constitution.

An Arab Constitutional Court

What then is the role of a Constitutional Court in Egypt or the other Arab states, given the still unsettled issues of legal modernization, including the conflicting claims of the Sharia and the Constitution on the legal system as a whole?

Judicial review was an issue in Egyptian legal circles as early as the adoption of the first constitution in 1923 which was silent on the subject. Legal scholars came out in support of the right of the courts to review the constitutionality of legislation on the grounds that the judiciary is obligated to respect all the laws of the country and the constitution being the highest among them, any law not in conformity with it must give way to its provisions. But the courts were reluctant to venture into these untested waters, not until 1941 when a court of first instance decided it had the competence to declare a law unconstitutional. In justifying its decision, the court said that "if all three powers of Government are equally bound by the Constitution, the judiciary is free not to follow the dictates of the Legislature when the latter contravenes the Constitution. A judge must adjudicate in the case before him in accordance with all the laws of the land, including the Constitution which is superior to them all."[19] Three years later however the Court of Appeal reversed that decision.

The reluctance of the courts, including the Court of Cassation, to accept the doctrine of judicial review continued to plague the judiciary until the establishment of the Egyptian Council of State in 1946. As the highest administrative judicial body, the Council was compelled two years into its life to deal with the issue in a case involving the constitutionality of a legislative decree enacted by the Executive at a time when Parliament was in recess. The Council took the position that there was nothing in the law which prevented the Egyptian courts from exercising their competence in judicial review; and contrary to those who claimed that judicial review undermined the separation of powers doctrine, the courts helped in fact to bolster this constitutional doctrine by ensuring that the Legislature acted in compliance with the Constitution.[20]

The example of the Council of State was later followed by the Court of Cassation when for the first time since its inception it refused to apply a criminal procedure law which failed to respect the constitutional principle of non-retroactivity of penal laws. But this proliferation of judicial review among the courts raised the concern of the Egyptian Parliament which moved in 1969 to centralize judicial review in a single judicial body, the Supreme Court. The Explanatory Memorandum of the Supreme Court law justified the move on the ground that "it was not appropriate to leave the matter of deciding such an important issue to the courts of various levels, and [thereby] create conflicting opinions [among them]."[21]

Without competence to declare a law unconstitutional, the courts were nevertheless obligated to respond to the petition by the defense that the law in the case before them did not conform to the constitution. All they could do under the circumstances was to refuse to apply the unconstitutional law, a decision which was by no means obligatory on any other court or that court in any other case. The absence of the doctrine of *stare decisis* in the civil law system was remedied in the case of the Egyptian Supreme Court when the Legislature required all courts to abide by its decision regarding the constitutionality or unconstitutionality of a law. Still the Court decision did not abrogate the law which is a matter for the

Legislature to do; but the Court was required to publish its decisions in the Egyptian official gazette as a matter of public notice.

As mentioned earlier, judicial review in Egypt has since 1979 been the responsibility of the Constitutional Court. It superseded the Supreme Court in this function following the adoption of the 1971 Constitution which provided for such a court. The law establishing the Court[22] gives expression to the constitutional purpose in designating it the only court with competence to review the constitutionality of legislation. But this does not mean, according to Egyptian constitutional experts,[23] that the ordinary courts have lost all authority in this regard. These courts must still decide when a plea is made about the non-constitutionality of a law in the case before them whether the pleading has sufficient merit to be heard by the Constitutional Court.

The law establishing the Court has given the ordinary courts the ultimate say whether a question regarding the constitutionality of legislation may be brought before the Constitutional Court and under what conditions. It is only when these courts are presented with a plea of unconstitutionality of a provision in the law pertinent to the case before them and are convinced of its merits, that they are required to adjourn the case, and give the defense three months time to seek a ruling from the Constitutional Court.

Review of the constitutionality of legislation is only one of three areas in which the court has exclusive jurisdiction. The other two are: to decide conflicts of jurisdiction between two courts, or the execution of two contradictory judgments in the same subject matter; and to interpret legislative acts and Executive decrees when necessary to put an end to various interpretations in their application.

But the Constitutional Court's most important role, and perhaps its *raison d'etre*, according to the Explanatory Memorandum of the law establishing the Court, is its ability to centralize judicial review and thereby bring about a consistency in the application of the rights guaranteed by the Constitution through the Court's uniform interpretation of its provisions. A draft proposal granting the

Constitutional Court direct original jurisdiction over the constitutionality of legislation failed when the law establishing the Court was adopted. Consequently the Court is denied the right to entertain a petition seeking to test the constitutionality of a law or decree prior to becoming an element of contention in a case before the lower courts. The only exception to this rule is when the Court itself, seized with a question concerning conflict of jurisdictions or contradictory judgments, decides that a law related to the matter under consideration is contrary to the constitution, takes the initiative on its own to declare it unconstitutional.[24]

The record of the court has been impressive.[25] From the start of its tenure in 1979, it had to deal with some of the basic issues confronting a country in the process of modernizing its legal and political systems. Having assumed its jurisdiction at about the same time that article 2 of the Constitution was amended making Islamic law the source of legislation, one of the earliest questions it had to answer was whether certain laws, such as the provisions in the Civil Code which legitimize the payment of interest on loans and compensation for moral harm from unlawful acts, both of which are prohibited by Islam, did not in fact conflict with the amended article 2 of the Constitution. In its decision, the Court avoided the virtual demolition of the 1949 Civil Code by holding that the amendment to article 2 of the Constitution had no retroactive effect and could not therefore apply to legislation enacted prior to its adoption.

Neither did the court shrink from giving its opinion on sensitive political issues, such as the freedom of association and the formation of political parties, fair compensation for private property expropriated or nationalized for public use, guarantee of the legal rights of the accused and the immunity of the homes from illegal entry and search, in a country undergoing a transition from the unitary, socialist, regime of President Nasser to the more liberal and pluralistic rule of President Sadat, the Court was instrumental in guiding the country on the new democratic path by invalidating some of the restrictive laws inherited from the Nasser regime.

But not all the Court's decisions had this salutary effect. A 1979 law of domestic relations with hard fought for benefits for Egyptian women was struck down by the Court on the ground that the Presidential legislative decree which enacted it when Parliament was in recess, had neither the justifiable urgent circumstances for its enactment by legislative decree nor the endorsement of

Parliament within fifteen days or immediately upon resuming its sessions as the Constitution demanded.

More troubling however was the Court's refusal to permit the Bahai sect to exercise its religious rites on the ground that it is not a recognized religious community. The court surveyed at length the history of the constitutional provisions which guaranteed the freedom of faith and the exercise of religious rites from the 1923 Constitution to the current 1971 one, to arrive at the conclusion that while the Constitution guarantees the freedom of faith to every one, the exercise of religious rites is restricted to the three recognized heavenly faiths, Islam, Christianity and Judaism. It said that the constitutional intent expressed in previous Constitutions that the exercise of religious rites should not contravene public order and morality, remains valid even if the present Constitution is silent on it. In other words, because Islam does not recognize the Bahai faith, and Islamic values define the public order in Egypt, then the Bahai exercise of their religious rites is contrary to public order.

ENDNOTES

1. For a discussion of the interaction between judicial review and the democratic process in the United States of America, see John Arthur, *Words That Bind: Judicial Review and the Grounds of Modern Constitutional Theory*, Boulder (1995).
2. On Germany, for example, see Gerhard Casper, "Guardians of the Constitution," 53 So. *Cal. L. Rev.* (1980) 773.
3. See Mauro Cappelletti, *The Judicial Process in Comparative Perspective*, Oxford (1989).
4. According to article 1 of Law No. 48 of 1979, the Court has jurisdiction for (a) Review of the constitutionality of laws and regulations, (b) Resolution of conflicts of jurisdiction between two competent judicial bodies, and (c) Settlement of conflicting decisions by two competent judicial authorities. It is also entrusted by article 2 with the interpretation of legislative texts and executive decrees when differences in their interpretation or application occur.
5. *Al-Hayat al-Niyabiya* [Parliamentary Life], Beirut, vol. X (March 1994) 46-51.
6. Abdel Rahman al-Qadir, "Al-Tajriba al-Maghribiya fi Majal Muraqabat Dusturiyat al-Qawanin," [The Moroccan Experience in the Review of the Constitutionality of Legislation], *Al-Majalla al-Maghribiya lil-Qanun wal-Iqtisad wal-Tanmiya* [The Moroccan Journal of Law, Economy and Development] No. 4 (1983) 4.
7. Allal al-Fasi, *Difa' 'An al-Shari'a* [In Defense of Sharia], Casablanca (1966) p.17.
8. Muhammad al-Khamlishi in *Tajdid al-Fikr al-Islami* [Renewal of Islamic Thought], Proceedings of Colloquium at the Academy of King Abdul Aziz al-Saud for Islamic Studies (April 3-4, 1987), Casablanca (1989) 75.

9. Al-Fasi, *Difa' 'An al-Shari'a*, op.cit. p. 141.
10. Kairawan Court dock No. 51883, dated December 24, 1989. Text in *Al-Majalla al-Qanuniya al-Tunisiya* [*Revue Tunisienne du Droit*], Tunis (1988) p. 24.
11. See Mabruk Ben Musa, Dawr al-Qadi wa Makanatuhu fil Dawla wal Mujtama' [The Role of the Judge in State and Society], *Majallat al-Qada' wal Tashri'* [Judicial and Legislative Journal] Tunis, vol. 32 (May 1990) 7 at 30-34.
12. See Rafi' Ibn 'Ashur, "Mas'alat Muraqabat Dusturiyat al-Qawanin wa Tatawwuriha fi Akhir Sanat 1987," [The Question of the Review of the Constitutionality of Legislation and Its Progress at the End of 1987], *Majallat al-Qada'*, Id. 9.
13. For a more detailed discussion of the Saudi Grievance Board, see George N. Sfeir, "An Islamic Conseil d'Etat: Saudi Arabia's Board of Grievance," 4 *Arab Law Q.* 2 London (May 1989) 128.
14. See Cappelletti, *The Judicial Process*, op.cit.
15. See M. Al-Ghazali, "Introduction to a Draft Islamic Constitu-tion," *Islamic Studies 2* (1981) 153.
16. See David Powers, "On Judicial Review in Islamic Law," 26 *Law and Society 2* (1992) 315, and Abdel Rahman Abdel 'Aziz al-Qasim, *Al-Nizam al-Qada'i al-Islami* [The Islamic Judicial System], Cairo (1972), p. 405-437.
17. See Emile Tyan, *Histoire de l'oganization judiciaire en pays d'Islam*, Leiden (1960), and "Kadi" in Enc. of Islam, new ed. Leiden (1978).
18. Tawfiq al-Shawi, *Siyadat al-Shari'a al-Islamiya fi Misr* [The Sovereignty of Islamic Sharia in Egypt], Cairo (1987) p.22.
19. Cited in Ramzi Taha al-Sha'ir, *Al-Nazariya al-'Amma lil Qanun al-Dusturi* [The General Theory of Constitutional Law], Cairo, 3rd. ed. (1983), p. 525.
20. Id. p. 527.
21. Cited in 'Adil 'Umar Sharif, *Al-Qada' al-Dusturi fi Misr* [Constitutional Adjudication in Egypt], Cairo (1988) p. 78.
22. Law No. 48 of 1979.

23. See Al-Sha'ir, *Al-Nazariya al-'Amma*, op. cit. p. 565-66.

24. Id. p. 588.

25. For a record of the Constitutional Court's important decisions in the first ten years of its tenure, see Muhammad Nasreldine Kamil, *Ikhtisas al-Mahkama al-Dusturiya al-'Uliya* [The Competence of the Higher Constitutional Court], Cairo (1989).

BIBLIOGRAPHY

Works in Western languages on the law in the Arab states, have concentrated mainly on Islamic law. Two recent bibliographies, that of John and Marianne Makdisi, "Islamic Law Bibliography: Revised and Updated List of Secondary Sources, 87 Law Library Journal No.1 (Winter, 1995) 69-191, and that of Laila Al-Zwaini and Rudolph Peters, A Bibliography of Islamic Law, 1980-1993, Leiden, 1994, include many of these works. Very few, however, if any, address the process of modernization or take a comparative, historical view of the transformation which has taken place in the Arab legal systems in the last one hundred years. There is also considerable literature in the Arabic language, whether in the form of books or articles in legal journals, dealing with the contemporary state of the law in the Arab countries. But here too little has been devoted to the cultural significance of the legal change and the process of modernization.

In reviewing this bibliography, the reader is reminded that the transformation of the legal system in the Arab states which began in earnest in the third decade of the 19th century, took essentially the form of borrowing, adaptation and assimilation of Western law. Comparative works on the formation and development of that law are therefore as important to the understanding of the modernization of Arab law as are works on the subject at the receiving end, in the Arab states themselves.

Abdel-Raziq, Ali, *Al-Khilafa wa Usul al-Hukm* [The Caliphate and the Bases of Governance], Cairo 1923.

Abdul Hakim, Kalifa, "The Natural Law in the Moslem Tradition," in Edward F. Barrett (ed.), *University of Notre Dame Natural Law Institute Proceedings*, (1951), 29-65.

Abu-Talib, Sufi Hassan, *Mabadi' Tarikh al-Qanun: vol.I Takwin al-Sharai' vol.II Al-Sharai' al- Qadima fil-Bilad al-'Arabiya)* [Principles of Legal History: vol.I Formation of Law, vol.II Ancient Laws in the Arab Countries], Cairo 1971.

Abu Zayd, Nasr Hamid, *Al-Nass, al-Sulta, al-Haqiqa: al-Fikr al-Dini Bayna Iradat al-Ma'rifa wa Iradat al-Haymana* [The Text, the Authority, the Reality: Religious Thought Between the Desire for Knowledge and the Desire for Hegemony], Casablanca and Beirut 1995.

Ahmad, Muhammad Sharif, *Fikrat al-Qanun al-Tabi'i 'ind al-Muslimin* [The Notion of Natural Law Among the Muslims], Baghdad 1980.

Ahmad, Muhammad Sharif al-M, *Nazariyat Tafsir al-Nusus adaniya: Dirasa Muqarana bayn al-Fiqhayn al-Madani wal-Islami* [The Theory of Hermeneutics: A Comparative Study of Civil and Islamic Jurisprudence], Baghdad 1979

Anderson, J.N.D., "The Shari'a and Civil Law: The Debt Owed by the New Civil Codes of Egypt and Syria to the Shari'a," *The Islamic Quarterly* 1 (April 1954) 29-46.

Anderson, Norman, "Modern Trends in Islam: Legal Reform and Modernization in the Middle East," *Int'l & Comp.L.Q.* 20 (1971) 1-21.

Anderson, J.N.D., "Codification in the Muslim World: Some Reflections," *Rabels Zeitschrift fur Auslandisches und internationales Privatrecht* 30 (1966) 267-289.

Anderson, J.N.D., "Recent Developments in Sharia Law," *The Muslim World*, 40(1950):244-256; 41(1951):34-48, 113-126, 186-198, 271-288; 42(1952):33-47, 124-140, 190-206, 257-276.

An-Na'im, Abdullahi Ahmad, *Toward an Islamic Reformation: Civil Liberties, Human Rights and International Law*, New York, 1990.

An-Na'im, Abdullahi Ahmad, "Human Rights in the Muslim World: Socio-Political Conditions and Scriptural Imperatives: A Preliminary Inquiry," *Harvard Human Rights J.* 3 (1990) 13-52.

An-Na'im. Abdullahi Ahmad, "Religious Minorities under Islamic Law and the Limits of Cultural Relativisim," *Human Rights Q.* 9 (1987) 1-18.

Antonius, George, *The Arab Awakening: The Story of the Arab National Movement*, New York 1938.

Awdah, Abdel-Qadir, *Al Tashri' al-Jina'i al-Islami Muqaran bil-Qanun al-Wad'i* [Islamic Criminal Law Compared to Positive Law], Cairo 1985.

Al-'Aysami, Shibli, *Al-'Almaniya wal-Dawla al-Diniya* [Secularism and the Religious State], Baghdad 1986

Al-Azmeh, Aziz, "Islamic Legal Theory and the Appropriation of Reality," in Al-Azmeh (ed.), *Islamic Law: Social & Historical Contexts*, London and New York 1988.

Badawi, Ibrahim Zakiy al-Din, "Nazariyat al-Riba al-Muharram fil-Sharia al-Islamiya" [Theory of Forbidden Usury in Islamic Law], *Majallat al-Qanun wal-Iqtisad [*Revue du Droit et Economie Politique] Cairo 9 (April 1939) 387-446 and (May 1939) 533-566.

Badie, Bertram, and Birnbaum, Pierre, *The Sociology of the State*, Chicago 1983.

Badr, Gamal Moursi, "Islamic Law and the Challenge of Modern Times," in J. Piscatori & G.S. Harris (eds.), *Law, Personalities, and Politics of the Middle East: Essays in Honor of Majid Khadduri,* Washington, D.C. 1987.

Badr, Gamal Moursi, "Islamic Law: Its Relation to Other Legal Systems," *The American J. of Comp. Law* 26 (1978) 187-198.

Ballantyne, W.M., *Commercial Law in the Arab Middle East: The Gulf States,* London, 1986.

Ballantyne, W.M., *Legal Development in Arabia*, London, 1980.

Beccaria, Sezare, *On Crime and Punishment*, 1764 (Engl. transl. David Young) Indianapolis 1986.

Beetham, David, *The Legitimation of Power*, Atlantic Highlands NJ 1991.

Berkes, Niyazi, *The Development of Secularism in Turkey*, Montreal 1964.

Berman, Harold J., *Law & Revolution: The Formation of the Western Legal Tradition,* Cambridge 1983.

Brinton, Jasper Yates, *The Mixed Courts of Egypt*, rev. ed. New Haven, Connecticut, 1968.

Cappelletti, Mauro, *The Judicial Process in Comparative Perspective*, Oxford 1989.

Chadwick, Owen, *The Secularization of the European Mind in the 19th Century*, Cambridge 1975.

Chehata, Chafik, "Les Survivances Musulmanes dans la Codification du Droit Civil Egyptien," *Revue Int'l. de Droit Compare* 17 (1965) 839-853.

Chehata, Chafik, *Al-Ittijahat al-Tashri'iya fi Qawanin al-Bilad al-'Arabiya* [Legislative Trends in the Laws of the Arab States], Cairo 1960.

Chehata, Chafik, "L'Influence du Code Civil Francaise en Egypte et le Nouveau Code Civil Egyptien," *Majallat al-Qanun wal-Iqtisad* [Revue Droit et Economie Politique] 21 (1951) 415-423.

Comair-Obeid, Nayla, *The Law of Business Contracts in the Arab Middle East: A Theoretical and Practical Comparative Analysis* (with particular reference to modern legislation), London and The Hague, 1996.

Corm, George, *Ta'addud al-Adyan wa Anzimat al-Hukm: Dirasa Susiulugiya wa Qanuniya Muqarana* [The Plurality of Religions and the Systems of Governance: A Comparative Sociological and Legal Study], Beirut (2nd pr.) 1992.

Coulson, Noel J., *Conflicts and Tensions in Islamic Jurisprudence*, Chicago & London, 1969.

Coulson, Noel J., A History of Islamic Law, Edinburgh, 1964.

Christelow, Allan, Muslim Law Courts and the French Colonial State in Algeria, Princeton 1986.

Demerath, N.J. III, "Religious Capital and Capital Religion: Cross Cultural and non-Legal Factors in the Separation of Church and State," *Daedalus* 120 (Summer 1991) 21-40.

Djait, Hichem, *Europe and Islam: Cultures and Modernity*, Berkeley & London 1985.

Durham, W. Cole Jr. & Dushku, Alexander, "Traditionalism, Secularim, and the Transformative Dimension of Religious Institutions," *Brigham Young Univ. L. Rev.* (1993) 421-465.

Dwyer, Kevin, *Arab Voices: The Human Rights Debate in the Middle East,* Berkeley, Los Angeles, London, 1991.

Eaton, Richard M., "Islamic History as a Global History," in Michael Adas (ed.), *Islamic and European Expansion: The Forging of a Global Order*, Philadelphia 1993.

Enayat, Hamid, *Modern Islamic Political Thought*, Austin 1982.

Fareed, Muneer Goolam, *Legal Reform in the Muslim World: The Anatomy of a Scholarly Dispute in the 19th and the Early 20th Centuries on the Usage of Ijtihad as a Legal Tool,* San Francisco, London, Bethesda 1996.

Al-Fasi, Allal, *Maqasid al-Shari'a al-Islamiya* [The Objectives of Islamic Sharia], Casablanca 1977.

Al-Fasi, Allal, *Difa' 'An al-Shari'a* [In Defense of Sharia], Casablanca 1966.

Fawdah, Faraj, *Hiwar Hawl al-'Almaniya* [Discourse on Secularism], Cairo 1987.

Foda, Ezzeldine, *The Projected Arab Court of Justice*, Leiden 1957.

Friedman, Lawrence M., *The Legal System: A Social Science Perspective*, New York 1975.

Friedman, Lawrence M., "On Legal Development," *Rutgers Law Rev.* 24 (1969) 11-64.

Friedrich, Carl Joachim, *The Philosophy of Law in Historical Perspective*, Chicago 1963.

Friedrich, Carl Joachim, *Transcendental Justice: The Religious Dimension of Constitutionalism*, Chicago 1964.

Gierke, Otto, *Natural Law and the Theory of Society 1500-1800* (Engl. transl. by Ernest Barker), Boston 1957.

Glendon, Mary Ann, *The Transformation of Family Law: State, Law and Family in the United States and Western Europe*, Chicago 1989.

Goadby, F.M., *International and Interreligious Private Law in* Palestine, Jerusalem 1926.

Guttman, Egon, "Reception of the Common Law in the Sudan," *Int'l. and Comp. L. Q.* 6 (1957) 401-417.

Hallaq, W.B., "The Logic of Legal Reasoning in Religious and non-Religious Cultures: The Case of Islamic Law and Common Law," Cleveland State Law Rev. 34 (1985-86) 79-96. Hill, Enid, "Comparative and Historical Study of Modern Middle Eastern Law," *The American J. of Comp. Law* 26 (1978) 279-304.

Hinsley, *F.H. Sovereignty*, Cambridge (2nd.ed.) 1986.

Horwitz, Morton J., *The Transformation of American Law 1780-1860*, Cambridge 1977.

Horwitz, Morton J., *The Transformation of American Law 1870-1960: The Crisis of Legal Orthodoxy,* New York & Oxford 1992.

Hourani, Albert, *Arabic Thought in the Liberal Age 1898-1939*, Cambridge 1962.

Jadirah, et al., *Al-Tajriba al-Dimuqratiya fil-Mamlaka al-Maghribiya* [The Democratic Experiment in the Moroccan Kingdom] Proceedings of a Symposium of Moroccan Scholars and Professionals, Dar al-Mustaqbal al-'Arabi, Cairo 1987

Kamali, Muhammad Hashim, "Methodological Issues in Islamic Jurisprudence," *Arab Law Q.* 11 (1996) 3-33.

Kelley, J.M., *A Short History of Western Legal Theory*, Oxford 1992.

Kerr, Malcolm H. *Islamic Reform: The Political and Legal Theories of Muhammad 'Abduh and Rashid Rida,* Berkeley 1966.

Khadduri, M. and Liebesny H.J. (eds.), *Law in the Middle East, vol. 1: Origin and Development of Islamic Law,* Washington, D.C. 1955.

Al-Khamlishi, Ahmad, "Manhaj al-Fikr al-Qanuni fil-Fiqh al-Islami" [The System of Legal Thought in Islamic Jurisprudence*], Al-Majalla al-Maghribiya lil-Qanun wal-Siyasa wal-Iqtisad* [The Moroccan Journal of Law, Politics and Economy] 16 (December 1984) 11-37.

Al-Khamlishi, Ahmad, "Kayfa Naqra' Dhahir al-Iltizamat wal 'Uqud" [How to Read the Code of Obligations and Contracts], in *Al-Majalla al-Maghribiya li-Qanun wa-Iqtisad al-Tanmiya* [Revue Marocaine de Droit et D'Economie du Development] 7 (1984) 7-29.

Al-Khamlishi, Ahmad, "Al-Tajdid am al-Taghallub 'ala 'Aqabat al-Tariq" [Renewal or Overcoming Obstacles on the Road], in *Tajdid al-Fikr al-Islami* [Renewal of Islamic Thought], several authors, Mu'assasat al-Malik 'Abdel-'Aziz Aal Sa'ud lil Dirasat al-Islamiya wal 'Ulum al-Insaniya (Colloquium 3-4 April, 1987), Rabat 1989.

Al-Khudari, Muhammad, *Tarikh al-Tashri' al-Islami* [History of Islamic Law], Cairo 1925/1985.

Khuri, Fuad I., *Imams and Emirs: State, Religion and Sects in Islam*, London & Beirut 1990.

Le Goff, Jacques, *Intellectuals in the Middle Ages*, Cambridge & Oxford 1993.

Liebesny, Herbert J., The Law of the Near & Middle East: Readings, Cases, and Materials, Albany 1975.

Mahmassani, Subhi, *Al-Awda' al-Tashri'iya fil-Duwal al-'Arabiya, Madiha wa Hadiruha* [The State of Legislation in the Arab States, Its Past and Present], Beirut 1957.

Makdisi, John, "Formal Rationality in Islamic Law and the Common Law," *Cleveland State Law Rev*. 34 (1985-86) 97-112.

Mattai, Ugo, "Three Patterns of Law: Taxonomy and Change in the World's Legal Systems," *The American J. of Comp. Law* 45 (1997) 5-44.

McIlwain, C.H., *Constitutionalism Ancient and Modern*, Ithaca 1947.

Merryman, John Henry, *The Civil Law Tradition: An Introduction to the Legal Systems of Western Europe and Latin America,* Stanford 1969.

Moneger, Joel, "Biographie du code des obligations et contracts: De la reception a l'assimilation d'un code etranger dans l'ordre juridique marocaine," *Al-Majalla al-Maghribiya li- Qanun wa-Iqtisad al-Tanmiya* [Revue Marocaine de Droit et D'Economie du Development] 7 (1984) 15-65.

Mundy, Martha, "The Family, Inheritence, and Islam: A Re-examination of the Sociology of Fara'id Law," in al-Azmeh (ed.) *Islamic Law: Social and Historical Contexts,* London 1988.

Mustafa, Mahmud M., *Tatawur Qanun al-Ijra'at al-Jina'iya fi Misr wa Ghayriha min al-Duwal al-'Arabiya* [Development of Criminal Procedure Law in Egypt and the Other Arab States], Cairo 1969.

Mustafa, Mahmud M., *Usul Qanun al-'Uqubat fil Duwal al-'Arabiya* [The Foundations of Criminal Law in the Arab States], Cairo 1970.

Mustafa, Zaki, *The Common Law in the Sudan*, Oxford 1971.

Mutwalli, Abdel-Hamid, *Mabadi' Nizam al-Hukm fil-Islam* [The Principles of Government in Islam], Alexandria 1966.

Najjar, F.M., "Egypt's Laws of Personal Status," *Arab Studies Q.* 10 (1989) 319-344.

Noonan, John Thomas, *The Scholastic Analysis of Usury*, Cambridge 1957.

Ostrorog, Leon, comte, *The Angora Reform*: three lectures delivered at the centenary celebrations of University College on June 27, 28, and 29, 1927, Westport, Conn. 1979.

Pogi, Gianfranco, *The Development of the Modern State: A Sociological Introduction*, Stanford 1978.

Rahman, Fazlur, *Islam and Modernity: Transformation of an Intellectual Tradition*, Chicago 1982.

Ravndal, G. Bie, *Report on Capitulations by the American Consul at Constantinople to the U.S. Senate* [Doc. No. 34, 67th. Cong., 1st. sess., 1921].

Reid, Donald M., *The Odyssey of Farah Anton: A Syrian Christian's Quest for Secularism*, Minneapolis & Chicago, 1975.

Ren, Xin, *Tradition of the Law and Law of the Tradition: Law, State, and Social Control in China*, Westport, Conn. & London 1997.

Rheinstein, Max (ed.), *Max Weber on Law in Economy and Society*, Cambridge 1954.

Rosenfeld, Michel (ed.), *Constitutionalism, Identity, Difference and Legitimacy*, Durham & London 1994.

Al-Sadda, Abdel-Mun'im Faraj, *Muhadarat fil-Qanun al-Madani: Nazariyat al-'Aqd fi Qawanin al-Bilad al-'Arabiya* [Lectures on the Civil Code: Theory of Contract in the Laws of the Arab Countries], Cairo 1960.

Sajo, Amyn B., "Islam and Human Rights: Congruence or Dichotomy," *Temple Int'l. & Comp. L.J.* 4 (1990) 23-33.

Salam, Nawaf, "The Emergence of Citizenship in Islamdom," *Arab Law Q.* 12 (1997) 125-147.

Al-Sanhuri, Abdel-Razzaq, *Al-Wasit fi Sharh al-Qanun al-Madani al-Jadid* [The Intermediate in Explaining the New Civil Code], Cairo 1952.

Al-Sanhuri, Abdel-Razzaq, *Masadir al-Haq fil-Fiqh al-Islami: Dirasa Muqarana bil-Fiqh al-Gharbi* [The Sources of Right in Islamic Jurisprudence: A Comparative Study with Western Law], Cairo 1954.

Schacht, Joseph, *An Introduction to Islamic Law*, Oxford 1964.

Schacht, Joseph, "Problems of Modern Islamic Legislation," *Studia Islamica* 12 (1960) 99-129.

Sfeir, George N., "The Saudi Approach to Law Reform," *The American J. of Comp. Law* 36 (1988) 729-759.

Smith, W.C., *Islam in Modern History*, Princeton 1957.

Tanaka, Hideo, "Legal Equality Among Family Members in Japan: The Impact of the Japanese Constitution of 1946 on the Traditional Family System," *So. California L. Rev.* 53 (1980) 611-643.

Tibi, Bassam, *Islam and the Cultural Accommodation of Social Change*, Boulder 1990.

Toynbee, Arnold (ed.), *Survey of International Relations: The Islamic World*, vol. I (1925).

Tucker, Judith, "Gender and Islamic History," in Michael Adas (ed.), *Islamic and European History as a Global History: The Forging of a Globel Order*, Philadelphia 1993.

Al-Ulaymi, Rashad Muhammad, *Al-Taqlidiya wal-Hadatha fil-Nizam al-Qanuni al-Yamani: Dirasa Muqarana* [Tradition and Modernity in the Legal System of Yemen: A Comparative Study], Cairo and Beirut 1988

Ungar, Roberto Mangabeira, *Law in Modern Society: Toward a Criticism of Social Theory*, New York & London 1976.

Van Caenegem, R.C., *An Historical Introduction to Private Law*, Cambridge 1992.

Van Caenegem, R.C., *An Historical Introduction to Western Constitutional Law*, Cambridge 1995.

Von Mehren, Arthur Taylor (ed.), *The Legal Order in a Changing Society*, Cambridge 1963.

Watson, Alan, *Legal Transplants: An Approach to Comparative Law*, Athens GA. & London (2nd ed) 1993.

Watson, Alan, *The Evolution of Law*, Baltimore 1985.

Watson, Alan, *The Making of the Civil Law*, Cambridge MA. & London 1981.

Wieacker, Franz, "Foundations of European Legal Culture," *The American J. of Comp.* L. 38 (1990) 1-29.

Wieacker, Franz, *Privatrechtsgeschichte der Neuzeit*, (2nd ed.) Gottingen 1967.

Wilks, Michael, *The Problem of Sovereignty in the Later Middle Ages: The Papal Monarchy with Augustinus Triumphus and the Publicists,* Cambridge 1963.

Ziadeh, Farhat J., *Lawyers the Rule of Law and Liberalism in Modern Egypt*, Stanford 1968.

Ziadeh, Farhat J., *Property Law in the Arab World*, London 1979.

Zweigert, Konrad & Kotz, Heinz, *An Introduction to Comparative Law*, Oxford (2nd ed.) 1992.

INDEX

R

S

T

www.ingramcontent.com/pod-product-compliance
Lightning Source LLC
LaVergne TN
LVHW090314210926
848480LV00001B/248